T0247698

REMEMBER,
YOU ARE A WILEY

REMEMBER, YOU ARE A WILEY

A Memoir

MAYA WILEY

GRAND
CENTRAL

New York Boston

Grand Central Publishing
Hachette Book Group
1290 Avenue of the Americas, New York, NY 10104
grandcentralpublishing.com
@grandcentralpub

First Edition: September 2024

Grand Central Publishing is a division of Hachette Book Group, Inc. The Grand Central Publishing name and logo is a registered trademark of Hachette Book Group, Inc.

The publisher is not responsible for websites (or their content) that are not owned by the publisher.

The Hachette Speakers Bureau provides a wide range of authors for speaking events. To find out more, go to hachettespeakersbureau.com or email HachetteSpeakers@hbgusa.com.

Grand Central Publishing books may be purchased in bulk for business, educational, or promotional use. For information, please contact your local bookseller or the Hachette Book Group Special Markets Department at special.markets@hbgusa.com.

Print book interior design by Marie Mundaca

Library of Congress Cataloging-in-Publication Data

Names: Wiley, Maya, author.
Title: Remember, you are a Wiley / Maya Wiley.
Description: First edition. | New York : Grand Central Publishing, 2024.
Identifiers: LCCN 2024008150 | ISBN 9781538739938 (hardcover) | ISBN 9781538739952 (ebook)
Subjects: LCSH: Wiley, Maya. | Wiley, George A.--Family. | Women political candidates--New York (State)--New York--Biography. | African American women lawyers--Biography. | Civil rights lawyers--United States--Biography. | African American television journalists--Biography. | New York (N.Y.)--Biography.
Classification: LCC F128.54.W56 A3 2024 | DDC 340.092[B]--dc23/eng/20240331
LC record available at https://lccn.loc.gov/2024008150

ISBNs: 978-1-5387-3993-8 (hardcover), 978-1-5387-3995-2 (ebook)

Printed in the United States of America

LSC-C

Printing 1, 2024

For Naja and Kai, who make me a better Wiley

CONTENTS

REMEMBER,
YOU ARE A WILEY

CHAPTER 1

THE MOVEMENT FAMILY

IT WAS A SATURDAY, but not an ordinary Saturday. On this particular day, Mommy's fully open face was like a conductor's baton, and her enthusiasm inspired our own giddy expectations. My brother, upon hearing her mention a picnic, darted into the sort-of sitting room in our DuPont Circle row house. This room connected the front living room to the dining room and kitchen, as well as the staircase to the upper floors. This was our main gathering place. Its walls had little to do with holding up the house; they were there mainly to support the picket signs leaning on them like shields at the ready.

My brother grabbed a sign. He started marching around the room, thrusting it above his head to the rhythm of his march. "PICK-ET, PICK-ET," he chanted. My mother laughed wholly and deeply, with a unique fullness. When she laughed, she would scrunch up her long, thin, "ski-jump nose," as she called it, with dramatic effect. Wrinkles rippled like waves of joy at the bridge of this one small but prominent feature, calling more attention to the gleam in her eyes. This was all elevated by thin lips that framed a smile so large and warm, it was as if her whole face were an open gateway to some wondrous new land. It drew you in. When she let rip this particular squeal of laughter, I wasn't sure of the joke. Still, we all laughed anyway until she explained that she had said "picnic," a familiar word but an alien activity.

I know we went on one that day, but I don't remember the picnic itself. Even at that young age, our family time was made up of protests. Much of Dad's life was spent on trips to protests and fundraising opportunities around the country, so he was on the road a lot. Every time Dad traveled, he came home with a stuffed animal as an apology, which led us to expect a gift whenever he returned. He was away so often that my brother and I probably had more plush souvenirs than the rest of the kids on our block combined. My favorite, for reasons I've long forgotten, was a stuffed lilac cow that stood on all fours and had its head swiveled in warm regard, as if it had just taken a break from grazing in the pasture and was glad to see me. I named her "Purple Cow." I loved that cow and took her everywhere. Eventually her color was more gray than lilac, and her neck became a floppy thing. I still had her when I left for college, and she was discarded, grudgingly, only because my mother was sick of storing her and, well, she was less than sanitary after so many decades.

Dad's tokens of affection had more power because of his absences. Though I missed him, these absences made me proud, given his important work. I was once asked, when I was still a child, what I thought of my dad. I said he was perfect and had no faults at all, which my mother lovingly scoffed at. She never wanted us to have Dad on a dangerously high pedestal; it could fall on and crush his two little adoring children, who missed him so much.

Despite lionizing my father, I am my mother's child. I always have been, even when I didn't know it. Or maybe I pretended not to know it. In contrast, even now, my father hangs around me like the early-morning dew that clings to the grass. Droplets of Dad don't come every day, but always return unbidden, simultaneously comforting and uncomfortable. He clings in a presence neither gentle nor tormenting, which makes me feel everything from hopeful to hampered. It is not that I loved him more than my mother, or that I miss her any less. In fact, I am sure I miss her more because she was my constant. I loved Dad, but he was the parent who, like the dew, was somewhat magical in its metamorphosis from vapor to droplets. His presence hung in the air, but his appearances were unpredictable. I have probably always been searching for him even when I didn't know I was looking.

My parents were also literal giants. My mother always claimed to be precisely six feet one inch tall with her usual unflagging certainty. For that to be true, my father, a big man, had to be at least six feet two or three inches, though I never heard this confirmed by anyone other than my mother. This was a source of silliness in our family. As little kids, I remember my brother, Danny, and I sitting on the edge of our parents' bed as they teased each other about who was taller. They turned around, back-to-back, craning their necks and demanding we declare one of them vertically dominant over the other. Dad had a big Angela Davis afro, so my rail of a mother, with thin, limp locks that my father's sister once called "white trash hair" to her face, would inevitably proclaim he was cheating. It would make us giggle and shout, "Daddy is taller." The truth was, as kids, my brother and I had to tilt our heads back precariously far on our spindly necks to see into either of their faces. But Dad had the added benefit of that invisible pedestal; his absences from our days and most of our nights gave him a presence that had nothing to do with physical size.

He was a promising organic chemistry professor turned civil rights and economic justice activist. Either role made him iconic. But the public knew Dr. George A. Wiley as the latter. A rising leader toward the end of the civil rights movement of the 1960s, he started by fighting school segregation. But when Black housing was going to be torn down to "revitalize" downtown Syracuse, New York, that really kicked off his journey into the deep roots of Black poverty. His central purpose became organizing low-income Black people. For Dad, ending poverty became a critical civil rights goal: Decent housing, all basic needs, and freedom from hunger are things every Black person, and every person, should have. In his view, Black women would be the primary leaders in creating a multiracial coalition attacking poverty. He founded the National Welfare Rights Organization, which was at the forefront of what we now call the movement for economic justice. He and his organization were major players in the 1968 Poor People's Campaign that led to Resurrection City, the three thousand wooden "tents" built on the National Mall to protest poverty. These tents, filled with mostly Black people, and the corresponding Poor People's march protested both poverty and the failure of real economic transformation in low-income communities of color.

For me he was also the daddy of the airplane game. He would lie on his back at the foot of their bed, and give Danny and me turns hovering on his outstretched feet. We grinned in anticipation, then we each burst into laughter as we "flew," buoyed by his black-socked flat feet, as Dad kept his knees to his chest and over his growing barrel belly. My long, skinny outstretched arms and wobbly, lanky legs, ashy and scarred from my day on our "playground" of concrete sidewalks and alleys, flapped in the air as I struggled to balance. That was the game. The balance. It was the treasured and too-short fun that followed a long day without him. A long day without balance.

It was also Daddy who, exhausted and compensating for lost time, would wrap us in a sheet, one at a time, and swing us by our ankles in that same foot-of-the-bed spot. It was exciting to be swung, but the sheet's white, whirling blindness made it all the more electrifying. I would get brief and kaleidoscopic glimpses of the room through the billowing fabric. A corner of the TV. A section of the two street-facing windows that I would sometimes hang out of to watch people walk by. The red wall, which Mommy painted while wearing a bandana on her head and a plaid workshirt with cut-off sleeves.

While we played, my mother would laugh and grin along with us. She was usually propped up on her pillows, her lengthy legs stretched out with one ankle comfortably crossed over the other, watching the nightly news, a football game, or whatever else was on in that dark hour. She would often have a dinner plate in her lap because she'd waited for Daddy to come home so they could eat dinner together. My brother and I would have eaten many hours earlier, a meal that marked the beginning of the interminable wait, as we wondered if this night would provide another short trip to Daddy's amusement park.

Mommy was a doer all day long, so at night, she reclined in bed with the TV. I'm now a working mother myself, so when I look back I see her relishing the role of witness rather than waitress to all our needs, and I understand how important she must have found these too-rare moments.

The four of us were seldom all together because we were a movement family, a family of activism in the late 1960s and 1970s, and activism has no business hours. Daddy worked day and night. Weekends marked a change in our routines but not his.

Mommy had an office gig and was the family breadwinner. She also rented out various rooms in our three-story, redbrick row house to help pay the rent and manage our costs of living— something, I guess, my parents' paychecks could not cover by themselves. Women had been entering the workforce in greater numbers, but Mommy was in that historic generation of professional women making greater demands for women's rights and who were, and still are, paid less than their male counterparts. Daddy was an organizer, which was a low-paying job.

In those early years, I understood none of that. In my neighborhood, all the mothers worked. My best friend, Charlene, lived around the corner. She didn't have a father, and her mother was a cashier at the Safeway supermarket a few blocks down the street. The mothers on welfare I knew growing up worked constantly, with Dad. Everyone worked.

I had all I needed, and I never heard my parents worry about money because, honestly, they were not concerned. My parents were risk-takers who jumped from the top of the waterfall knowing they would eventually land feetfirst, ready to be carried in their chosen direction. I would later learn I had that sense of comfort because my scholar-with-a-dollar mother was also a deeply confident and optimistic manager of the family financial affairs.

If anything, I felt quite wealthy. Our house was lovely thanks to Mommy's artistic eye and flare. Our sofa and canvas butterfly chairs were not expensive, but they were made more inviting by her ability to thoughtfully arrange them. She was also a bibliophile, and we had one first-floor room with a wall of books that gave color, depth, and even warmth despite only a single window. Sculptures, entrusted to her by her artist friends for storage, increased the sense of wealth and privilege, especially as Mommy so carefully arranged them. One was a life-size sculpture of a woman sitting on a stool. It was so realistic that people were often startled by it, convinced that it was my mother keeping watch. Her single red bedroom wall was another example of her taste. It drew the eye, contrasting with the more traditional eggshell walls that accompanied it and setting off the whole room in a fashionable wash of color without overwhelming it. That seemed the embodiment of my mother's physical presence in the world.

Even surrounded by Mommy's comforting style, my entire focus after 3:00 p.m. was on these evenings with Daddy, which were never promised. When he wasn't traveling, the wondering and watching for his return home was a nightly routine. When he was, it was counting the days until he would be home. The wait intensified my hunger for his hugs, for the sound of his laugh that reminded me of keys jingling in his pocket. I longed for his "mushy kisses," as I called them. He would instinctively lick his lips before planting a kiss on my cheek and I would predictably scream, "Eeeew!" and giggle loudly.

Family outings were a rarity, unless it was a protest or rally. As young children, though we did go to rallies, we were kept out of the most exciting action. One of the last and most remarkable moments of my father's leadership in the movement was the aforementioned Poor People's Campaign.

The year was 1968. In the midst of the planning, Dr. Martin Luther King Jr. had been assassinated while protesting working conditions in Memphis. The war in Vietnam had ended the lives of tens of thousands of Americans and more Vietnamese civilians in US airstrikes, and President Lyndon Johnson's obsession with it was also suffocating his war on poverty in its preschool years. The civil rights movement was actively turning its eye toward an issue my father was already promoting: ending poverty. The National Welfare Rights Organization was a cosponsor of the campaign with Dr. Martin Luther King's Southern Christian Leadership Conference, which was not without its tensions—but I would not come to understand those until years later. Like all major protests, the Poor People's Campaign was a coalition of groups and individuals who marched and constructed and inhabited Resurrection City for more than a month in the nation's capital.

Resurrection City marked a period of my childhood without playtime and good-night songs, as my father spent hours in the makeshift city under the unseeing eyes of the massive statue of Abraham Lincoln. But the power and persistence of protesters couldn't change the weather. It mercilessly rained for days in May and June 1968, for much of the forty-plus-day action. At one point, the storm was so bad that it knocked down the makeshift dining hall, and about a third of the protesters were forced to leave. One participant, Laura Jones, said in a remembrance, "It was mud and rain and very uncomfortable."

I didn't witness any of it except through my dad's absence. My eldest cousin, Jacob, was participating, and he was the only interesting thing happening, from my perspective. The firstborn child of my grandparents' firstborn child had been forced by the weather from the tents to the refuge of our home. I remember hearing the door and taking my four-year-old's one-step-at-a-time trot downstairs, then seeing my grown cousin in the doorway below. From the top of his afro to the bricks on his feet, he was caked in mud. Mommy was striding, with her very long legs, swiftly down the hall beneath me. It stopped me in my tracks.

The whole scene was strangely exciting, as all adult commotion usually was. In my short time on the planet, I knew Mommy to be patient and loving and clear about cleanliness as a critical virtue. Our house, outside of my and my brother's bedroom closet—which was the monster we would feed with mounds of toys and clothing whenever my mother would yell at us to clean up—was an oasis of order. Everything had a place, and cleaning happened regularly and punctually. Mommy sternly halted Jacob's muddy progress into the house, since it apparently hadn't occurred to him that he looked like a statue come to life.

I was too young to understand what this scene represented about the waning of the movement. It was big. It was in pain. It was trying to face down the poverty of Black people, and of all people. And it was mired in the mud and muck of a country exhausted by the war in Vietnam and a presidency mired in it. The tide of public opinion and will was turning away, once again, from people who couldn't pay the bills because they were Black.

My world was that of a child, and my mommy was its central organizing principle. As normal as she seemed to me, Wretha Wiley was graceful and elegant while managing to be completely without arrogance, comfortable in her own alabaster skin and seemingly in complete command of all around her.

My mother was both sun and moon. We orbited daily around her light and warmth, and when she wasn't at work, she was reading a book, both of which she did as often as she could. To us, her little mismatched children, she bathed the whole world in bright light when she was excited, while Dad swam in his big, public-facing activism that was itself exciting. Dad's power was loud. Mom's power was quiet. She focused us on the beauty of little things, like a drawing we had made or the color of a cloudless sky. She would call such things "glorious," a word I often heard her use, and she always meant it. It created an important, if not unintentional, yin to Dad's yang in our whirling world.

In addition to the precious nights of playtime with Dad, we looked forward to our one-night-a-week family dinner, which we enjoyed for a glorious period of our young family life. We went out to a neighborhood spot, the Copley Plaza Restaurant, just a few blocks from our house. It was an Italian-style diner, and we loved it. It was the finest restaurant imaginable to me. Each weekend, we sat in a booth. My mother would order the same thing for my brother and me: a wooden bowl of iceberg lettuce with store-bought Italian dressing and a white ceramic boat of spaghetti with two massive meatballs. So entranced was I in this meal that I have no recollection of what my parents ordered.

Daddy would always grab a toothpick at the cash register, and I would watch in fascination as it rolled its way across his lips from one corner of his mouth to the other, periodically gripped in his teeth if he smiled, which he did frequently. Danny and I would grab toothpicks, too, because he did. I would concentrate, trying hard not to look like I was concentrating, on making the little sharp-edged stick roll on the wave of my uncontrollable lips as smoothly as Daddy.

Going to the Copley Plaza was a special event, not just because of the luxury of eating out but because it was a stark contrast to the weekday meals, which Danny and I ate alone. On the nights Daddy didn't make it home early enough to see us, Mommy would let us join her while she ate. We'd plant ourselves on the floor at the foot of her perch, her dinner plate on her lap, and we'd watch the news with her until she announced, "Bedtime." We would usually beg to stay up a little longer in hopes that Daddy might get home to say good night. Pretty soon after she came home from work, our questioning would start. "When is Daddy coming home?" Many times her answer was "I don't know." My mother never believed in telling us what we wanted to hear and was always gentle but direct. Sometimes, after a few hours of us begging her to answer a question she could not, she would say, "Why don't you call him and ask him?"

We would run to their bedroom. On the table by Daddy's side of the bed (the side closest to the bedroom door, probably because of his late-night arrivals) was the black rotary telephone common to the era. We knew his office number by heart. Our little fingers were small compared to the big, round plastic holes that revealed the fading white numbers beneath them. I remember the effort and the concentration I had to put into pulling the dial around the face of that Bell telephone. Danny and I would be perched on the edge of the bed, our spindly legs dangling over the side, phone cradled on a shoulder, our small heads pressed together so we could both hear. When we heard his distinctive "Hello," our mournful and whining "Daddy, when are you coming hooooome" would begin. Unlike my mother, who was direct and refused to make promises, Daddy would simply say, "Soon." We knew better. We had experience with "soon" translating into hours or never. So, we would press, almost in unison, "But wheeeeeen?" This questioning was as much a part of our evening routine as anything else.

When bedtime inevitably came, my brother and I trudged to our shared room down the hall from my parents. It had one little window that looked out on the back alley and two twin beds, which were periodically rearranged to keep life a little interesting. What I remember most about those nights was my mom singing "You Are My Sunshine" when it was her turn, and Daddy singing, "Que Sera Sera." To this day I can't hear "Que Sera Sera" sung by Doris Day in Alfred Hitchcock's film *The Man Who Knew Too Much* without being transported back to the dark and to Daddy's voice and silhouette. It was a song that seemed not only a foreshadowing of our future, but also a poignant statement of our existence as a family, which was dependent on forces we could not control. We had little control over our life as a family of four because of the ongoing fight to give other families, families with single mothers, some control over their lives.

CHAPTER 2

REMEMBER, YOU'RE A WILEY

IN HIS SENIOR YEAR of high school, George Wiley was still Black, still short, still skinny, and still confident. He was the fourth of six children, all of whom attended an all-white high school. Encouraged by his chemistry teacher, he entered a statewide science competition. As the story goes, Dad worked day and night on a massive contraption to turn milk by-products into rayon. His close-knit, large family was terrified. Apparently, the monstrous machine took up an entire room, and his family didn't believe he could finish the massive experiment in time, let alone win the statewide competition.

My grandmother, Olive Wiley, known simply as Nana to her large brood of grandchildren, wanted to lessen the blow of failure for her eager and self-assured son. She tried to tell him that it was okay if he couldn't finish it or if it failed to operate properly. Dad's response was simple and swift. Of course he would finish. And he would win the competition. Because he was a genius. It was 1949, and he had recently scored 150 on an IQ test. The family had already agreed that in a family of smart children, George was the smartest, the budding scholar.

Nana, a deeply religious Christian woman, took him to task on his self-praise. Both his parents maintained a strict, fundamentalist family where the word of the Bible was the gospel, and no one should raise themselves up as superior. George responded that his genius was a fact, the truth. Simple. He wasn't bragging, he was merely explaining why she need not worry. Dad finished the science project and won the competition, earning a college scholarship in the process.

We now have research that tells us the IQ test is as much a measure of motivation as it is any raw intellect. Dad had both, but motivation seemed to be his distinguishing quality, along with his positive attitude. It is hard for me now to imagine a white community tolerating an arrogant Black boy. A charming and funny one, seen as promising and who minded most of the boundaries, must have been acceptable.

This was the child who would become Dr. George Wiley, chemist, activist, and father. I was aware that these details were of his making, even as I rejected the notion that his road was mine or his map my guide. I don't remember exactly at what age Daddy became "Dad," but in time I knew him as the Dad of the R-rated movies my Mom yelled at him for taking us to see. He was the Dad of the top-down car rides in his red roadster, a beat-up Austin Healey, a once-fancy British sports car that was always breaking down. They were no longer being manufactured, and Dad couldn't get parts for repairs. It seemed half the time he was underneath that car with Campbell's soup cans and other creative fixes. I loved and hated it for being exactly what it was, a fun but broken little treasure my father adored; it was a mirror reflecting back to me the joys and challenges of being Dr. George Wiley's child.

It had two little seats in the back that were the perfect size for my brother and me, so we always rode back there as Dad chauffeured us around in it. One of our best days was spent chasing the Goodyear blimp as it floated silently, like a massive water balloon waiting to drop. The trunk of the roadster contained a folding lawn chair that Dad would pull out at a phone booth to sit and make long work calls. My brother and I waited in those two little tailor-made seats that in those minutes, and sometimes even an hour, felt like detention. He owned not only the booth but the sidewalk during these curbside phone calls, his feet stretched out as if he were in his own backyard.

Dad had no self-consciousness about these publicly odd moments that drew stares from, well, everyone. The lawn chair, the afro, the dashiki, and the sunglasses. But most of all the hole-filled orthopedic shoes that he prominently displayed. He seemed oblivious to the stares that made me shrink into the back seat. "Daddy let's goooooo." But there was power in his personality, his confidence, and his absolute refusal to be anything less than he was or do anything less than he wanted. He was not "normal" and didn't care who knew it.

I, in contrast, was spending my young years trying hard to be as normal as I could be, and that proved impossible. A mentor and friend of mine, john powell, whom I worked for at the American Civil Liberties Union, just a few years out of law school, once told me that his children wanted to fit in. He suggested to them that their lot in life might not be to fit in. I remember feeling he was speaking to me. When I asked him what he wished for them, he said, "Engagement." It was a simple, illuminating moment. I needed to find a way to be engaged, without fitting in. Or maybe even because I didn't fit in.

Neither of my parents fit in, but for different reasons. Dad's origin story, and what it meant to be a Wiley, involved a silent expectation and imagination. That expectation was achievement. The imagination was changing society. The message on repeat was "Remember. You're a Wiley." It also had its contradictions, especially when it came to this Black man in a white world. The man who loved red roadsters and hated poverty was an iconic iconoclast. Understanding how he came to embody both these high expectations and imaginings was the challenging legacy he left me with, a challenge as to whether I was worthy, better than the man, or someone totally different despite the familial relationship. But what was that legacy that shaped and explained him? One thing his early days did teach me was that we don't know what we will become, and we are shaped as much by our experiences as our expectations.

Dad's life seemed to direct him both toward marrying a white woman and a career in chemistry, but not necessarily a radical white woman or a future parading through the streets sporting a black-fisted afro pick in his pocket and holding a bullhorn to his mouth, flanked and followed by fist-raising Black women and mostly white organizers. His own story seemed a puzzling contrast between this reality and the world he came from.

To understand that story, and try to find my own, I had to first understand what shaped Dad's upbringing. George Wiley grew up in a white, fairly rural suburb of Providence, Rhode Island, the aforementioned fourth of six children in a Black family that was a fundamentalist Christian pillar of respectability: a successful, working-class family with a reputation that outmatched their economic position or the hue of their skin.

My father's father had to work hard all his life. Through luck and fortitude fueled by faith, Papa, as all us grandchildren called him, had some important breaks in his life. William Wiley had dreams the world denied him as a descendant of Black people enslaved in South Carolina. He wanted to be a journalist and edited the high school newspaper. He couldn't afford college, but in the 1920s he passed the civil service examination to land one of the few civil service jobs available—mail clerk. Even in the Northeast, Black people were rarely allowed this type of employment.

Then, in a move that was unusual and based in principle, not financial security, Papa quit his catch of a job and went on to study the Bible and become a missionary. By the time Olive Wiley, my nana, was pregnant with my father, he had become a Bible salesman to support the family.

It was 1931 and the Great Depression drilled holes in everyone's boat that kept them afloat. This included Papa's Bible-selling income. The family was struggling to make ends meet. Dad would be born a Depression baby.

My grandparents couldn't afford the birthing costs that would come with Nana's labor. Doctors and midwives had to be paid, and they had barely enough to subsist, as they already had three other young mouths to feed. They were barely making it. The only reason they had any resources was that they rented out the family house they owned in Warwick, Rhode Island, a rural suburb of Providence. My father's parents, two older sisters, and one older brother were living in a small, underheated rental apartment in the Black ghetto on the South Side of Providence.

Nana had to go to a midwife she knew in Bayonne, New Jersey, who was a member of their church. There, with the unpaid help of this midwife, her frail fourth baby, George Alvin Wiley, was born. He almost died in his first year of life in that chilly slum apartment. Dad survived, though, and my grandparents believed that miracle was a literal and divine one.

Papa then had another stroke of good luck. He landed a job as an undertaker's bookkeeper. Business was still thriving there because the Depression did not end death nor the need to bury loved ones. The family moved back to their house in Warwick. In that house, my father grew from a frail baby into the young man who would be a chemist.

Papa had some unique training that I suspect helped him with the "luck" he had. My great-grandfather, George Washington Wiley, for whom my father was named, had been a cook in Charleston. Papa lost his mother when he was only five. I don't think he ever knew what took her life. He was so little. At the age when I was flying like an airplane on my father's flat feet, my grandfather had been farmed out to other family members to be cared for, until his father gathered him up to go north. My great-grandfather escaped the harshness of Southern racism to the racism of the North, when he married and followed his second wife to Providence, Rhode Island, in 1905. Papa's stepmother was a servant to a wealthy white family who summered in the North and wintered in Charleston.

Rhode Island had few Black people, and its racism was more "genteel" than in the South, perhaps because the small numbers bred less fear of a mass retribution for the sins of slavery. As a child, Papa was trained as a butler by a Brown University professor to whom he delivered laundry. This professor taught Papa the fine points of marching into the sitting room to bow and announce that supper was served, setting a formal table, and pulling back chairs for the family to occupy.

When I learned this detail after his death, it explained Papa's formal bearing. But he was never arrogant or self-important. Papa expressed it more as gentleness and contemplation rather than vanity or airs. He was a quiet and diminutive giant, who was balding, with a head of close-cut, very white hair. I adored him because his sweetness was so enveloping, and yet he seemed half the size of his towering son. Papa would stand, feet turned out duck-like, always wearing a jacket over a collared shirt, which added to his air of formality. Hands clasped behind his back, he would contemplate all that happened around him, including a very large pack of grandchildren running about.

Part of my grandfather's heroism, in my eyes, and his formative role modeling for my father and his siblings, was Papa's own form of activism. Despite the racism and economic insecurity that had denied him his dream of a career in journalism, he became the editor of the Providence edition of a Black newspaper. Papa had the tenacity to secure political advertising dollars from Democrats in the 1932 presidential campaign and Senate races that produced Franklin D. Roosevelt among others. But he didn't leave it at that. He used his newfound political network to get his job back in the post office. Nana could be a homemaker, making her children's clothes and participating in the Parent-Teacher Associations and other clubs and activities for her little Wileys.

White people in Warwick did not like having their mail handed to them by Black people, though. For years, Papa had to battle through that racism with his gentle and deeply religious elegance to arrive at the overearned position of mail clerk.

Before Papa worked in the post office at night, he wrote for his paper, farmed a small plot on the family property, and kept chickens. Papa used the pages of his paper to challenge discrimination. He also founded the Providence chapter of the National Urban League, one of the oldest civil rights organizations in the country. And he used both to advance the cause of racial justice for Black people in Providence. So being a Wiley meant working hard, pitching principled fights, and engaging in respectable forms of quiet tenacity.

By extension, their children grew up in an unusually white world with the advantages and the discrimination that came with it, but in a significantly milder form than would have been their lot in the South. Warwick meant better public schools. George was teased as "Alvin the Chipmunk" because of his middle name, according to my mother. But he was not teased, apparently, for his race, despite the singular nature of their Blackness in the sea of white neighbors and white classmates.

That didn't mean they didn't experience overt racism. When my aunt Shirley, Jacob's mom, wanted to join the Girl Scouts, my grandparents saw no reason she couldn't. They packed their four children (my father's youngest two siblings had not yet been born) into their car to drive Aunt Shirley to sign up. When they got there, they were turned away because she was Black. The car ride home was one filled with my father's and his siblings' tears. My grandfather was stone-cold silent. Papa was a quiet man, and when he was angry, he was a pot silently coming to a boil on a high flame. I never saw him blow like a kettle, but he knew how to use his voice.

He returned home and typed out an article titled "Girl Scouts Are Segregated." It worked. The Girl Scouts reached out immediately to welcome Aunt Shirley into their ranks. But this was not integration and acceptance. It was a bribe, and Papa wouldn't take it. This problem was not one to be solved just for his firstborn or even for his children alone. He wrote a second scathing article and did not relent until they agreed to integrate. He was the Wiley his son would emulate.

The Wileys were active in racial justice and also lived relatively insular lives in their white community. There were only three Black families in Warwick, and one of the two others were my grandmother's people, the Thomases.

Our family on Nana's side had been enslaved on the Eastern Shore of Maryland, a plantation near the one Harriet Tubman escaped from, as near as I can tell. But our forebears moved north less than a decade after their emancipation and landed in Providence. Nana grew up similarly insulated in Warwick, and she insisted the family be close-knit. They studied the Bible together. All her children contributed to the household, with the older siblings taking care of the younger ones. Dad and my uncle Al, his older brother and closest sibling in age, delivered newspapers and worked harvesting at the nearby vegetable farms, along with other jobs that helped financially. Fighting wasn't allowed, all-day church on Sunday was a requirement, and respect was not optional. In many ways, they were a community unto themselves, the brown foam in a sea of white, that bobbed above the waves, despite any efforts to drag them under. As my aunt Shirley said in a biography of my father, *A Passion for Equality* by Nick and Mary Lynn Kotz, "Wileys...don't fit the Black skin/white masks mold. We don't fit the black middle class socialite mold. We had no ties with family in the Deep South. We didn't belong to one of the established black churches...We didn't yearn for, strive to be in the American mainstream. We were always in it."

"Remember, you are a Wiley." That is what my nana said to her brood when they were leaving the house for school, but it was never repeated to me. And my aunt Shirley said it was never defined for them in words. She just knew that you didn't break rules. You didn't go out like other young people. You didn't dare come home without honors. My grandparents exemplified those expectations, rather than verbalized them.

Dad was the eager-to-please child. He was very social and therefore very much out in the white world, despite its racist limits. Dad was dutiful, despite not minding all the rules. His streak of challenge to authority and norms was already apparent at an early age. Dad's friends were all white with nicknames like "Squeaky," "Turkey," and "Ham." Dad's name was "Bonny." It was a kind and loving nickname, rather than a teasing one. Friends from his childhood described him as fun-loving. He would join the rampaging boys in committing minor acts of vandalism, like throwing tomatoes at streetlights and building bonfires in the middle of the street. They were troublemakers. Dad said once in an interview that they just liked to be chased by the police as sport. Given his status as a Black boy in a white town, it's astonishing to me that he could feel so comfortable and cavalier. My grandparents, however, understood better. These boys were getting to an age old enough for prosecution.

Being "Bonny" to his white friends wouldn't protect George. His skin color would make him a target of police brutality while theirs might serve as a shield. Dad's behavior would have landed him in jail and perhaps with some bumps and bruises, or worse, as a lesson in knowing his place. That didn't happen. Or more accurately, it hadn't happened yet, and Nana and Papa ensured it didn't. My uncle Al talked about the leather strap that Papa kept in the basement. When Papa went down there, you knew you had done something really wrong. I assume Dad got the basement-strap treatment. George's antics were unacceptable behavior for any of their children on moral grounds, and they were also well aware of the possible consequences.

Growing up in a white suburb and attending an all-white public school produced a difficult reality for my father. His relationships blurred lines in the sands of racism. He could have white friends and play baseball on the high school team. But he could not gain entry to all public venues with his white friends or date white girls. He couldn't ignore that the world was racist, and yet he searched for ways to live fully in its limits by burying himself in his own sense of sameness despite the obvious contradictions. George Wiley wrote of his childhood, "I did not think of myself as a Negro, but simply as a person who was essentially equal with the other people in the neighborhood." His confidence surpassed this sentiment.

That included a stubbornly aggressive attempt to transcend race. Nana and Papa taught their children to know what they could achieve but also to refuse to hate others or even consider all white people racist. That would have been blasphemous to them. Nana once said she lived by and taught her children a motto she had heard elsewhere: "I will let no man belittle my soul by hating." That seemed to me to include self-hatred, as well.

Racism was an ever-present reminder that despite his best efforts, the devastating and senseless boundaries remained. My father's first reported memory of being discriminated against because he was Black was at the white barbershop. He and my uncle Al could walk there from their house and so as small boys they would go for their haircuts. But one day the barber told my grandparents that people had been complaining about the little boys coming to the shop and asked them not to come back. Being respectable didn't translate into being treated equally. Instead, they were met with Northern racism. The kind of racism that said, *I'm not racist. It's just the way things are.* From then on, they had to travel seven miles to downtown Providence to the "Negro" neighborhood to go to a Black barber.

My father recounted another story of going to the pool with his white friend who so completely accepted Dad that he was stunned and confused about why they were not let in. For whatever reason, the white man at the door didn't make an explanation for turning Dad away, even as his white friend argued against it. Dad just wanted to get out of there. He never even bothered explaining to his baffled friend what had happened. The pain and shame of these moments had to affect him, hurt him. And yet, he demonstrated, as all his siblings did, amazing resilience, a deep capacity to love and accept others, and, most important, a continued belief in himself.

Dad was in an undeniably Black family. I was not. Once, my brother and I stood together staring in a mirror that was in the hallway on the floor, leaning up against the wall. It had the perfect dimensions for our little bodies, matched in height and little else. Danny, my brother, was smiling widely with the innocence of his forming mind. He chanted, "I'm White and you're Black." I would respond, as if we were singing a duet, "I'm Black and you're White." We were smiling, giggling, unaware of what made this so funny.

We were stating what was to us the obvious truth. It was a description, not an identity. An observational truth in a world that had already made clear to us, two nursery schoolers, that these color schemes had some practical use we still didn't fully grasp and weren't necessarily accepting. Looking back, my grown self just sees it as two little ones reveling in ourselves and challenging each other as if we were playing a game of "I Spy."

We were not quite prepared for my mother, who happened to be walking by at some point during our chanting. She stopped and, with an angerless but serious gaze, said, "You're both. You are both Black and you are both White." Her tone, stillness, and intensity told us what her words did not: We had done something incomprehensibly wrong. I didn't know what. I don't know if my brother, fifteen months my senior, knew, either. I felt ashamed to think that a part of our chanting, while loving and playful, had an inaudible whisper reverberating just beyond my hearing that told me this was no game. My conscious mind might not have heard, but it responded, *Mommy is wrong. I am Black and Danny is White.* It was, of course, a phenotypic fact. Probably sensing our anxiety and confusion mounting, Mom began to joke about which half of me and Danny was which color. The upper half of me was Black and the bottom half of Danny was Black, she said. The laughter had come back, and the absurdity of it all has remained in my bones.

Dan's complexion didn't mean he was left with no mark from my father's gene pool. Mom's bone-straight hair was no match for Danny's shiny curls. His larger and beefier nose bore no true resemblance to her narrow ski jump of a proboscis. Mom's eyes were light blue-gray pools. Dan's large and generously lashed dark ebony eyes matched mine and Dad's. To an eye that searched for more than complexion—and even that was not a match—our Mom's beach-sand skin was a subtle but discernible contrast to Danny's olive undertones. He might have looked "white," but he would burnish in the bright sun to a coppery brown, while Mom would turn a kind of pink that could explode into a violent red. I often thought these things might have at least raised a fleeting question about Danny's origins with strangers. They never did.

My sienna-brown skin was incontrovertible, and my dark kinks were too stark a contrast to see my mother's bones under my living palette or her expressions on my face. I had her cheekbones, her chin, and her long legs, and my very gait was hers. Danny bit his lip like Dad, and I flashed my hands in the air as Mom did. None of that mattered.

Our little family was very different from Dad's. We were growing up in a Black city in a Black neighborhood that was gentrifying, compared to his rather rural and very white community. He was also raised in a strict Christian home. Religion was a clear part of Dad's resilience, and it became a point of tension as the Wiley children grew older. Dad attended the white and fundamentalist church that Nana and Papa took their children to, but his older sisters, as they grew old enough to make their own choices and required more of a full social life denied them in a white community, chose to find a Black church. My aunts were also denied modern signs of vanity, from lipstick to straightened and curled hair, because of my grandparents' fundamentalism. Aunt Lucille ventured out first, although she was the secondborn. She joined the choir at a Black Baptist church in Providence. Aunt Shirley and even Uncle Al followed, meaning all of Dad's older siblings went in search of a more Black social life. But Dad stayed behind and sat for hours at a time on a wooden pew, unmoving, as the pastor must have intoned things I know Dad could not have completely believed.

This was a turning point of sorts as my father stayed on the path of being what his biographers would label "the White Negro" rather than finding his fellowship in the Black community. He didn't stay at the white church for its social life, which didn't permit drinking or dancing or, from what I could tell, any fun whatsoever. As a grandchild who had to attend a similar church service whenever we visited my grandparents, I can only assume that George continued to attend the white fundamentalist church as a dutiful son who stubbornly refused to go to the refuge of the Black church.

In a chapter of Dad's biography, the authors gave him the aforementioned name, one I could not abide: the White Negro. How I hated and still hate the title. To my ears it was a criticism, a charge that had to be challenged. It seemed to me that this label erased his modest means and his experience with racism. It obscured my father's self-possession and pride but also his outrage at injustice, which personified his life and choices. If I'm honest, it also felt like a challenge to me and my own sense of place in the world, and my claim to my own roots of ancestral struggle.

Yet he stayed the course, as I understand from the biography. Far from the nerdy science kid, he buried himself in sports as well as in books. Sports were allowed, making baseball and tennis acceptable ways to have a social life. The thing is, he was small for an athlete, weighing only 125 pounds. He was a less than impressive five feet six. I imagine that would have been hard for any boy. Boys, particularly athletic ones, need to be seen as physically dominant. But a "White Negro" boy? He stuck out like a sore thumb not for his athletic prowess but for his color and his size. This White Negro, as a teenager, had to pretend not to be interested in girls, despite his crush on the class cheerleader. The White Negro had to feel psychic pain, and constant contradiction seemed to produce a relentless drive to do as much as he could in the white world.

Dad was living not strictly as middle class but was in a very middle-class and working-class community. People had to work hard, but they were not crushed under the boulder of poverty. He and I both ran unfettered with friends growing up. His streets were much less mean, and he was not the privileged one in them, as I was. Nana had been unique, a Black woman homemaker. In my low-income neighborhood, Mom as a bread-winner did not stand out. What was odd was the size of her pay-check and the fact that she put on professional outfits to go into an office. And then there was her white skin.

My brother and I were growing up in the fast-rising waters of gentrification, which were sweeping away Black people like an unforgiving ocean. The houses were mostly owned by white absentee landlords. Ours was. An unseen ghost named some-thing I could only remember as Mrs. Shoemaker. I remember every time I heard the name, I thought of the old lady who lived in a shoe, who had so many children she didn't know what to do. But we were also floating in an integrated family, surrounded by adults beyond our parents who were Black and white, profes-sional and poor. For me, it was a Black neighborhood, even if white people were sprinkling themselves about.

This pre-Metro DuPont Circle in downtown DC of the later part of the 1960s and early 1970s was our hometown. In 1966, the northern side of what we simply called "the Circle," as if there were no others, was still part of an abandoned core. White resi-dents had taken flight to the suburbs, except for the smattering of gay white men brave enough to be out of the closet. They popu-lated a small strip on the western side of the Circle that was blocks away and another world entirely.

My earliest memories are of the contrasts between segrega-tion and my very Black-and-white personal life. There was also the contrast between poverty and wealth. Those were the days when you could run out your front door and spill onto the sidewalks or roam the back alleys, which were the arteries of a circulatory system for garbage trucks and cars that prowled their way to the backs of building parking spaces. All the children in a one-block radius would ebb and flow in periodic and unpredictable tides; the cacophony of laughter, screeches, and fights rang through the alley like it was a dry riverbed, and we were the bubbling rainwaters streaming from the streets.

Charlene, my best neighborhood friend, lived right around the corner. She was the only girl in a large family of brothers, and the only girl my age on our block. Their mother had to support them. Charlene was so beautiful. Tall and slender, her skin was the color of the highest-quality milk chocolate bar my sugar tooth could imagine, and it looked just as velvety. She usually wore her hair in well-greased squares of twists with candy-colored barrettes holding the stubborn tresses in place. Usually, one of them was always cast to the right side of her slender face, gracing her high cheekbones. Her almond eyes were not large, but they were perfect, and she often had a stunned, incredulous stare, with a slack mouth that seemed to be always slightly agape. It gave her a look of always being unpleasantly surprised by the world around her.

I, on the other hand, had a massive, unkempt afro because I would scream like I was being beaten whenever my mother approached with the black pick with its power fist handle. I knew that pick meant pain. My knees would invariably be ashy, and I had a massive gap between my two front teeth to match my brother's. We used to have contests to see who could shoot water the farthest from between our gaps. He usually won, but that was just because he did everything better than me.

REMEMBER, YOU ARE A WILEY

When we played, Charlene and I would usually meet up on the corner between our houses. We had no playdates. I just showed up, and if she wasn't there, I would ask her brothers where she was. If we came inside, it was always into my large and comfortably appointed row house. I remember vividly a small poster that had a black-and-white photo of a little white girl who was looking straight into the camera. The words floating around her angelic face said something about how difficult it is to love unconditionally. Charlene had a greater claim to that statement.

Once, and only once, I went to Charlene's house. It was dark and felt almost like entering a cave. What struck me even more, though, was that it was almost empty. My child's mind couldn't understand where a family with a mother, a grandmother, and something like eight kids could sit or even sleep. Her brothers were not home, but her grandmother was. She sat silently, barely acknowledging our entry or exit; her stillness was an ominous kind of heaviness. It was a weight in the dark space that I could not quite carry. The weight of abject poverty, I felt, as a huge boulder. It seemed to hold her grandmother in place, with no hope of escape.

I could feel the shame and embarrassment that washed off Charlene. I had never wondered all that much why we never went to her house, but once I saw it, I knew without having the words. I also knew I would not come back, and I never did. It was too painful for both of us, too difficult to manage the vast gulf between our experiences.

I couldn't understand how they could have so little, knowing how hard her mother worked. Her mother was a cashier up the street at the neighborhood Safeway grocery store. We would go in on occasion to steal candy we had no money to buy. It was scary, but desire overcame our fear. One day the white manager watched us and kindly and gently came over, bent down on one knee to look us in the eye, and gently reached into our pockets to pull out the chocolate or the coveted Now and Laters. He said, "Now you girls don't want to take these," and gently sent us on our way.

I was deeply embarrassed and ashamed, and yet it took little prompting from Charlene to return again the next day to try again. After all, it had worked a few times, and the gentle admonishment wasn't so bad. He watched us and now, angry at our recidivism, yelled at us and tossed us out. I was horrified. Mom had sometimes sent me to the store to grab an item for her, and now I felt expelled for life. And what would Charlene's mother say? Her mother was a ghostly apparition. Like Charlene's silent and statue-like grandmother. I don't recall ever having exchanged words with her. The heaviness of what she bore seemed to suck the breath from her body and limit any ability to make motions beyond those required to slide groceries on a motionless belt. I knew my family was rich. We had to be.

Far from my father's almost rural, small-town upbringing, there were no playgrounds nearby; the Circle was the territory of "winos" and white hippies who might be tripping on something. We usually went there only if a parent took us. The alleys nearby allowed a kind of random play without the fear of cars. We would run there with Charlene's brothers, who varied from teenagers to boys around my brother's age. The boys, particularly the older few, were always a bit frightening because they shouted without smiling and had been hardened in a way I could feel. They felt dangerously reckless. I never thought they would hurt us intentionally, but I did have the sinking feeling that bad things could happen around them. They always seemed to search for something to break or throw. The air would feel different in their presence, as if it could whip up fast enough to lift me off the ground and toss me like a cartoon superhero character, only I could not fly or bounce back from a brick wall, and I knew it.

I loved my neighborhood, despite all the contradictions it created that made me feel at times like an untrained gymnast asked to perform a backflip on a balance beam. Like the Wileys of Warwick, we were both a part of the neighborhood and outside it. I looked for land mines without even knowing it. Dad's boundaries growing up were much clearer, and he seemed to run over the ground of segregation with a hero's forward offensive. He wore the white hat against the evil of anti-Black racism. I didn't have clear boundaries, only the fog that came with an interracial gentrifier.

Despite this liminality and the pain it often caused me, I loved my family and our home. In the end, the greatest pain came from the search for how to be a Wiley. Dad just *was* a Wiley, and he and Mom were redefining what that meant in this new era. Even as we bore Dad's last name, Mom was just as much a part of shaping me if not more. She would be the one to guide me.

CHAPTER 3

THE ARROGANT INTELLECTUAL

As MUCH AS I saw and experienced Black poverty as a child, I also saw white poverty. This was because my mother insisted on having a house in the mountains. On weekends we would often go to the four-room shack that my parents bought in the beautiful Blue Ridge Mountains in West Virginia. It was Appalachia in every sense, including the poverty it was known for. Mom wasn't looking for luxury. She was looking for beauty in solitude, a break from the city.

Wretha Frances Whittle, my mother, came from deeply conservative and evangelical West Texas. Compared to my father's upbringing, my mother's childhood stories made her exotic and inscrutable. It was cattle and wildcatting oil country, the kind of place that had a constant boom-and-bust cycle due to the fragile economy based on exploiting natural resources. Mom's grandparents owned a cattle ranch, and that colored her life. She grew up drinking clabber, the fat in the unpasteurized milk from their cows that rose to the top of the bucket. She told me her grandmother would scoop it off for everyone's artery-clogging delight. By thirteen, Mom was driving a tractor.

Family summers meant Bible camp, but also road trips out west. There, Mom experienced the contrast from flat, dry West Texas and fell in love with the high peaks of the Grand Tetons, where she would spend summers in college working as a waitress in the lodges of Wyoming so that she could hike. She never lost her love for mountains.

She'd organize us all for the three-hour drive from Washington, DC, to what she called "our mountain," although it wasn't all ours and I never knew its name. Its foot was in Virginia and its crown was in West Virginia. We knew when we crossed the state line because the short stretch of paved road ended abruptly and the deeply rutted dirt road began. At the top a panoramic view spread out all around us, including an undulating ocean of blue waves at the farthest point. It was breathtaking. I remember Mom asking Dad if we could buy it—that part of the mountaintop and the forest that cascaded below. He said yes and we clasped hands and danced in a circle, our cheers ricocheting among the trees.

The house had been built by the current owner. He was elderly and had raised eight children in its four rooms. There were two bedrooms over a living room and dining room; a screened-in back porch lay behind the house. There was electricity but no running water. We used an outhouse that terrified me at night. Mom would leave rusted juice cans in our room in case we couldn't make it until morning. In the mornings

Mom would send us off down a hill with a bucket each to bring up water from the well that she could use to wash dishes and clean up.

We were an even stranger family in the Appalachian Mountains than in our gentrifying neighborhood. On that mountain lived the Jesses and the Doves, who could have been called the Hatfields and McCoys given the legendary tension between them. But what was most striking was the depths of white poverty I saw there. Mom would always pack up our old clothes and be sure to stop by the small trailer at the bottom of the mountain, where a woman lived with six children. The parallels to Charlene's home were not lost on me. My parents treated our neighbors with respect, and they seemed to get it in return. We did not, however, have poor white friends on that mountain. Not even Dad.

My parents let the neighbors hunt rabbit and deer on the property because, as my mother explained, they ate what they killed. That didn't stop me from crying about it, thinking of my pet bunny I unimaginatively named Bugs. And I remember always feeling a bit terrified of the rifles when I saw them. Once hunters came marching over the ridge of our property, carrying a rabbit for Dad. It was a thank-you and an act of kindness. I was mortified and cried, cowering in our little house, peering out through the window screen in a crouch. I made Dad take the limp creature away after the hunters left. I remember Dad marching off dutifully toward the woods holding the limp creature by its hind legs. I hoped he would give it a proper burial.

The world of our weekends in West Virginia clashed with that of DuPont Circle. Danny, who loved frogs, kept one he had caught in West Virginia in a very large cage my father built for him in his room in DC. Mom put a small washing basin in the cage, and they gathered moss and sticks to make a truly impressive habitat for the creature. It was such a happy experiment that on another trip, we gathered a massive garbage can of pond water swimming with tadpoles to bring back to DC. We showed Charlene and her brothers the exciting horde of little swimming, not-yet-legged tadpoles. The garbage can sat outside our kitchen door, at the top of the steps that led down to the back alley. We ran down the next morning to excitedly check on Danny's mass of small charges to find that the bucket had been spilled and the tadpoles ruthlessly crushed into the cement. It was heart-stopping. We were inconsolable. We ran crying for Mom to come see. She said, "Oh! Oh!" in the distressed and empathetic way she had. It had to be Charlene's brothers. They knew the tadpoles were there. To others it would just have been a regular plastic trash can on a back stair that would not have attracted attention. It felt personal; their reckless, usually undirected anger seemed trained on us. I wondered what we had done to become targets, because I couldn't understand undirected anger.

It wasn't easy to reconcile the Mom who married Dad and lived in a mostly Black neighborhood, an activist in her own right, with the Mom who could be comfortable in Appalachia, carting back tadpoles for her son. But she was never one to shy away from all the world's contradictions, and she never tried to spare Danny and me from them, either.

Nothing in her background or her geography explains why in 1957 she hopped on a plane bound for New York City and then went straight to Harlem, having never been either to New York or a Black community. She had just finished college in her hometown of Abilene, Texas. Hardin-Simmons University, a Southern Baptist school, was as fundamentalist as most everybody who lived in Abilene. Her upbringing was segregated and politically conservative, and yet she did not hesitate to step right into both Spanish and Black Harlem. There she worked to reduce teen pregnancy and joined Students for a Democratic Society, an activist youth organization that was a prominent force in opposing the war in Vietnam with a strong socialist bent.

My mother's appearance made this path as improbable as her upbringing. She looked like a model. She was long-legged and rail-thin, with that ski-jump nose, high cheekbones, and a large grin, which was stunning despite her impossibly large and imperfect teeth. Her intelligence was matched by an open and easygoing nature. She was a bookworm and so composed, yet when she smiled, it was as if she drew back a red velvet curtain to reveal an infectious spirit of joy. In all her school pictures, she is the center, drawing all eyes, the tall peak with others flanking her in descending slopes on either side. She was the debate champion and the senior class girl voted "most liked." Very much like my father in terms of her popularity and the recognition she won with her smarts, but also with her smile. She was not a flirt, however. She was a competitor, but, like Dad, she was a kind one and was well-liked in a society she would eventually shun.

My grandmother was a stubbornly rigid, controlling, and unhappy woman. Diminutive in stature compared to her eldest daughter, Grandmother stood at just over five feet. A bulldog in granny glasses, she was the grammar-school teacher whom everyone knew and feared, as tough and unforgiving as the dry Texas dirt on which she trod. She even returned letters I wrote her corrected with a red pen.

She and her six sisters were "frontier women." My grandmother was the second youngest, a baby when her parents moved southwest in a covered wagon from the plantation part of the Confederacy to the dry and flat ranching part of it. My mother would embrace our lineage for their strength and toughness. She wanted me to know that we came from a hardened stock of people who made a way, but she did not put them on a pedestal. She described her aunts (and her mother was implied here) as mean.

In contrast, my mother was warm and loving and judgmental in appropriate ways. If anything, she was a very forgiving person who always looked to understand the transgressions of others, even when she denounced the behavior. So, her condemnation of these aunts was telling.

Still she would remind me I was a Texan, too, even as I would recoil from the label. This was made more confusing by her refusal to ever let us visit her hometown, something I had no deep desire to do anyway. I always wondered if my mother's forebears owned slaves. My mother, always honest and direct, said that some must have. On her father's side she could confirm it. No one on my father's side lived in Alabama as far as we knew, making it unlikely that my mother's ancestors directly owned my father's, but that was no real solace.

When she was young, growing up in West Texas, my mother looked forward to her family vacations, which involved driving cross-country. One summer, the Whittles' family vacation was a trip to visit her father's distant cousin in Alabama. This branch was revered in family lore as wealthy and successful, but the two groups had never met. So when the family made the drive from Abilene, it was with a mixture of excitement and anticipation.

She told me that when they turned from the main road to the long, straight drive, lined with trees as an arch of wondrous welcome, they saw Black people sitting underneath them, the survivors of its plantation past. Mom described the house as a dilapidated Tara from *Gone with the Wind*. Once they got close enough to see the mansion, they saw parts of the roof were clearly caving in. A desiccated shell of its former racist and violent glory, the house had been falling in on its own putrefying commitment to the past. When they entered the home, it was clear that the condition of the house mirrored that of the people in it. When I asked what happened next, she simply said, "We got back in the car and left."

While there is something very disorienting and upsetting about knowing I was related to people who colonized the West, I felt more disturbed by the fact that my mother was born to parents who admired this antebellum heritage and were eager to visit it. I had no doubt that had their wealth from slavery been preserved, my grandparents, including the little pit bull of a grandmother whom I loved and who loved me, would have stayed and relished that aforementioned visit to the old family home, which had been built on the backs of the forebears of the people who were sitting under the trees on the long, formerly majestic, plantation driveway.

My grandfather, who was a stranger to me, had been a middle-level manager of a savings and loan bank. He and my grandmother had married "late" in life for the times they lived in, when my grandmother was twenty-six years old. My mother was their firstborn and a Depression baby. She told me years later that after the Depression her father became an FDR Democrat because his bosses at the bank ran off, leaving him to foreclose on friends and neighbors. So many families had the bank take their homes and ranches, and my grandfather, Herman Whittle, the tall, blue-eyed, quiet giant, became the face of that loss. He became a pariah for a time but stayed in his post and later went into insurance.

I heard only one real story about my misty apparition of a white grandfather. In Texas, tornadoes posed a real threat to people's lives and livelihoods. People had storm cellars of the type I only knew from annual airings of the film *The Wizard of Oz*. Mom said that they didn't even have a storm cellar. If a tornado appeared on the horizon, Herman Whittle would simply fling open the front door, stand on the porch, and watch with amazement and wonder at the brewing storm. Fear and hiding were not in his nature. In stark contrast, one of my mother's aunts would awaken all her children, roust them from bed, and rush them to the cellar.

Her father's daring seemed a perfect mirror for my mother's own seemingly fearless and wonder-bound steps out of the front door of a closed and claustrophobic West Texas town. Mom, definitely her father's daughter, would walk right out on that porch to look for the social and political storm brewing, but she wouldn't just watch. She would walk with determined strides right into it.

Abilene, Texas, was in Taylor County, which was a dry county when Mom was growing up, and even dancing was not permitted in many towns. My mom was forced to attend church three days a week for Bible study, church activities, and, of course, worship services on Sunday. During the summers she went to Bible school. Church was an unspoken social obligation in that strict society. Despite that, she said, her parents were not all that religious. Her father had stopped attending altogether, perhaps one of the casualties of his dismal foreclosure experience during the Depression.

But in all my mother's history, of which I still know

precious little, there is one part of her story in particular that she never discussed and barely acknowledged, which felt rare and unusual given her openness. She had a younger brother who died at the age of two. She was four, so his illness and death must have been deeply painful. I remember the depth of my love for my brother even at that tender age, and because of it. He was the most central person in my life other than my parents. Her little brother must have been the same for her, but I don't remember her even telling me his name. I looked it up later—Michael. He died from some child-killing disease not uncommon in the 1930s. Was it scarlet fever that took him? Or diphtheria? I can't be sure. I asked my mother very little about him and have always regretted it. It was almost as if her very reticence kept my questions at bay. This was a stark contrast to how she handled the traumas of others, including mine and my brother's. My mother never took any hard discussion off the table, and I knew she would always be honest with me.

It was strange to consider what a brother of hers might have been like. She and her sister, my aunt Sandra, were not close. In fact, they were polar opposites, socially, politically, and even in terms of their interests. It was difficult to imagine that they were born to the same parents and attended the same schools. Only when I was deep into adulthood did my mother agree to answer my questions about how she diverged from what her parents and community raised her to be. Largely that story is about my grandmother. Wretha Whittle Sr. wanted intellectual independence and educational advancement for her daughter, just not the direction Mom took it in. Grandmother wanted her daughter to have a clear path to success and aggressively felled anyone who even remotely threatened to interfere. I often wondered if some of Grandmother's anger and belligerence was about the limits her world placed on her. Her controlling nature seemed to be about taking what power she could claim from within the confines of an extremely oppressive community.

There were a few ways my mother found her freedom, and one was as a competitive debater. This gave her permission to vigorously question the strictures and persecutions of society out loud. Even in 1950s Texas, my mother did not debate women. Oh no. She debated in the men's division where, she said, the competition was better. And she excelled. She described herself as "an arrogant intellectual" who argued against school segregation and for recognition of Red China. She was a fierce competitor on the debate stage and a fierce fighter at the dinner table with her family. To my grandmother's pride and chagrin, she had raised a truly independent daughter who knew her own mind and used it.

Debate, which was a sport second only to football in the competitive landscape of Texas back then, was a permissible tool for my mother to consider and challenge conservative thought. Her debate coach in college was a rare liberal thinker, a personal injury attorney, who saw his role in society as a form of wealth redistribution. He encouraged her, becoming an advocate similar to my father's high school chemistry teacher. She always spoke of him as a key person in her development in liberal thinking in a conservative society.

According to my mother, my grandmother's insistence on her education was not a selfless act but a controlling one. Mom was meant to stay in Abilene, be successful, remain a part of the social fabric, and care for her mother. This was the path Grandmother dictated, and she used her power in the community to pave it for her eldest daughter. And her power was not inconsiderable within the acceptable boundaries.

Back in the days before supermarkets and living in cattle country, Grandmother was accustomed to going to the store and choosing one of the grazing cows in the pasture behind it to claim as her own. It would be butchered and kept in the freezer so Grandmother could come throughout the year to claim parts of her cow. Supermarkets ended that system, but my grandmother didn't care. There was still a pasture out back with cows in it, at least for a time, and she demanded to choose her cow. My petite grandmother was so formidable that the butcher at the supermarket would keep up the pretense of her chosen cow when she came periodically for cuts of it.

At some point, my mother stayed too long in the library to read at her Southern Baptist college, breaking a rule, and she was sanctioned as a result. (She was always an avid reader, so much so that when she passed away, I was confronted with the task of deciding what to do with forty boxes of books in the basement, not including the ones filling several bookshelves in the house.) My grandmother, upon learning of this challenge to my mother's intellectual pursuits, pushed the downturned corners of her mouth even further southward, marched into a dean's office, and ordered him to rescind the sanction. The dean did as he was told.

In Southern Baptist West Texas there were still rules that could not be broken. Racial segregation was one of the big ones. In Abilene, there was a small and mostly poor Black population, but the largest community of people of color were Mexican Americans. They lived, literally and figuratively, on the other side of the tracks from Mom. But the best Mexican food in town was there. One day, my mother and her friends decided to go patronize one of these eateries. They were spotted heading in the impermissible direction. This set off a phone-tree chain reaction that strictly enforced the social order that you did not mix with denigrated "Mes-kins," as the Texas drawl of her time intoned. When word reached Grandmother, my mother was in a world of trouble, but she nevertheless would later cross that racist boundary by escaping to the east. There, she would continuously teach me that social rules and norms that are wrong should be broken, and she would demonstrate just how directly and aggressively one could break them. She would be a Wiley.

CHAPTER 4

PERSEVERANCE

WHEN I WAS YOUNG, I refused to do things that made me feel less than perfect. It started when I demanded ballet lessons after I visited my friend's class as a nursery-schooler. I was too shy to participate but watched jealously as the all-white class of girls pliéd, relevéd, and swooshed their little arms above their golden and mousy brown heads. Mom refused, saying, "It will ruin your legs!" She didn't want me physically tortured with impossibly demanding contortions and the strict regime that came from ballet. Dance, however, was good, and modern was a great choice, according to my mother. I had no idea what modern dance was and refused anything less than my vision.

Mom's friend and our housemate, Harriet, took me when I was a middle-schooler to see Alvin Ailey at the Kennedy

Center. I hadn't been to the high-ceilinged, golden stage of that theater before. My only familiarity with it was its namesake. I was awed by the vaulted, red-carpeted halls, but it was the performance that made me realize my devastating mistake. I watched the grace, power, and beauty of the much more familiar and human movements, which had an emotionally transporting, elegant, and deeply human vibrancy. I had shut myself off to modern dance and I knew I only had myself to blame, though I wouldn't admit it.

I went home and begged to take modern dance classes at a small studio in Tenley Circle. I went one day a week and felt gawky and stiff the whole time. I constantly compared myself to a girl my age, who was in the junior company and had been dancing since she was, well, five. After about a year the teacher announced to Mom that I needed to come at least three days a week to catch up to my peers, since I was of age for the junior company but was lacking in flexibility and strength. My response was to drop out of dance.

That refusal came not out of arrogance but out of a deep sense of inadequacy. I felt average my whole childhood because everyone around me was so astounding. This capitulation to my sense of mediocrity represented something deeper. In my own mind, I could never measure up or bear the weight of responsibility of being a Wiley—to make a difference and be remarkable at what I did. My parents were strong and determined. All Wileys were. I could not see myself having the power and confidence to face the challenges they had.

Wileys made a way for themselves, no matter the odds. Dad's persistence became his pathway. His budding career in science began with the role modeling of his older sister, Lucille, who was a top student at their all-white high school. She loved

46

sciences and wanted to go to nursing school, but Black students weren't welcome. Instead, she won a scholarship to pharmacy school and ultimately became the chief biologist at the state hospital. She encouraged her younger brother's path, as did his high school chemistry teacher.

Among my dad's family, it wasn't just Lucille who had a successful but divergent career path because of race. Shirley, the firstborn, had two fingers stolen from her in a factory accident. She attended Brown University and wanted to be a journalist, like Papa. Denied the typing jobs white women in her position had, to earn her way through school she got one of the jobs allowed a young Black woman, and it was a more dangerous one. She worked in a foundry that made the switch plates for electrical outlets. After she lost parts of two of her fingers, and therefore her job, she joined her father's paper and eventually earned her way back to college and a career as a special education teacher. She finished college at Syracuse University, which was where she would meet my mother. Mom was a new graduate student looking for an apartment and found Aunt Shirley, whose apartment she took over. Aunt Shirley would connect my future parents to each other, not knowing where that would lead.

Dad went to the University of Rhode Island, where his track star brother, Alton, had already been making a name for himself. Both Wiley boys were among the less than a handful of Black students. George, who hadn't yet had his full growth spurt and looked much younger than his age, shot up to over six feet his freshman year. And so began a journey he shared with his brother into being "firsts." Dad quickly went from "Bonny" to "Smiley Wiley" and was the first Black man accepted into his white fraternity. A former classmate of Dad's from college,

Professor Paul Abell, described him as a person "who just had an aura of an interest in life." He was outgoing and always able to talk to everyone about everything. Chemistry, religion, politics, sports, cars.

Always the fun Negro, he would keep his friends' rapt attention with his staged rendition of "Casey at the Bat," the poem by fellow New Englander Ernest Lawrence Thayer, rather than any poems by Harlem renaissance poet Langston Hughes, who intoned the reminder that "Dreams" are something Black people cling to in an America that is not an America to them. In college he continued to wrestle with his inability to date white women. After all, except for family, he was surrounded by peers who were exclusively white. He had to find Black women to escort to the college social events, at which he could be a brother but not a brother-in-law.

The stories I was told about his time in college feel in stark contrast to others I heard. My father and my uncle Al both earned their way through college thanks to the Reserve Officer Training Corps (ROTC), which helped pay for some of their tuition in exchange for service at ROTC camps. Dad got his red roadster in college, having saved up for it through paper routes and other odd jobs. He drove his two white friends from URI to the ROTC camps. But this meant traveling to the segregated South.

The drive from Providence to Washington, DC, which would later become his home, was simple enough. However, the Washington, DC, of the early 1950s had no integrated hotels, so Smiley George Wiley could not stay with his white friends. Dad's response was always to shrug off the racism and then confront it, gently but firmly, even when it came from his Southern cohorts in the ROTC camp. He would talk to them, push them on the wrongs of racial segregation. He himself was the embodiment of the lie that was Black inferiority. It was a powerful tool, and he used it gently but directly.

The Southern recruits would come to him quietly and alone to confess their view that segregation was wrong. But they were never willing to do it out loud, in a group or in any way that might get them shunned. My mother would tell me that Dad would stop at segregated restaurants along the drive to DC and insist with a huge smile that he be served. She joked that he could make a Klansman a friend. He didn't get served, but he was always rejected much more nicely than others might have been because he was so disarming.

Dad was not only a friendly and fun student, he could also be extremely irreverent. Dad didn't want to go to the corporate side of chemistry. He wanted to conduct research and teach. He entered a postdoctoral program at Berkeley in 1959, after a postdoctoral stint at UCLA. This was an important career step to the teaching market, but it did not curb Dad's cheeky humor. My dad apparently jumped onstage, impromptu, at an orientation for freshmen and began to parody the university chancellor, boldly joking in the president's voice, "And I feel that one of my greatest responsibilities as president is to provide sex for the students!" That kind of irreverence would have been boundary-pushing humor for any white student, let alone a Black one. A white colleague from those days described Dad's civil rights activism as "being atypical." At that point in his life, he seemed to challenge all the orthodoxies as his own personal activism. Dad could be comfortably confrontational despite the costs to his rare privilege.

Early on, Dad had rejected the more lucrative corporate chemistry path. During a summer internship at DuPont, Dad thought the employees were too conforming and the job was too limiting. He was eventually accepted to Cornell University's PhD program in organic chemistry. He wasn't the first Black man to get an advanced degree in organic chemistry, an honor that went to Elmo Brady, who, in 1916 earned his chemistry doctorate from University of Illinois at Champaign-Urbana.

According to his Cornell roommate, Malcolm Bell, Dad "could survive anything and work his way through any problem. He had enormous intrinsic confidence." And still, he failed German eight times, which was an unfortunate record, especially as language was a requirement of his degree. That was not the kind of first I imagined he was striving for, and it had to be at least a little humiliating for a Black man in a racist and elite school studying a subject that few Black people take up even today. Bell also said that when Dad wanted to do well, he did very, very well. I can't imagine German being something he cared much about doing well in, but I also can't imagine he wouldn't take a required course seriously. Had it been me, I imagine it would have destroyed me the first time and there would have been no second. In the end, this was a story of Dad's herculean persistence, even in the face of humiliation.

One of the lessons I would later learn about George Wiley was that even someone outwardly confident and charismatic must still grapple with failures and fears. He hated Cornell, according to my mother. Maybe its form of elite racism produced some deeper rebellion or insecurity that made for a shameful performance. He was also a human, capable of succumbing to the pressures of a white social world that was never completely accepting. Being a Wiley, to me, always seemed to include assuredness—how else could a Wiley become "a first fill-in-the-blank"? In all this, Dad was in the top tier of his field—the top 10 percent, according to one colleague from Berkeley, although his so-called white male friends debated this statistic. Whether he was top-tier or not, I know he got where he was despite the obstacles and because of his self-confidence, motivation, and resilience.

Whatever contradictions or perverse challenges drove my dad, they didn't change what being a Wiley meant. It made for a pride-filled family whose name produced successful "firsts." My uncle Al became the first Black state District Court judge and then the first Black Superior Court judge in Rhode Island. Dad was a budding chemist. Decades later the University of Rhode Island built a new dormitory and named it "Wiley Hall" after Uncle Al and Dad, and their "many and varied contributions to the nation, the State of Rhode Island, and the University of Rhode Island."

In sharing this history, Danny and I understood not just our father but where he came from. We were Wileys, too. The thing was, I had no direction or drive. By the age of six, Danny was a talented artist and put all of himself into everything he was learning. His concentration and patience were preternatural. I was the exact opposite. I was concerned just enough to earn a solid but lackluster B average, mostly by excelling at literature and history, to counterbalance my struggles in math and science.

I'll never forget high school chemistry. My brother and I were in the same class, taught by a man I and my friends unaffectionately called Mr. Piggy. He was a terrible teacher, and many of us struggled to understand the material. My brother still excelled, but I got the first (and last) D of my academic career. It was particularly demoralizing when my mother said in response, "Your father was a chemist. You're not supposed to fail chemistry. It's in the genes!" It was a chastisement from a woman who rarely harangued us about grades and never compared us to Dad.

In response I asked my mother, "Well what did *you* get in high school chemistry?" I don't recall her answering the question, but I do see some of my mom in my academic performance. She, too, focused on literature, but it wasn't enough to make me feel I had a direction or a path to follow. My grandmother created a monster of an intellectual and independent daughter who fled at the first opportunity, became a radical lefty, married a Black man, and never looked back. Mom graduated college with honors, unlike her high school classmates and her younger sister, who found husbands to marry in college and started families soon after. Instead, my mother won a prestigious Rockefeller Brothers Fund Scholarship to attend the storied Union Theological Seminary in Harlem. She wouldn't be a seminarian, but a scholar. An intellectual, she was deeply interested in understanding society.

She would describe her way of approaching this pursuit as reading everything, from literature that captured philosophical and theological contemporary thought, like George Orwell and Norman Mailer, to psychologist and dream analyzer Carl Jung, as well as philosopher and activist Jean-Paul Sartre, along with radical theologians. At least, these were among the many authors whose books filled shelves in our home. She had no career path in mind but was committed to serving others and making society a better place.

Texans were not supposed to leave Texas, and the rest of her family stayed put. Mom could get away with it because she was attending a religious institution. But Union was the kind of seminary that included radical thinkers. It was the school of intellectual theological and ethical giants like ethicist Reinhold Niebuhr, whose classes she took, and socialist theologian Paul Tillich, who had only recently retired. Niehbur and Tillich were public intellectual giants of their day, committed to addressing the social questions posed by a mid-twentieth century that had witnessed the near extermination of six million Jews in Europe. Niebuhr, a "Christian Realist," argued, "However large the number of individual white men who do and who will identify themselves completely with the Negro cause, the white race in America will not admit the Negro to equal rights if he is not forced to do so." Mom, like Dr. Martin Luther King Jr. and other activists, was influenced by his realist philosophy, which undergirded so much ethical activism.

Mom was searching for a way to make a better world; she learned that it might not just be good works, as she had been raised to believe. She seemed to have questions that led to more questions, but the exploration was the point, which was why she wasn't particularly interested in a degree. Her days at Union were transformative, a turning point that interrogated her past assumptions and determined her future.

She would learn the contradictions of the left's subtle conformism, and the one upside to the oppressive regime she had fled. In Texas, the rules were clear and the consequences for their violation were, too. She hated them but appreciated the honesty of it all. At Union she would feel manipulated into conforming to unspecified rules, which led her to rebel.

The committee that granted her fellowship was premised on unfettered academic study. In fact, you were not to know your path or have a very clear plan for your course of study. It was an open curricular offer, and she accepted gleefully. The catalog itself promised an extensive experience that would allow her to traverse the intellectual terrain without boundary. However, the Fellowship Committee changed before her fall entry into those ivied halls in Harlem. The president of the seminary now sat on the committee, and he hauled her in for failing to sign up for newly required courses such as Practical Theology, which was a more traditional class designed for the mostly men who would seek ordination and find a flock to shepherd.

Union was changing the rules on her, and she refused to take the required courses. This fight extended for the following two years. The story Mom told was that eventually the dean of women hauled her in to ask about her "personal problems" and suggest psychiatric help. It was sexist and mind-boggling, but my mother was unflappable in the midst of such abusive manipulation. According to her, they won in the end, but it seems to me she did. She stood her ground, and while she stayed the full two years of her fellowship there, she did not earn a degree. Still, the victory was in her getting what she wanted out of the seminary and not succumbing to the seminary's demands of her.

Equally important to the experiences she had at Union were those in East Harlem, where she threw herself into community work. For two years she worked for a religious service organization called the East Harlem Protestant Project. It was not proselytizing, but mentoring girls as young as ten and as old as thirteen. She was not given any materials or instructions other than to help them. It was about education and recreation, and she had a head full of ideas about getting them off their block and seeing the city.

Theirs was one of the poorest blocks in New York. The lithe and liberated young twenty-two-year-old Wretha had set herself up on a block of four thousand residents that were evenly divided among Puerto Rican, Black, and Irish Catholic groups, none of which were people with whom she had previously interacted. And this block had been completely cut off from all city services. No social workers, counselors, or even New York City police officers committed themselves to that single block on East 100th Street between Second and Third Avenues. She was undeterred.

She quickly learned that she would be the student and these young girls would be the teachers. They would not go on outings around the city. The girls refused. It was dangerous for them to leave their block, where gangs battled for turf. She successfully got them to travel only two times, and each time it was only for a walk over the bridge to Welfare Island to sit on blotchy grass and look back at Manhattan.

What tortured my mother was not that these girls rejected her recreational plans for them, but the reality of their lives. They were desperately poor, with some very traditional and controlling fathers. They had a deep interest in sex, which the conservative, particularly Puerto Rican parents forbade as a topic of discussion. They knew more about the practice of sex than she did, coming from her religious background, as she readily admitted. But they needed sex education. They needed to know about contraception and sexually transmitted diseases.

She found it excruciating that these girls were sexually active at such a young age. At the same time, she worried about their experiences, which produced expressions of their hatred for their domineering fathers, who had old-school beliefs about the role and value of girls. Despite a shared conservatism, this was very different from her experience with her own father. She also felt the painful contradiction of the ludicrous loving-father image that the church was presenting these girls each Sunday. It completely contradicted their lived experiences.

My mother decided to put the needs of the girls first. So, they spent most of the next two years talking about boys, sex, and contraception, sitting in a storefront on one of the nation's forgotten and feared blocks. Maybe this was what she meant about that frontier women stock we came from.

In this, there were glimmers of her strength in the face of male authority, but it was only the beginning. There was a block party organized by a gang, which was mostly a social club. The dances happened every Friday night. Despite the more social nature of the gangs, violence still broke out occasionally. A neighboring gang crashed the party and shot it up. A few kids were shot and one stabbed. The first time Mom met with her girls after that incident, the police tried to barge in to question them. They were bullying, demanding in a way Mom described as abusive and domineering. She was angry and she was ready for them. She was not a rude woman, but she was no doormat, either. She refused, telling them she would speak to them when she had completed her activities with these girls. She was stern but reasonable, and they left the storefront. I always hoped that the girls saw some possibility of defiance for themselves in her behavior.

Her time in Harlem set my mother on a path to reconciling not just the good and the bad of her upbringing, but also the manipulation of liberal authority and the ignorance and naivete of her ideas about society. Wretha Whittle the Second left Abilene believing good works could change injustice. Now she knew that she did not and could not completely understand the experiences of the Puerto Rican and Black girls who made up her flock. She could not, despite her two years of commitment and effort, make any real inroads into the harms and challenges they faced, including bad fathers, no fathers, deep poverty, and unresponsive government.

Mom would say that her time at Union and in East Harlem made her a "pessimist." This was not a negative word to her; it was Christian realism. She learned to believe in the innate evil of "mankind" and the relative insufficiency of good works. Mom's clear-eyed view was that society was not fair, and it would likely be impossible to make it so. I never experienced my mother as a pessimist, though. That might be because she also deeply believed in the fight for fairness and justice. Rather than make her give up, this pessimism empowered her to fight, even if the struggle failed. As she put it, "I'd rather work for some goal that I valued, rather than giving up because I can't win." Whatever she called it, I experienced it as a motivating hope bound up not in outcomes but in the possibility of struggle.

After leaving Union Theological Seminary, Mom headed to Syracuse University, where she and Dad found each other. Syracuse University had promised a course catalog that she could traverse seamlessly, which was no truer than the promise of her fellowship at Union. Nevertheless, she continued to take courses in philosophy, literature, and religion. In the Black ghetto, she found and rented the apartment of a student who had recently finished her graduate degree in education, Shirley Wiley—Dad's oldest sibling. It was the fall of 1957, and Mom had a paying secretarial job with the deeply conservative county clerk's office. But, as she had done much of her life, she also found ways to serve. She joined a small neighborhood organization, the Eastside Cooperative Council, a Black neighborhood group fighting bulldozers felling the apartment buildings, filled with Black and largely struggling families, as part of its urban renewal program to remove the "blight," which was code for removing Black people. *Make it white and make it right* was the unspoken mantra.

At that point, Dad was in his postdoctoral program at the University of California, Berkeley, aware that they would not hire him into a tenure track faculty position. His job search eventually landed him a faculty position at Syracuse. A couple years after she'd arrived, in the spring of 1959, Mom went to a party of graduate students and young faculty members, who were what she called a social "cabal." A young chemistry professor announced, "Well, we just hired our first Nobel Laureate." Mom expressed her disbelief. It was a stunning statement because Syracuse had a mediocre chemistry department, and she knew it. He couldn't deny it, but said it was "a guy who would be one soon." This prodigy's name was George Wiley. Mom knew it was Shirley Wiley's brother, and that meant she had no interest in meeting him. My aunt was a strong-willed person and could be a combination of domineering and demanding, so Mom likely assumed Dad would be, too. It wouldn't be a stretch to think that a Black man who had made it through an Ivy League chemistry PhD program and was presumed by the white chemistry faculty to be on the road to a Nobel Prize might be obnoxious. Mom was not a person to tolerate obnoxious people, especially obnoxious men.

Aunt Shirley, of course, didn't know that, and she gave her little brother a list of names of people to look up when he got to Syracuse. That fall, when Dad got to campus, he, unlike my mother, found a place in a white neighborhood. He rented an apartment with a few students on the opposite side of campus from Mom and began to run down that list.

Dad was persistent, which is to say, he was undaunted and

undeterred when he had a mind to do something, in this case create a social life in Syracuse. It wasn't that he had any particular reason to meet Mom. Aunt Shirley wasn't trying to set them up. In fact, the family did not encourage interracial dating. She was just trying to help Dad make a home and find a community. Mom was simply on the to-do list, and Dad wouldn't stop trying to check her off. Despite my mother's best efforts to avoid him, Dr. George Wiley tracked her down. When he called, she felt obligated to have lunch with him because he was new to campus. She decided to just get it over with.

It was a cold, clear, sunny January day in 1959 when they first laid eyes on each other. Wretha Whittle was quickly and very pleasantly surprised. He had come to her office job, where she was doing secretarial work for the dean of the Maxwell School. They walked two blocks to a nearby greasy spoon, and both knew they liked each other by the time they arrived at the restaurant. Dr. George Wiley was easygoing and open. Wretha Whittle was not only intelligent, but she was also an excellent reader of people. I would learn the hard way that she was usually right about my friends or boyfriends. Her impression of George was that he was smart, yes, but he was also infinitely kind, gentle, and honest. She quickly concluded, "He was the finest man I had met in a long time." She was attracted to him, and that was that.

Mom was never focused on Dad's Blackness. She didn't pretend to be color-blind, the way so many race deniers do. Of course, she was conscious of the fact that he was a Black man, but he was immediately familiar. They were both raised in similar, strict Christian traditions and with similar rules and assumptions around what those Christian values required. As she would say, there was no cultural difference between them, only skin color, and that was just appearance. His darker skin was a societal disadvantage and an incidental problem, but not a fundamental one for her.

Naturally, their first date, which was not intended as one, was steeped in politics and that would mark their differences, minor though they might be. It was 1960, a presidential election year and one that would become historic. John F. Kennedy, young, Catholic, rich, a playboy and a US senator, had just announced his run for president. The dean for whom Mom worked was the head of a group supporting Kennedy, which made the group the most left-leaning of organized campus groups that included university leaders. Neither Dad nor Mom liked Kennedy. They agreed that Kennedy seemed an opportunist politician who did not understand the issues of the times and therefore would not be likely to provide the leadership they both agreed the country needed.

The agreement ended there. Dad was a Hubert Humphrey man. Humphrey was a civil rights candidate who understood the importance of addressing racism. As a senator from Minnesota, who had also been a mayor of Minneapolis, he had pushed unsuccessfully for a strong civil rights plank in the 1948 Democratic Party platform. Dad was not yet a political organizer or leader, but he was an engaged participant, carrying a sign and marching for Humphrey. Mom supported Adlai Stevenson. She was the debater who had roiled conservative West Texas by pushing for recognition and relations with Red China, grasping the international problems coming out of the cold war, and she liked Stevenson's comprehension of that greater landscape. Adlai Stevenson was dragged into presidential politics after staring down McCarthyism.

Her favorite Stevenson story was one from his time as

governor of Illinois. Apparently, there was some uproar about stray cats, and some silly proposed law required them to be trapped. Many politicians with aspirations to higher office might have simply signed "the cat bill," which in Mom's view was taking the path of least resistance. Stevenson vetoed it, but he did so in a tongue-in-cheek way, stating that the government had enough to do without trying to control "feline delinquency." There were practical reasons for said veto, but she just loved that it included a statement she remembered years later as "It is the nature of cats to wander about." His actual quote was pretty close: He called it "unescorted roaming," which was even better. He wasn't calculated, and that appealed to her. Stevenson was a lefty, but he was practical and grounded and authentic.

What really mattered to Dad was civil rights. Things were bad for Black people, and Humphrey, for Dad, was the candidate who recognized and addressed that reality, so he had an emotional investment. Mom agreed, of course, but Humphrey was too abstract about what he would actually accomplish.

They also talked about Dad's time at Berkeley and his dislike of the president of the University of California system, Clark Kerr. Kerr was an economist by training who in 1958 ascended to the presidency after being Berkeley's chancellor. Dad saw Kerr as a "pretender to the throne," a power seeker who cared more for his own position than for what was right. Dad was the faculty advisor to an informal group of students at Berkeley who were trying to support the Southern civil rights student movement. A state law blocked them from raising money on campus for political causes. Knowing that law, the Berkeley students intentionally organized a fundraising effort anyway—which put Dad in a difficult position, as they had not consulted him about it, and rightly so. Like all civil disobedience of the movement, it required the breaking of unjust laws as a direct attack on them.

Dad didn't yet understand that the violation of the law was part of the point. He had gone to negotiate a waiver from the requirement and believed he had worked it all out, allowing the students to fundraise for college scholarships to Black students who were expelled from school for participating in sit-ins. The administration had accepted the compromise in principle. The students, however, refused. Dad left before it was resolved, but the students won their fight. This was the beginning of progressive student organizing that, within another few years, would become even more aggressive in protesting the war in Vietnam. Kerr would suggest expelling the students for their antiwar protests, proving Dad's dislike for him was justified. His students' uncompromising activism was also evidently warranted. Those white students taught Dad that you don't necessarily get more if you compromise, and as they talked, he admitted to his future wife that he had been wrong. It made her admire him all the more.

By the time Mom had spent a few hours with Dad, she knew two things. First, his politics and beliefs were not as left as hers. Second, he was a remarkable and admirable person. What had been a routine social engagement for Dad and an obligation to be fulfilled for Mom instead became a date. Dad knew that this was serious, and the pursuit began. He was relentless, according to Mom, calling and seeing her every day. Apparently, she was enjoying it.

Almost immediately, he declared that he wasn't going to fool around with her, this white woman, if she was not open to marriage. He had dated a few white women and his race was always quickly a barrier. He wouldn't be disappointed again. It wasn't a flat-out proposal of marriage, but it was pretty close. She needed to tell him her intentions, specifically whether she could marry a Black man. She understood his need for clarity, but such serious conversations were still very unnatural to her. It wasn't that she hadn't contemplated marriage with a boyfriend before, but the luxury of taking time to consider was one a racist society didn't afford. Psychologically, the decision that she could marry a Black man meant a decision to pursue a very serious courtship within a few weeks of having met him. She resented the pressure but was always pragmatic. Three dates in, she said yes. Mom was not a rash woman, but like my father, she was not ruled by fear. She was decisive her whole life, leaping effortlessly into change as if she were taking an obvious and easy step.

CHAPTER 5

SCHOOL

WHEN I WAS YOUNGER, I often felt adrift, tossed about as my parents sailed on an angry sea with unblinking concentration, following a bright north star so they seemed steady and intentional. I now look back on that perception and realize commitment and clarity are not always connected. I was growing up in an easier time, relatively speaking. I was growing up in a Black city and not their white towns, and was trying to understand how I fit into the color palette they intentionally mixed into grays. They did that by sending little yellow me, for all the politically principled reasons, to the Black neighborhood public elementary school. In my public school the students and teachers were Black, and most of the students were from families struggling with poverty.

But before the overcrowded and hypersegregated Black school, I attended a small, experimental preschool in a posh neighborhood, which we would later move to. It was in a Victorian house in fashionable Cleveland Park, not far from our DuPont Circle home but a world apart. Even my enrollment there was a contrast to my parents' upbringing. My parents had been cared for by their mothers when they were too young for kindergarten, whereas my mother had to send us to preschool because she worked. Somehow, she convinced the nursery school to take me even though I was not yet four so I could attend with my five-year-old brother. The first day my mother deposited me in this foreign land, she also gave me a snapshot of that side of the world, although as soon as I was fully acclimated to it, I would leave to see the other side of this country's racial tracks.

The National Child Research Center, as this nursery school was known, was a massive place to my young eyes. The school was in a large Victorian house, and the yard seemed massive with its real playground, including a sandbox and a slide and a large swath of grass. By comparison, our DuPont Circle row house had no real yard to speak of, just a little patch of grassy dirt, surrounded by a short, black wrought-iron fence with a little gate. It wasn't really fencing at all, just a decorative expression of protectiveness. If we wanted grass to play on, we had to walk to DuPont Circle with its grass lawn encircling a big fountain.

It was the waning years of the 1960s. On my first day of preschool, Mom drove Danny and me in our fire-engine-red boat of a Plymouth station wagon. Danny, dutifully without tears, was peacefully delivered into the hands of a looming white lady, who walked him from the foyer to his classroom. I was not to follow him. That was my first big red flag. He was my constant companion and best playmate. I hadn't planned on separation. The hallway seemed long, dark, and foreboding. I firmly grasped my mother's hand. When the woman returned, my mother tried to deliver me into her outstretched hand, but I refused! Both my mother and this stranger emitted high-pitched tones meant to comfort me but instead simply sounded like warning sirens. I was going to be swallowed by a gaping door into a strange room that did not contain my brother.

We arrived at a compromise: My mother would walk me down the hall herself. Once we arrived at my classroom, I could see light and children getting games and activities off of shelves inside, taking them to little rug squares, and happily sitting on the floor with them. Still, I wrapped my arms around my mother's long, stockinged leg. She was so tall that I was attached only at her thigh. She had to get to work, so she gently tried to pry my viselike grip loose, which only loosened my tongue. The nice white lady bent over and tried to convince me to take her hand. There was only one white lady I was having, and she gave birth to me. I howled louder. As my mother tried to pull my crab pincers off her leg, I slid down that long pole to rest on her foot like a fireman who had not yet decided to run into the burning building. Eventually, they pried me off. Mom told me she loved me and would see me after she got home from work, then made her escape. I watched her rush away down the hall.

I stood there in the doorway, still crying, as another white lady, the teacher, tried to coax me to enter the room. I remained near the door. Some little girl walked up to me and asked me if I wanted to play. It was the icebreaker I needed. It wasn't immediate—I was still reluctant and sniffing tears of fear and loneliness—but it slowly started to thaw as we sat and found the universal language of play. It was a nice place.

I was the only little brown-skinned preschooler. I was the only brown kid at home, too, as home life did not yet include the neighborhood. My life was also very different from that of my classmates. I remember being very little and Mom putting us in bathing suits and walking us down the few blocks to that fountain so we could splash in it. It was against the law, but Mom was unapologetic. Occasionally police ordered us out, and I would feel ashamed and embarrassed.

One of my shame-filled early memories is of three-year-old me in a bubble bath. My mother bought the bubble bath to entice her young ruffians, who ran wild in the back alleys of downtown DC, into the tub to clean up. As I sat with a wash-cloth, it suddenly occurred to me that if I scrubbed myself hard enough, the deeply embedded dirt would dissolve off of me to reveal the slightly beige-tinted white skin of my gorgeous brother or the gently pink skin of my beautiful mother. Maybe then, I wouldn't be ugly. It is a difficult memory, and hard for me to admit.

There were Black girls I thought were beautiful, but I didn't think I was beautiful, and my mother's beauty was undeniable. I desperately wanted to look different, even at that very young age. It's impossible to distinguish the self-loathing I experienced from the larger, quieter messages about race and beauty, and my own efforts to belong to my mom and my brother. All my earliest memories are of feeling different. Dad's Blackness was not contested when he grew up, and it would only be challenged during the Black power movement of the 1970s. Dad had demanded to be seen as raceless in his youth. I was conflicted, determined in my otherness that was also my Blackness, and I was less confident about any of it.

Kindergarten was a different experience but a good one. It was the redbrick lunch box of a building I still view as a quintessential school. I was too young to know that Morgan, a short walk from my home on Eighteenth Street, had been built as a whites-only elementary school. The elementary school for Black children, called Woodrow Wilson, sat on Seventeenth Street, a short distance away. In the 1930s, the Morgan building was deteriorating, so the simple-minded segregationists who ran the district decided to build a new elementary school a few blocks farther from the all-Black school. They named the new school Adams Elementary. Wilson was closed and, as all things racist in America, these administrators moved the Black children to the deteriorating Morgan building. When I sat in a classroom decades later, Adams had become an all-Black school because white residents had long before fled to the suburbs.

All my classmates were Black and, while I didn't know it at the time, there were probably many more kids than was appropriate for a kindergarten. But, like my fancy nursery school, I had more than one teacher in the classroom, which I didn't realize was unusual. As we ran into the square room, our teachers' smiles brightened the place, despite the dingy walls. I can still feel myself sitting in my little chair at the square desk, beneath the big Black upper- and lowercase alphabet letters affixed to the walls well above eye level. We would look up every morning and recite the alphabet after the Pledge of Allegiance and a round of "My Country 'Tis of Thee." My teachers seemed happy, and so we were happy.

I can't remember their names, only that they were relatively young and white. My mother would later explain that

Morgan had an experimental program. In 1967, just a few short years before I would attend, Morgan became a "community school," a model that Black and some white parents demanded to advance school integration. A community leader, Bishop Marie Reed had led the reform movement, and Antioch College offered support. The community model meant that parents and teachers had the opportunity to innovate. Students learned and their performance improved, as measured by testing, but white flight that refused to trust either the program or the abilities of Black students continued to plague the school. I was the beneficiary of this wondrous experimentation, but for only a year.

The model had not failed. Leadership waned, especially after Bishop Reed passed away. The DC Board of Education closed Morgan and merged the students with Adams. In both schools, we all came from the same neighborhood. Both schools were all Black, so the student populations were basically the same. The experiences were not.

Adams was a hard place. It was bursting at the seams and felt hostile. Teachers scowled. The playground was a physical manifestation of the experience inside the institutional building. It was concrete and contained one very rusty, rickety, colorless merry-go-round that was terrifying to ride, especially when too many of us would jump on. The crush of bodies made me feel like I could fly off at any minute and split my head open on the concrete. I vaguely remember a jungle gym that had only a few bars to swing from, but there were no swings and no slides. It was no playground, but kids would find a way to play on it anyway.

Despite its size and the fact that there were white people living just on the other side of Connecticut Avenue, the massive boulevard that connects downtown DC all the way to Maryland, the school building only held two white boys, who were brothers. Like most of my classmates, they had a mother receiving welfare benefits. They lived across the street from me in a basement apartment I never saw. We were not friends, not because they were white but because they, like many of us, were wary. All young children can be mean, sorting each other in inexplicable ways in an effort to find power in relatively powerless lives. This was truer in my neighborhood because of the depredations of policies and biases of others. Government programs and the decisions of landlords, banks, or seemingly well-meaning individuals could offer a hand in help that rose to a slap in the face. Sometimes instantly.

By the second grade, Charlene still could not read. I knew Charlene to be smart. I also knew that lots of smart kids had to have special help to learn to read because my brother, deprived of oxygen at birth, was one of them. But unlike my parents, Charlene's mom didn't have money to send her daughter to the private school on the other side of Connecticut Avenue, less than six blocks from their home. I look back and wonder if our beleaguered teacher had any idea that Charlene was unable to read. Did she know—and with such an overcrowded classroom, was she just forced to batch-manage us? Were there just too many of us for her to know?

Charlene bore the brunt of hard teasing by classmates too angry about their own pain to express compassion. To this day, I am still ashamed of my own childhood paralysis in these moments of vicious mockery. I remember once sitting around in a circle, where we were each supposed to read a few sentences from a shared book. It was a brutal exercise for Charlene. The others were harsh. When Charlene was being teased, I sat, as I often did, in pained silence, fearful that the tidal waves of anger might change direction and sweep me under. I didn't come to Charlene's aid and she, in turn, came to school less and less.

Attacks were inevitable, but not predictable. My paralysis stemmed from that unpredictability. I could be accepted and a playmate one day and become a target of attack the next. More often, a good day meant I was just ignored. It was mystifying and debilitating. I did not feel hated, but I knew I was not accepted, either.

I was an ashy-kneed, white-talking tomboy in frilly, laced plaid dresses sewn by my white, West Texas grandmother. I had an Angela Davis afro to match my dad's, but the other girls had hot-combed braids or pulled-back puffs. I was lighter-skinned than most, but truthfully wasn't the only light-skinned student. It wasn't just my skin color, though. I understood that my mother was a liability for me in my neighborhood from a young age. Her height, style, and grace made her stand out in any crowd, but in an all-Black neighborhood in a segregated city where my classmates lived on welfare checks and school lunches, she didn't make sense. As a result, I had a target on my back.

It didn't help that I did well in school. I had educated parents who read to me at home, and I was learning to read well thanks to my special preschool. I wasn't smarter; I was more privileged. My being at the top of the class meant the teacher would use me—the strange kid with the white mother, who dressed differently, talked differently, and had hair untamed by the hot comb—to "encourage" my classmates through humiliation by comparing their efforts to my shining examples. My teacher held up my wide, ruled green-gray paper with the alternating broken and unbroken lines that we used to practice writing the alphabet. I was a perfectionist with a genius of an artist brother at home and was eager to gain her praise. As a result, I worked extra hard to ensure straight lines and perfect curves. My teacher would berate me for being slow, but then turn around and berate the rest of the class for not being me. No one won.

In first grade, I had some protection. Carlos, a green-eyed, sandy-haired, and very athletic classmate, had a crush on me. Carlos would never be called "light bright," even though he was. He was too strong, too beautiful, and too undeniably able to kick ass. To me, he was a shy friend who would ring my doorbell and quietly walk with me to school. It was sweet and I had no idea that he was my "boyfriend." I received a jealous reverence from the others because Carlos liked me and for no other reason. If anyone started teasing me in class, Carlos was on them like white on rice. The following year, I would learn how much he had protected me.

By second grade, Carlos disappeared. He just stopped showing up at my door, or at the morning bell. He was gone. I had friends like Charlene, of course, but she was an increasing rarity in class. There was also Donna, a nice and pretty girl, light-skinned like me and living in better conditions than Charlene, but still in a visibly less-stocked apartment than my home. I could feel her shame, too.

On the playground, when recess had ended, each class had to line up in its assigned spot to be escorted back into the building by our teachers. One particular recess, I was invisible. Donna had not been playing jacks with me but I found her in line, where she turned toward me with the girls around her egging her on. Her full lips were pursed, her eyebrows furrowed. Her eyes, though, were not angry. I could somehow see that she was pretending despite the fists curled by her sides.

I was so confused and scared. The crowd of kids was gathering around us in anticipation of a fight. A fight over I knew not what with my dear friend, with whom I had not shared one angry word. I tried to talk to her, although I have no idea what I was saying, but she wasn't responding. I was sure she was going to swing a balled-up fist at me. This tore a new hole in my already battered heart. I knew I would not be able to hit her back. In truth, I was not able to hit anyone. It wasn't in me. So I was sure I was going to get beaten up. Luckily, the teacher came and broke up the crowd with a stern threat and the promise that the only beatings that day would come from her. That wasn't an idle threat. In those days a ruler to the arms, legs, and even the behind was still permitted and even approved by parents and principals alike.

I sometimes vaguely complained to my mother about school. But once or twice I did express fear. I remember once asking her what I should do if someone hit me. In her strictest tone, she told me not to hit anyone, ever. Now, if you are going to put your child in a public school like mine, there is only one right answer: Hit back harder. You might even need to hit first, depending on the circumstances. If you land a good punch, it won't last long. If you aren't so good at fighting, at least your challengers might think twice before the next attack. Fighting was expected and the teachers were rarely seen on the playground. In fact, I don't even recall them being on the playground, except when they came to retrieve their charges at the end of recess.

When I asked Mom what I should do instead of landing a blow, she instructed me to tell a teacher. I am rolling my eyes just writing this. It was one of the few memories that I look back on as a reminder that my glorious mother was an imperfect being. I did as she instructed. The next time I was threatened on the playground, I went into the school building, which was forbidden during recess. My teacher was sitting at her desk. She scowled just seeing me walk into the classroom, which was frightening. I remember her pulling one boy's pants down and spanking his behind with a ruler in front of the whole class. I had received raps on my knuckles once or twice, although I have no memory of why.

When I told her why I was there, she became angrier. She looked at me with such derision, I began to shrink at her withering stare. She called me a tattletale in disgust and told me to get right back out on that playground and to never tell on any of my classmates again. I was now doubly humiliated and in much more danger because I'd told. Trembling, I slowly cracked the door and peeked out, searching for an opportunity to slip out unnoticed and hide in a corner of the playground, praying for invisibility until the bell rang and we had to line up to march back in the building. Thankfully, I escaped that day, but I now knew Mom could not, or would not, protect me.

Without thinking very consciously about it, I believed implicitly that I needed Dad to come to school and be seen so that I would become more acceptable to my classmates. Mom made me more foreign, which was the difference between invisibility and a beatdown. I discovered the hard way that it wasn't that simple. I was desperate to feel at school the same way I felt when I was sitting on Dad's lap in his office. Adults entering the room would all remark how I looked just like him. He would wrap me in his arms, and I would feel owned, understood by others, and accepted.

Elsewhere, I felt like a dim, fluttering, faulty bulb next to the high-wattage lamp lights of my parents and brother. Strangers were always trying to understand me. It was like living in a *Sesame Street* segment where Kermit the Frog sang, "One of these things is not like the others." No one had to try hard to guess "which thing" was not like the others. Life as members of an interracial family in the late 1960s and early 1970s made us unicorns or swamp monsters, depending on your point of view. To the general public, we looked unrelated. There were times when I was with my mom in public and someone, most often another white woman, would ask her if I was adopted. The questioner never intended to be hurtful—the need to make my mother and me make sense was all about the questioner and our society's distorted sense of race. It still struck me like a hard slap across my face. But when I sat on my dad's lap, I felt lighter, freer. Even proud.

I begged Dad to come to my school for some event or meeting that the teachers had invited parents to attend. I had to beg him. My busy parents didn't come to my school very often, and anyway, it wasn't the kind of school that had very much reason to invite parents to witness there. I didn't explain why I needed Dad, but I am not sure I could have. Dad agreed to come. It would be the only time.

He arrived as his full and iconic self. I expected no less. He was in his daily uniform, which I didn't see as something that stood out. I knew that kids who were poorer got teased more. It seemed the most important thing was to not look poor, to look as distant as possible from that humiliating and bone-crushing poverty. Dad wore holey shoes because they were more comfortable. They teased me mercilessly after that. I heard taunts of "Light, bright and damn near white" and sometimes threats about whippin' my ass.

My classroom and the lives of my classmates, their anger and the anger of some of my teachers, would create lesson plans the school did not intend, lessons my father began to experience when he went to jail after four little girls were murdered in Birmingham. I would be two years behind grade level by the second grade, despite my parents' graduate education, despite my reading readiness thanks to books at home and early childhood education before kindergarten. My schooling and its depredations would teach me that racism could not be contained, even though we had rid ourselves of the guard at the pool door that barred my father or the women who told my aunt that she couldn't be a Girl Scout. I would learn that gaining entry to these places would not tear down the walls my father had attempted to bulldoze.

My mother would later remind me that I had six teachers in one year and there were teacher strikes periodically because the conditions in the classroom were untenable. It was a broken school system. Beyond addition and subtraction and a bit of long division, I received very little math education, and I recall no science of any kind. There would be a delay in my own educational attainment despite my privileges. I would also feel the loss of my classmates like Carlos and, even more devastatingly, Charlene, as they disappeared into the abyss of gentrification. Loss was becoming normal. I would know what "structural racism" felt like, not just the book learning about it. I had my mismatched parents in my outcast family that fit in nowhere to thank for that.

Neither of my parents attended a Black, segregated school, like I did. The irony would be that fighting school segregation would have a massive impact on the formation of my very family.

CHAPTER 6

SYRACUSE

In October 1963, Mom's contractions started. As far as she and my father knew, there was nothing unusual about my mother's labor. Dad had work to do. At the time, he and other members of their fledgling Syracuse chapter of the Congress on Racial Equality (CORE)—the nation's largest, activist civil rights organization fighting racism and segregation—were deep in a fight to integrate Syracuse's schools. My mother herself had been a part of the struggle, as she always was. In fact, she had helped to start it.

Mom saw a notice in the paper about a public hearing on a geographic change for school assignments for Sumner, their neighborhood school. The new boundary meant that many of Sumner's white students would be reassigned to a predominantly white school, making the Black student population of Sumner, which was fairly integrated racially, increase from about 25 percent to 40 percent. This transition to a predominantly Black school happened as the neighborhood was changing. As white residents fled to the suburbs after World War II, the Black ghetto was growing. My parents' house was in a neighborhood in so-called decline. The ghetto was encroaching. It suited them just fine. They loved the house, and it was close to the university.

My parents had been married for about a year, and Mom was about five months pregnant with Danny, when she saw the opportunity in this issue. They had recently formed the fledgling Syracuse chapter of CORE, which focused on tackling racial discrimination in housing, jobs, and schools.

Cofounded by James Farmer and a multiracial group of leaders, the Congress of Racial Equality began in Chicago with lunch counter sit-ins in the 1940s. CORE was very much a Northern organization, but a pivotal one in the civil rights movement down South. It organized the famous Freedom Rides of 1961, during which future congressman John Lewis, along with many others, was badly beaten. It sent Black and white bus riders to push for enforcement of a Supreme Court decision that proclaimed racial segregation of public transportation unconstitutional. CORE was one of the more confrontational civil rights organizations because its focus was organizing demonstrations, protests, and other conflict-based means of ending segregation and winning voting rights; it would come to rely on a chapter structure, much like the National Association for the Advancement of Colored People.

Syracuse was a hypersegregated city in the 1960s. It was so segregated that almost six out of every ten Black children attended two of the thirty-three elementary schools, and a third school was almost entirely Black. These were not good schools, and Black parents were angry about it. In the full bloom of her pregnancy, Wretha Wiley stood on the steps of a public school, gathering data about the children entering the building so she could make the case that the boundary change would increase racial segregation.

With only a few days before the public hearing, my parents hastily called a meeting at their house. It was attended by as many leaders as they could collect, including the head of their neighborhood association in Thornden Park. They all agreed they needed to fight the boundary shift. There was no time to follow the decision-making procedures their various organizations usually required, so they drafted a statement of opposition and signed only their names. The end of the statement went beyond simply opposing the boundary change of the school—it demanded integration. This was just the beginning.

In May 1962, Dad had locked horns with David Jaquith, a very conservative member of the school board. Jaquith was rich, the owner of Jaquith Industries, and a Barry Goldwater Republican who would challenge Governor Nelson Rockefeller's reelection bid two months later. Jaquith made it clear that he didn't see how Black children were harmed by the boundary change in any way. He said: "I don't accept the premise that racial imbalance creates any kind of missed opportunity. I don't think the school should accept responsibility for solving what is basically a housing problem." The board refused their request to form a study committee, and so the activism through direct action began.

The small group of individuals became a coalition of the Syracuse chapter of CORE, operating through the ad hoc committee my pregnant mother helped form in her living room.

Through the summer, they loudly and, according to Jaquith, rudely, shouted outside of the school board meetings, rallying and picketing, and successfully delaying final decisions on boundaries. The fight continued into the fall, with my mom a central part of the organization alongside my dad, who had become the prominent face of the protests and Jaquith's public sparring partner.

But several months later, on that October day, she went into labor. CORE's, and therefore Dad's, fight with Jaquith was at a pivotal point. She went to the hospital by herself, a white woman pregnant with a Black man's child. She was given drugs to speed the labor and then left alone with her contractions, ignored by medical staff for hours with no husband there to demand attention. Lying there during her first labor, it was clear to my mother that she had been abandoned because her husband was Black. Her baby would be brushed with the paint of a racist society from the start, and this was her first true experience with the life-threatening consequences.

When my brother was born he wasn't breathing, and he was without oxygen for several minutes. My mother always told me it was ten minutes, which feels unfathomably long. Regardless, the actual number is irrelevant—the outcome was all that mattered. The doctor told my parents that their newborn might not survive. Despite the fact that I was not even yet a possibility, this event would shape my childhood.

Luckily, my brother, Daniel, survived the difficult labor but still paid a price for the hospital's racism. My mother explained this to me with her preternatural calm, her eyes deadening a bit as the word slipped from her tongue with an unspoken and unbidden anger. Danny had brain damage that would challenge him significantly. It didn't rob him of his incredible intelligence or artistic talent, but he had great difficulty learning to read. His specialness, through no act or fault of his, would leave me feeling small and inadequate despite my size and forceful personality.

My mother was not a complainer, nor was she a worrier, and she never appeared stressed. She did stay quietly attentive because she believed Danny would require special education even though it didn't yet exist. The first "special education" law wasn't adopted until the 1970s.

My brother's needs resulted in his receiving the bulk of the family resources so he could attend a rarified and radically small, gentle, and supportive private school. This left me to be the "fine" child, as Mommy would not so reassuringly tell me, in my segregated, overcrowded school. This was a very rational decision for my parents to make, as Danny was the true victim of medical racism. That didn't make the contrast of our early elementary school experiences any less stark to me. I felt like an afterthought, not worthy of the love and support Danny received, even though none of my family felt that way about me. In fact, Danny would later tell me he thought I was the lucky one because I didn't have to struggle the way he did with a learning disability. He was right that we both had our challenges. They were just not the same challenges.

The greatest of ironies was that Daddy's absence from Danny's birth was the result of his efforts to integrate Syracuse public schools. This early and important story in my parents' civil rights activism and marriage would define much of the following decade, shaping not only our family life but also my sense of how the world worked.

Years earlier, Mom and Dad's marriage started with an integration victory. They had found a house before they tied the knot. It was in a neighborhood right near campus that was historically white, but the ghetto had been encroaching, making it somewhat integrated. They loved the house and the neighborhood, but the white woman who owned it refused to sell to a Negro, despite them presenting the best, and I believe the only, offer. Their broker was a white woman who was also a member of the local NAACP and, unlike most white brokers, spent a lot of energy trying to ensure Black people could live where they pleased. She was swimming hard against a fast current. Dad was up for the challenge. Dad set out to organize the fight to win the house.

Dad showed up on the owner's doorstep, charming and with his sweet, open smile, wearing the suit of his academic position. He was the picture of respectability. Dad's strategy was simple: Confront this white woman head-on. He simply asked her flat-out why she wouldn't sell to him. She denied her own racism, of course, confronted by this respectable professor, soon to be a family man, who would be a wonderful neighbor, he assured her. This owner insisted that the neighbors were the only reason she wouldn't accept his offer. Now he had her! He made this racist woman a deal: If he could get the neighbors to agree to have him as a neighbor, she would sell to him.

The next step was to use his complete self-possessed security and confrontational nature to gently but directly take advantage of the neighbors' politeness and inability to express their racism to his face. He went to every neighbor's door, rang the bell with a natural sense of belonging, introduced himself and his considerable credentials, and then asked if they objected to him moving in next door. As my mother put it, "Every last neighbor swallowed their feelings and their property values." They found themselves completely incapable of admitting that yes, they objected to someone Black moving in next door. And Smiley Wiley was a hard man to say that to. Dad had won.

The owner of the house was furious when he called her bluff and emerged with the consent of neighbors who she was certain would protect their silent conspiracy. My parents now had a house, one that would become the organizing grounds for a civil rights crusade bent on protesting racism, which was just as prevalent in Syracuse as in Selma. But in that moment, in that victory, the plan was only to be a married couple, have some kids, and watch Dad make breakthroughs in organic chemistry, while Mom pursued whatever intellectual endeavors and interests she could sustain as a wife and mother.

Mom was adjusting to her single-minded husband turning his attention back to chemistry, having achieved his heart's desire to marry Mom and to buy a home. Now it was back to his research. He still had that Nobel Prize to win. Mom continued her campus organizing. She started a chapter of Students for a Democratic Society (SDS). Founded just a year earlier at the University of Michigan, SDS was a radical student movement that challenged war, racism, and poverty, and demanded a new form of participatory democracy.

She turned their modest, four-bedroom, shingled home, with its backyard, into a gathering place for activists and intellectuals. Dinner parties were political salons for exploring societal and global issues and their solutions. Their community included Eduardo Mondlane, a faculty member teaching history and sociology who would, in 1962, became the president of the Mozambican Liberation Front (FRELIMO), which fought to oust Portuguese political rule over the colonized country. Dad said to Mondlane, on hearing his plans to liberate his country, "You can get killed for that." Mondlane's reply was, "I expect to be." He would be murdered in 1969. This was a familiar story to many Southern Black organizers.

It also meant houseguests like Tom Hayden, an activist and the first field organizer for SDS. Hayden would later marry actor Jane Fonda and become a congressman from California. But my parents met him in the early days of his activism and not long after he wrote SDS's manifesto, which adroitly described my parents. Hayden had written, "We are people of this generation, bred in at least modest comfort, housed now in universities, looking uncomfortably to the world we inherit." He wrote those words, or at least began to, in an Albany, Georgia, jail cell in December 1961.

Hayden was not someone my parents knew personally, but in early 1962 he was traveling the country, visiting chapters to fundraise for the work in the South. In those days, people made their homes available to traveling activists. Mom described Hayden as exhausted after his grueling but historic year of brave protests and abusive responses that came to be called the Albany Movement.

While SDS has been known for its anti–Vietnam War activism, in the early 1960s, SDS was an organization for white allies in the civil rights movement. The famous and impactful Student Nonviolent Coordinating Committee, founded by Diana Nash, Julian Bond, John Lewis, and Marion Barry (later my city's mayor), was the primary organizing arm of Black students in the movement. SNCC had focused its attention on organizing in Albany, Georgia, in the fall of 1961. It garnered more national support and attention after nine local Black college students began a sit-in at the bus station. The NAACP, Martin Luther King's Southern Christian Leadership Conference, and other organizations followed their lead and formed the Albany

Movement to engage in an all-out direct action campaign to break the back of racial segregation in the small Georgia city. Hayden and SDS joined, and he was part of the mass arrests.

The police chief there knew to avoid the most brutal of public violence, which would only earn protesters more supporters. Nonetheless, the jail conditions and treatment were horrific. Hayden was not only exhausted from the activism, the arrest, and being on the road, he was actively harassed by FBI agents along the way. A call to each FBI field office from national headquarters would precede him, and he would be contacted for questioning at each stop.

Agents knocked on my parents' door late the night Hayden arrived. Mom, angry about this game of harassment, answered the door and firmly told the agents that Hayden was not available. I don't know the exact words she used, but I can just see the taut downturn of her mouth, her thin lips pursed tight, and her eyes glaring as she defied them. She would be extending her Modigliani neck. Hayden rushed to the door, telling my mother it was all right. He would speak to them. His unspoken message to her, it seemed, was, *This is wrong, but it will be worse if we don't cooperate.*

Once, years later, the electricity went out at our house as Mom was hosting an event for Dr. Benjamin Spock. The "real" Dr. Spock, as I liked to think of him given my love for *Star Trek*, was a famous pediatrician who saved my behind. Literally. He single-handedly stopped my spankings with his book on parenting. Dr. Spock was also a political lefty and was running for president as a third-party candidate in order to push the Democratic Party (Chicago) to the left. Mom was an active supporter. When the electricity went out, my mom told my excited brother and me that the FBI cut our power. I completely believed her, though she was probably joking. Even as a child I knew the FBI was not an ally in the fight for our rights.

There was some tension for me decades later when, as an MSNBC legal analyst, I defended the FBI from Donald Trump's troubling "deep state" conspiracy theory attacks that were dangerous and without present-day merit. I knew that some FBI agents were themselves politically conservative and not very sympathetic to activism. If it weren't for the context and circumstances of Donald Trump's obviously corrupt, illegal, and often unconstitutional behavior, I would have been reminding people of COINTELPRO, the infamous program to spy on and disrupt the civil rights movement, which J. Edgar Hoover placed right up there on the enemies list with communists.

At the time of Hayden's visit, my parents were yet to fully leap onto a more activist path, but it was coming quickly. They had married in the spring, and by the fall they had helped form the Syracuse chapter of CORE. Black discontent with violent and humiliating racism in the South was building, spurred by activism like the 1960 Greensboro, North Carolina, Woolworth lunch-counter sit-ins; and by SNCC organizing, with young leaders like Bob Moses in Mississippi and John Lewis in Alabama. These events awakened a critical number of white college students. The waters of anger and moral outrage that built up behind the dam of fear and the silent acceptance of white privilege could not be held back any longer. In 1961, my dad would contribute to the dam breaking in Syracuse.

Rudy Lombard, a new graduate student on campus, was key to CORE's formation. A Black organizer from New Orleans, Lombard was tall, dark, and so damn fine, as my friends and I would later say. He could only be described as beautiful, even as I knew him in his fifties. Twice my age and still hard to resist. I remember Mom joking that when she met him, she wondered if she had picked the right man to marry. It was impossible not to be attracted to him, but his physical beauty was matched by his tenacious activism and intellect.

Unlike Dad, no one would question Rudy's Blackness, and, in parochial Syracuse, he was significantly more worldly for having been in the trenches in Louisiana, a dangerous state to organize in. Rudy had risen up as a leader inside of CORE despite his youth. At twenty-two, Rudy was the vice chairman of the National Action Committee (NAC), an advisory committee made up of the leaders of many local CORE chapters. He first met Mom and Dad at one of Mom's SDS meetings. Mom had always described him as an activist in exile—the realities of how dangerous Black activism was in the South were not lost on her. And Rudy would tell me later that he never married because he thought it would be unfair to a family. His assumption was he would be killed for his organizing.

In New Orleans, where Rudy grew up—and would later run for mayor, only to lose to a more traditional Black candidate—Black longshoremen had been organizing for labor rights since the turn of the twentieth century. Syracuse, on the other hand, was a place he found depressing in appearance and in personality. It was a working-class city, and the university campus lacked the ivy-covered, historical grandeur of other Northern universities. Black people were not "vibrant," by which he could only have meant that they were beaten down. The Black community wasn't large, either. There were only about fifteen thousand Black residents, and they mostly lived packed in a couple of neighborhoods. While the lack of charm, community, and activism in the city was a shock, the race discrimination was quite familiar.

A student invited Rudy to Mom's SDS meeting. Mom was already noticing a change in the incoming class of white Syracuse students—they were more militant. Rudy's arrival, and the founding of Mom's SDS group, coincided with Dad challenging segregation on campus. Dad was a popular young faculty member and had been a member of a white fraternity in college, which led campus fraternities to request he be their faculty advisor. They seemed to think he would be a relatively blind supporter of their social role and culture even though they were segregated. He agreed and immediately demanded they integrate. It caused an uproar on campus. There weren't many Black students on campus to integrate, but that was beside the point. He would win the battle, but it was also a demonstration of his willingness to rock the boat of campus racism, even without the protection of tenure. Dad was also awakening to something deep inside himself that couldn't be satisfied with simply making campus life a bit less racist.

Rudy was committed to the work in the South, so he wanted no part of leading a Syracuse CORE chapter, but he agreed to help found it. While Rudy was just passing through, Dad was a presence. As an organizer, Rudy saw immediately that Dad was a leader and held a unique position in the white community as an accepted Black man, one who had integrated his neighborhood and was pushing the campus to do the same. He was a natural choice, and the school boundary fight would establish their fledgling chapter.

In the midst of the fight, my pregnant mom was living and breathing the school boundary and integration fight morning, noon, and night alongside Dad. It was their shared passion and commitment. And they would move forward together, facing what might come, refusing to be resigned to the unfairness of the country and refusing to become complacent in the face of its injustices. Despite being pregnant, my mom didn't need coddling—frankly, she might have received the same poor medical care even if he had been present at Danny's birth. My parents blamed racism, not activism, for my brother's stolen breath. For both, this first and most significant experience of racism had deep emotional impact, and it would strengthen their resolve, not shake it. Syracuse CORE was born. And so was my brother.

They had been, very reasonably, demanding a study group to look at the impact of the boundary changes on Black children's education. The request fell on deaf ears. After months of protesting, in September 1962 CORE organized a massive rally outside the school whose boundary change they were fighting. Five hundred Black parents attended as my dad shouted to the crowd, "We have demonstrated today that Negroes in this community have the will and the courage to stand up for their rights." It was true and it was new. Black Syracusians were not beaten down that day. It forced Jaquith to agree to hear Dad out in the October 1962 semimonthly school board meeting. There Jaquith said that *if* my father could find a way to prove that segregation undermined the education of Black children, then he would support CORE's demands for integrating schools. In that public meeting and on the record, my dad looked at his nemesis and proclaimed, "I will convince you, all right."

My brother was born shortly after that battle between the white conservative industrialist and Dr. George Wiley began. Dad, and CORE, believed in truth as the best strategy to gain the support of opponents like Jaquith. He took a personal approach. Dad convinced Jaquith to test housing discrimination with him. They both saw the same apartment or house and Dad was denied the place Jaquith was offered. Afterward, the crusty conservative Jaquith couldn't deny discrimination was very real. Step one was complete. Step two required reviewing documented cases of racist expulsions of Black students without any real explanation, as well as instances of white teachers expressly telling children they were incapable of learning. When Jaquith blamed others outside their system, like the Southern schools Black children had come from, Dad showed evidence that they weren't taught to read in Syracuse schools. Dad methodically knocked down one delusional and unquestioned assumption after another. He didn't just present documented research; he took Jaquith to sit with Black parents and hear firsthand about the abusive treatment their children received, from unprompted explosions without cause to the humiliation of low expectations and racism.

The Barry Goldwater conservative conceded. They never became friends, but my mom said Jaquith and my father came to respect each other. Now Jaquith was leading a process to consider how to integrate Syracuse's schools. And by the summer of 1963, a year after Syracuse CORE's actions, the State Human Rights Commission would take up the call.

At the same time Dad was dueling with Jaquith, he and my mother were wondering if the racism they'd so recently experienced would result in serious developmental disabilities for my brother. Mom said Dad adored Danny and would stare tenderly at his newborn son when he was home. Both watched Danny like a hawk, but he seemed happy, lovable, and to be developing relatively normally. I don't think their guard ever completely dropped, but it certainly lowered after some time.

My parents would eventually conclude that they had come too late into the school desegregation fight. While they would win the battle and Jaquith would continue to champion school integration, Black parents were starting to turn away from the strategy, angry over the poor conditions their children found themselves in. Later, I would directly encounter this sentiment in my own work to advance quality education. My parents' lessons along with my own personal experiences would shape how I would respond to questions of school integration in my career as a civil rights lawyer and counsel to a New York City mayor, because the personal is the political and the political demands and decisions we make are always personal.

CHAPTER 7

AWAKENING

IT WAS MONDAY, SEPTEMBER 16, 1963. Rudy ran to my parents' home, where they and other CORE leaders were planning the second day of protests in their latest fight to stop the bulldozing of the Black neighborhood in Syracuse as part of what was known as "Urban Renewal." As always, our home also housed many meetings. Everyone was in the backyard. The weather was still balmy that time of year. When Rudy arrived, he shared the devastating news that the 16th Street Baptist Church in Birmingham, Alabama, had been bombed. Four little Black girls—Addie Mae Collins, Cynthia Wesley, Carole Robertson, and Carole Denise McNair—were dead. Like much of the rest of the country, everyone gathered was shocked, angered, and utterly destroyed by the news of the hateful murders. I doubt there was any question as to who the perpetrators were. It was more than a reminder that civil rights work meant accepting life-threatening violence. It meant any horror, every horror, was possible at the hands of hate.

The gathered group, my father at the helm, was in the midst of their greatest organizing campaign yet. Just two days earlier, Syracuse CORE led hundreds of people to protest the demolition of the Black community. The marchers included my mom, visibly pregnant with me and carrying Danny, who was just a few weeks shy of his first birthday. As part of the plan, several CORE members, mostly graduate students, had run onto the site of the condemned building, the demolition of which would make way for an interstate that would split the heart of the community, giving displaced Black residents no place to go in the segregated city.

Mayor William Walsh and the police department were having none of it. For the first time, the police responded by arresting those who climbed on top of the bulldozers and the buildings to be leveled. Fourteen in all were arrested. The news outlets took notice, and my father felt they were finally gaining momentum. I imagine his excitement was tinged with the danger and uncertainty of how the state might punish these protesters.

Dad was the behind-the-scenes guy: the strategist and negotiator. He also helped fundraise the bail for the jailed disruptors from distantly concerned white liberals who were unwilling to sacrifice more than cash. In addition to assisting with fundraising, Mom was the researcher and organized the volunteers who had agreed to be arrested.

But now, four little girls were dead. It was too much. Dad made a decision, a rational one that I nonetheless imagine was led by emotion. But it would have consequences I am sure he didn't expect. The violence in Birmingham called him out of himself. He would no longer just be the professor who worked as the behind-the-scenes strategist and public negotiator. He remained deeply committed to nonviolent action and now, more than ever, leaders had to prove that nonviolence, a method of protest Bayard Rustin had brought to the movement after his travels in India, was critical to the civil disobedience strategy and could produce results. It created images of contrast. Peaceful people simply asking for dignity in the face of brutality by the police officers who would arrest them. Dad decided to turn himself into a symbol of the action he so believed in.

The next day, Dad went from meeting with his doctoral students straight to the demonstration. The news cameras were there, too. The police were ready for them, having encircled the condemned buildings to protect the investment interests of wealthy developers and contractors against the Black residents long abandoned there, poor, policed, and now being displaced.

Dad waited for his chance, eventually spotting a way to break from the marchers and dodge past police officers. As he did, he yelled, "Remember Birmingham!" The police were incensed that he got past them. The picket line had been orderly despite the heightened emotions marchers likely felt, so his sprint must have surprised the police. Three policemen tackled Dad and angrily yanked his arms behind his back, spraining one, and he grimaced in pain. He wasn't just an angry white radical kid or a rough-and-ready Negro from the ghetto. The public witnessed the promising chemistry professor, the smiling, pleasant, and well-spoken Black man who wore suits and a lab coat, being roughly handled. The image of this pillar of the community protesting mattered in that moment, just as it had for Rosa Parks in Birmingham.

Not satisfied with the symbolism of his defiant act, Dad refused bail in hopes of spurring more action. The Willow Street jail was a horrible place. It was the first time he was not just treated as unequal but denied more basic humanity. The conditions were so horrific that the experience would profoundly change his emotional investment in the movement.

Upon his release three days later, he went straight to a rally at a Black church, where four hundred supporters waited to cheer him. He was ashy and bruised, and his arm was in a sling. He had not come with a speech to rally them, and his very physical condition must have stunned them. The handsome, congenial professor was now a shaken and disheveled man, slumped under the weight of his experience in jail. He now understood viscerally that human hearts could be harder than his gentle Christian parents allowed him to imagine. He did not begin his remarks with the bulldozers. He did not draw on the charge, electrified by his defiance, now radiating through the room. I have felt that kind of current, almost like a shared heartbeat, with a pounding that bounces off each person, rather than the walls, an echo that doesn't fade as it spreads across the room but radiates. Everyone is a semiconductor.

Dad's presence in that church could have become the tuning fork for the humming passion in that room, but his heart was broken. He began solemnly telling the audience what it was like to be in that jail, where rights as basic as being told your rights, given access to a lawyer, were denied. He described the conditions as "cruel and unusual punishment." "You sleep on a board without a mattress or blanket or springs. Your only protection from the cold is whatever clothes you happen to have on your back. Prisoners are fed survival rations, and I found people who were extremely hungry and underfed. No exercise is permitted. No books or writing materials are permitted. You couldn't read anyway. There isn't enough light."

He went on to talk about the beatings police delivered upon their charges. He broke down. Dad, Bonnie, Smiley Wiley, Dr. Wiley, George, shook and cried in front of those four hundred onlookers. I was not yet on this earth, and if I had been, I would have been shocked to see my father cry. The father I knew, already shaped and changed by that experience and others to follow, never cried in front of me. He always seemed to smile in the face of insults, persist in the presence of pugilists, and face down anyone at any level who got in the way of the movement. That night the intrepid, optimistic, confident man, as calm and steady as they came, could not contain the emotion of what he experienced.

When he stopped crying and composed himself, he said the words I repeat always, that my parents taught me to live by. "We have work to do." Dad, the activist, had been fully awakened. It would change everything.

My brother and I did not grow up like our parents. We knew about getting arrested. For the most part, it was something I considered as a normal part of the adult lives surrounding me and my parents, who rarely expressed fear. I remember a particular night when my brother and I were very young, which was otherwise typical. Mom was in my parents' bedroom with the nightly news playing on her television, the only color TV we had, which sat on a little stand at the foot of their bed. On Sundays, Danny and I would sit and watch our weekly Disney movie on that TV. But this was a weeknight, so we were playing in our bedroom down the hall.

With that air of excitement, Mom yelled out to us, "Kids, come quick, Daddy's getting arrested!" We ran down the hall on our toothpick legs and plopped down in our usual places, as if she was yelling, "Disney is starting!" Dad was handcuffed and being held by policemen, shrouded in his unwavering air of calm, composed with that sense of routine that comes with years of orchestrated arrests. My only question was whether he would be home before bedtime. He would not.

During my childhood, police were not our friends and did not protect us. "Officer Friendly" came each year to my elementary school to address us in the auditorium. It was always the same speech. "Don't talk to strangers. Don't take candy from strangers." And every year the police officer addressing all the Black students was also Black. I liked this ubiquitous Officer Friendly, who bore no resemblance to the ugly, angry, violent police officers on TV who didn't like protesters. The police officers who put Dad in jail were mostly white men. Intentional though that was, police remained a symbol of violence and reflected the power of politicians and business leaders who didn't like the protesters' demands. By being arrested you got TV cameras to draw the public's attention to the problems and their possible solutions. Politicians were more interested in stopping the disobedience. This was what we understood as children.

Even as we understood the possible impact being arrested could have, my brother and I were not raised to be disrespectful by our mother. Once, a police officer rang our doorbell. I answered, immediately yelling, "Mommy there's a pig here!" I said it like it was synonymous with "police officer." It was not a word that was used in our house, but it was one impossible not to hear out in our community. I heard her voice drop almost an octave and got a very stern, "MA-YA!" Whenever Mom empha-sized both syllables of my name, I knew she was angry.

I admit I was being a bit mischievous, but I also sincerely thought she would laugh or sneak a wink or a smile at me. Instead, she apologized profusely to the police officer, and I got the "we don't use that word" lecture. I would never use that word again. To this day, my brother still likes to remind me of that story on holidays.

As children we also understood that police could be dan-gerous, although we never experienced that danger directly. My mom did not have to fear the police growing up, nor did my dad because of his unique experience in his town. Mom did not shield us from the realities of the world, although as she explained them to us, her voice always flowed with the cadence of a babbling brook. One of the most disturbing stories she told was about Bruce Thomas, a CORE member, who was stripped naked and given a brutal beating in that same Syracuse jail.

Bruce was tall, and he had a dark chocolate complexion to match his deeply resonant voice, which was a baritone to my father's tenor. He used his voice as an organizing tool, often bursting into song to bring people to the moment, the emo-tion, the call to action. My mom once told me that in a skeptical church or community meeting, Bruce would just walk up to the front of the room and coax the group into the organizing action with a song, and eventually he would lead everyone in a march around the room.

I loved Bruce Thomas so much. He was like an uncle to me and was one of the few people who could have commanded me to any task or chore without a fight. When he called me "baby," it was like a warm hug that I didn't even know I needed. In some ways, Bruce made me feel what I wanted from my dad.

With Bruce there was no sense of distraction when he walked into my house and lifted me up. He was all there and just for me, even if just for a few moments. He would toss me in the air, and I would squeal with glee at the sheer height. I knew that he would always catch me.

My mother always spoke about Bruce with great tenderness, so I assumed everyone who knew him shared our love. One day, when I was much older, probably in high school, we fell into a conversation about him. Mom never hesitated to talk about the CORE days or what followed them, but she didn't reveal all the pain of it, either. It wasn't her way to dwell on the bad, even as she acknowledged it. The topic turned to the police in Syracuse. Mom, staring distantly, with slightly downturned thin lips, recalled how Bruce had been stripped naked and badly beaten in that same dungeon my dad spent time in. Her point was that it was something that happened to Black people. To Bruce.

She didn't share additional details. She didn't have to. Just the idea of him naked and being beaten in a basement was more than I could bear. Bruce was a powerful man who, as far as I was concerned, made a dark room bright. His brutal humiliation shook something deep inside me. I knew that he would never be in that jail for any other reason than having confronted racism with action. In my world, everyone went to jail at some point, and usually with purpose. This story was part of my education, as I came to understand that not all arrests were intentional. We were all equal, but we were not all treated equally. This reinforced what my mother always reminded me, "Life isn't fair."

Bruce worked in the General Electric factory, having never finished high school. In fact, he never finished the ninth grade, but I didn't know that as a child. He was a kid who became a "juvenile delinquent" and was incarcerated as if he were an adult. As a result, he grew up in prison. That was not who or what he was. But to the police, he was not a person. He was not a religious man or a beautiful singer or even worthy of love by all of us who loved him.

Housing discrimination was a primary focus for CORE, and Bruce, like every Black person in Syracuse, had suffered its humiliations. The urban renewal fight began because it was at the heart of how Black people were ignored at best and abused often. Dad had gone directly into Black churches to recruit community members to their cause. He asked Black pastors to allow him to speak from the pulpit on Sundays, and that was how he met Bruce, at the Missionary Baptist Church. Dad was not charismatic in the way of traditional Black Baptist church leaders, like Martin Luther King or Jesse Jackson, nor was he familiar with the anger of the streets that Bruce knew. But he made sense, was passionate, and had a vision and purpose Bruce could feel. As Bruce would say, it was Dad's smile that won people over, and his open nature that made Bruce feel accepted. It would change the course of both their lives.

Bruce and a powerful middle-aged woman named Anna Mae Williams became CORE's first recruits from the Black community of Syracuse, outside of the ivied campus of the university. Ms. Williams would later say, "George gave me a glimmer of what I have been looking for all my life…George lit the lamp in me and he stirred up something that has continued to burn."

Unlike graduate students and even faculty at Syracuse, Bruce had much more to lose than gain by joining the fight. Relatively speaking, he had a decent job and was doing better than many. The backlash against Black organizing could mean everything from losing a job to harsh police brutality and harder jail time. Still, Bruce became the chapter's most important organizer.

Dad and Bruce grew close in those early days. Dad saw in Bruce the face of the work they were doing. At one event with hundreds of people, Dad asked Bruce to speak. Bruce was incredulous. He was a factory worker, not a public speaker. Dad encouraged him to just speak from his heart about what he felt. Once Bruce did that, he realized that he, too, was a leader. Dad believed in Bruce, so Bruce started believing in himself. Dad elevated Bruce to chapter chairman, recognizing the need for leadership that was from the Black community of Syracuse, not the halls of the university. Dad would remain a researcher, a strategist, and a negotiator.

That night in jail changed my father, but it also fueled the fight.

Criminal justice reform was now on the agenda. The struggle to assist Black people displaced by urban renewal continued, and the fight to close the jail began. That jail was the City of Syracuse's most honest and unapologetic statement of how it viewed its Black residents. CORE started referring to the one-hundred-year-old building as "the dungeons." The cells might as well have not had toilets, given the condition of the facilities. But Black Syracusans like Bruce didn't need Dad's description. They had experienced the deplorable conditions, which Dad hadn't really believed were as bad as described. Most people behind bars in that jail were Black, and most had not yet stood trial. It was overflowing most days and, as Dad had learned along with the Syracuse students and staff, people could be housed there for two and three weeks.

The mayor disputed CORE's claims of the Syracuse police department's brutality. He called the charges a "complete fabrication." He claimed it was a national strategy to disgrace law enforcement, sounding very much like Southern mayors and police chiefs.

Ultimately, CORE won the fight to have the old jail demolished. It meant a new jail, but at least the conditions would be more humane, mirroring debates I would later be a part of on closing the infamous Rikers Island jail in New York City and the larger discussion about jails and prisons we're currently grappling with as a nation. However, the story that fascinates me the most about these efforts came about during the "Freedom Summer" of 1964. White college students from around the country were traveling to Mississippi and other Southern states to help Black people dealing with discriminatory voting laws and the constant threat of violence or unemployment for merely trying to register.

Riots were breaking out in Black neighborhoods in cities across the country, stemming from the murders of Freedom Summer CORE workers James Chaney and Michael Schwerner, along with a volunteer named Andrew Goodman, near Philadelphia, Mississippi. In Harlem about a month later, a New York police officer shot and killed James Powell, a fifteen-year-old Black boy. A rally focused on the Mississippi murders turned into a march on the local police precinct to demand Justice for James. That march morphed into the first major explosion of pent-up rage and pain that resulted in four days of brick throwing at police officers, smashed storefront windows, and looting. It would not stop in Harlem. That spark of justified anger flew, lighting a tinderbox that spread all the way down to Philadelphia and all the way up to Rochester, New York, just a short ninety miles away from Syracuse.

Black folks in Syracuse's Fifteenth Ward had just as many reasons to be angry as Black people in Harlem and Philadelphia. The CORE chapter heard that aggression was spilling out of neighborhood bars. Knife fights were bleeding onto the streets as the temperature rose that July. CORE leaders—again, largely white Syracuse graduate students, including my mother, who now had two babies at home—ran down to the neighborhood to do whatever they could to calm the unrest. They didn't hesitate, which a CORE member and graduate student, Ed Day, would later describe as "reckless." It clearly was. They, including Ed, were white. Neither my mom nor the other CORE members knew what to do, and Black people were pissed off. They were reckless but not naive. They understood that if violence was breaking out, they would become targets. The blinding nature of that kind of rage would not see the CORE people as allies. Black participants were not in the mood for white people to tell them to calm down.

This story always reminds me of the video of the hate-filled, brutal beating of Rodney King in Los Angeles by LAPD officers. I was a newly minted lawyer, just off my two-year federal clerkship with a wonderful District Court judge in Philadelphia. Now I was in a national fellowship at the American Civil Liberties Union watching the news in horror and anger, then in dismay as the violence erupted in South LA. A white truck driver named Reginald Denny would be a passing victim. That could have been my mom that July day in the Fifteenth Ward.

Dad rushed to the police department and met with Commissioner William H. T. Smith. He didn't hold back. He said,

REMEMBER, YOU ARE A WILEY

"Your policemen are about to start a riot!...Get those damn police cars out of here." Those would be eyebrow-raising words even today, but in 1964 a Black man talking to a white police commissioner like that was unheard of. But Dad knew that Black people were stoked into violence by the abusive behavior of police, whose idea of "peacekeeping" in the Black community was to assert their brutal authority. Their presence was its own provocation.

The police patrol cars had begun to roll in to prevent what was happening in nearby Rochester. Smith's leadership told Dad that he was crazy, but somehow Smith was moved to do as Dad advised. Maybe it was the shock of the passion and clarity Dad brought to that impromptu meeting, or the fact that George Wiley could move hundreds of Black people to protest, which meant he might be able to calm them. Maybe it was because Dad had earned the respect of the city's most prominent and deeply conservative Republican businessman and powerbroker. No matter the reason, he convinced Smith to ignore his own brass and take the risk.

Dad ran from the commissioner's office to the street corner. The police pulled out, and Dad convinced the gathering crowd to go home. There was no riot in Syracuse that day.

Ed Day later remarked that Black people in the Fifteenth Ward were shocked and impressed that Dr. George Wiley's white wife was in the streets. I seriously doubt that it ever occurred to Dad that she shouldn't be, or to either of them that she needed his permission. It was a joint mission, and they were committed.

I would not personally have a jailhouse awakening because I inherited Dad's. I didn't know the dungeon, but I knew it existed. I hadn't known Bruce had spent years of his young adulthood behind bars, but I knew how kids could be denied so much and end up there. I had not visited a jail or prison until I was in my thirties, but I knew they meant hard hearts and harsh conditions, especially for Black people. I would get an opportunity to see the way the political arm wrestled with questions of criminal justice reform.

In February 2014, I became New York City mayor Bill deBlasio's counsel. The mayor kept up with crime statistics almost daily. At the time, his opponents opposed any changes to the police's unconstitutional stop-and-frisk program, which targeted Black and Latinx New Yorkers. The police department, the business sector (particularly real estate), and many ordinary people believed that policing was working because crime rates were at an historic low. De Blasio understood that people would blame new policies and procedures for any spikes in crime. We all celebrated when low crime numbers proved what we believed. Stop-and-frisk did nothing to improve safety. Even if it did, that would not have been an argument for violating the rights of any human being. But politically it mattered.

But then Officer Daniel Pantaleo killed Eric Garner. While most of the attention focused on the chokehold Pantaleo used, the real question for me was: Why the hell were they arresting Garner in the first place? For selling a loose cigarette? Garner was denying the charge, and there were real reasons to question if the officers saw Garner selling a loosy, as they're called. But even if it was the truth, it was a low-level and nonviolent offense that merited, at most, a summons to appear in court. At most. To the extent it's a crime, it's a crime of poverty.

Rather than arresting Eric Garner, we should have been asking why he needed to sell cigarettes on the street at all. The shop owners who sell cigarettes that are taxed, and therefore more expensive, complained to the police, which was the only recourse they had. I wondered whether the government could provide other public responders to address these social problems. It was not a new approach. An academic I had met years before, Professor Herman Goldstein, challenged former police commissioner Bill Bratton's "community policing" with a vision for "problem solving policing." The takeaway for me was that police can respond differently to the problems they encounter—for example, by alerting or partnering with other agencies. It seemed so obvious, and there were already successful pilots around the country. Why weren't we doing that here in New York City?

But for those rightly enraged and traumatized by yet another inexplicable killing of an unarmed Black man as he cried out for air, analysis is no assurance that it won't happen again. It always does. George Floyd's killing on July 17, 2014, demonstrated that. But there were and are countless other stories from around the country before George Floyd could not breathe. When on December 3, 2014, a Staten Island grand jury declined to indict Officer Pantaleo, it was justice denied for those who had seen the video of a Black man, hands raised and walking backward. Again.

After the grand jury's decision, de Blasio visited Garner's father. Speaking about the incomprehensible pain of a father who lost his son in such a disturbing and needless act, de Blasio said, "I couldn't help but immediately think what it would mean to me to lose Dante. Things would never be the same again." He would pay dearly for such a simple and honest remark about his biracial son. Far too many in the police department interpreted that statement and the indignant reactions of those, including myself, who were appalled by the Garner video, as "anti-police."

Peaceful protests were popping up around the city in a prelude to the Black Lives Matter demonstrations, galvanized by Eric Garner's cries of "I can't breathe." It was both impressive and terrifying from the vantage point of City Hall. Many of us were impressed with the protests. They were peaceful and the sheer breadth was thrilling. What was terrifying was what might happen when police and protesters met. The police department was under strict instructions to stay calm and stay back, but that was no guarantee. The city was as taut as the rope in a tug-of-war battle, and if the contest became about who was stronger, the results could be devastating. The police could corral and billy-club protesters and arrest them for disorderly conduct, ultimately creating the conditions from which riots might burst forth.

It was strange not to be marching alongside the protesters chanting "I can't breathe." I felt simultaneously helpless in the face of the tensions of the moment, but I was also galvanized to search for creative ways to celebrate the ingenuity and peacefulness of the protests happening around the city. It was complicated. The mayor would be castigated as much, if not more, than the police commissioner if he failed to maintain order and restrain the police. The city council would erupt based on its constituency, and waning credibility could hamper a reform agenda.

The protests were peaceful. But on December 20, 2014, the situation became more volatile after the murders of two New York City police officers, Officers Wenjian Liu and Rafael Ramos. Ismaaiyl Brinsley, the shooter, traveled up from the Baltimore area after killing his former girlfriend and randomly picked these two officers, who were sitting in their patrol car. The police commissioner might be hired and fired by the mayor, but crime rates can strongly influence a politician's policies and pronouncements. It is one of the reasons that police unions in New York City have a tradition of protesting City Hall by simply engaging in a work slowdown. It's their way of saying, *You need us and if we don't like what you say or do, we can damage you politically.* Bratton confirmed that police had slowed their work after the two officers were killed, as had happened in the past. But instead of stoking the crime rates and, therefore, more demand to support the police, the public was rightly angry about public servants paid taxpayer dollars refusing to do their jobs. Crime rates also dropped. Although this statistic is only correlation and cannot be called causation, researchers have pointed to this phenomenon to argue that policing can beget crime.

We can be safer with fewer police, if we invest in reducing the problems that lead to so many unnecessary encounters. How police behave also matters, and too often they can, through their own fears, prejudices, or anger, create the very problems society has tasked them with solving. But the fear of crime makes politicians take positions voters want to hear. Black and Latino residents are much more likely to pay the price for both violent crime and the demands that we throw police at the problem.

The killing of Eric Garner and its aftermath would fundamentally impact my relationship with the mayor in a profoundly sad way, because he would not allow me to work on police reform. It also catalyzed my substantially deeper understanding of the troubles inside the New York Police Department. I was surprised when the mayor later requested that I chair the Civilian Complaint Review Board, which investigates police misconduct and makes disciplinary recommendations to the police commissioner. Through all these experiences, I formed strong opinions on *how* the police department needed to be reformed.

The night the killing of Eric Garner went viral, I was sitting in the bullpen in City Hall, where there was a large flat-screen TV perpetually tuned in to the news. I watched the video in horror and disgust, and I looked around to catch the eyes of my colleagues so I might feel less alone in witnessing such cruelty. We were watching a man strangled ruthlessly and with no regard for his life and well-being, all over a loose cigarette.

A police officer on the mayor's detail who happened to be there was more of a political operative. He understood the value of relationships and generally looked to see where he might need to smooth ruffled feathers, make a connection, or otherwise be engaged. It was his eyes I accidentally caught.

I looked away. He walked over, sat down at a cubicle behind me, and began talking softly and sympathetically. He was a very tall man with dark hair and bright eyes, and I suspected he was used to commanding attention with his size, his looks, and his charm. And as counsel to the mayor, I was a direct report to the person he had to protect.

I had decided I was not going to try and influence him. For one thing, I didn't know him well, so I wasn't sure how to do so effectively. I was also extremely upset and angry, and I was experiencing witness trauma. Floating around me like a mist was some dread, dusted with a tinge of hope that we might find some kind of mutual understanding, like Dad found with a Barry Goldwater Republican on school segregation. It was an unformed and very distant hope that I would not have been able to describe in the moment.

The police officer began to recount a story of a very dangerous situation he was in, one that made the news some years before. A mentally ill man had attacked people with a knife in Times Square. A rank-and-file cop at the time, this officer was one of the responders. As the man ran at him with the knife, he described pulling his gun from his holster as he yelled for the mentally ill man to stop. A police van intervened by ramming into the knife-wielding man, killing him. When the officer looked down, he realized his hand was empty. His gun was still holstered. He sincerely believed that he would have been killed. He had a family, children. He tilted his head in a half plead, trying to communicate how hard the job is, and that officers must make split-second decisions when life is on the line.

This was an emotional and complicated moment. I was a kid whose father died, and I was immediately glad this man's children didn't lose him. I could also imagine the terror of anyone at the mercy of a man wielding a knife. I would wish that on no one. But we still sat with an invisible chasm between us, with no bridge over it that I could see. The chasm was our respective abilities to put ourselves in the shoes of that mentally ill Black man. Did he not have family, too? How terrified must he have been by the delusional demons who commanded his violent actions? What traumas and experiences might have exacerbated his mental state? And shouldn't there have been less lethal ways of subduing him? In the moment, I was barely keeping up with his words, descending into my own self-defensive numbness, a common physical and emotional reaction to trauma. I had just watched a Black man killed by the actions of indifferent police officers.

What did this police officer's story have to do with Eric Garner's? Eric Garner had no knife, was threatening no one, and was backing away from officers in a situation that didn't even require an arrest. The whole thing was wrong. Eric Garner should still have been alive. Why couldn't he see that? Why was he defending the death of another father, even if he believed his story merited more sympathy for the dangers of policing? The police officer who put Eric Garner in that chokehold, Daniel Pantaleo, was going to go home to his children that night. Eric Garner was not. I wanted this police officer to have the same compassion for Eric Garner he was asking me to have for Daniel Pantaleo. I didn't know how to convince him when the plain truth seemed to be staring him in the face and he didn't see it, or wouldn't acknowledge that he saw it. I also felt completely inadequate because I could not debate him in my stupefaction. I had given up just watching his approach.

It was a numbness I would later recognize in my daughter's friend who became a godson to me. A tall and beautiful high school student, he loved to skateboard and could only sleep with the television on. He lived with us for some years after he had dropped out of high school. To this day he has never shared what it was like to be punched by a police officer for sitting in a park at night, or any of the other brutality he endured. I did know what it was like to go to court with him to get out of arrest warrants for doing the things young people do, like skateboarding in the subway, or turnstile hopping. For that, he got arrested. My daughter, who also did not pay, was not. These are the stories of unequal treatment and abuse that cause a heartbreaking limpness and acquiescence in those who experience them.

Despite my inability to debate the police officer that night, something more important would happen in the following days. I did something I had learned from my parents: I talked to people. I listened for the opportunities to make a connection, convince, or create a change. I had not been in City Hall long, but I had always greeted the police officers who covered the grounds gate and staffed the metal detector, and up the stairs I greeted the men at the front door, who stood in suits rather than the blue uniforms of the rank-and-file police officers. And then there were the police officers at the front desk, and those who stood outside the mayor's office door or at the top of the internal stairs that led to the hearing room for the City Council. By the time I had gotten to my desk I must have greeted and exchanged pleasantries with a bare minimum of a half dozen police officers on a slow day. Some were Black, and two were Latino—Puerto Rican and Cuban, respectively. Most were white and almost all were men. The majority may well have been politically conservative, and certainly many of them expressed views that supported my sense.

The day after my bullpen discussion, I stopped at the front gate and had my first real conversation with the Puerto Rican police officer who greeted me every morning, with the Irishman at the metal detector, and with some of my favorites who were Black and on the mayor's detail. A Black police officer I became friends with talked about trying to help white police officers understand why sitting on your apartment building's front stoop on a hot summer day was not a choice if you wanted a beer but lived in an overcrowded, un-air-conditioned apartment. He was a smart and sensitive person who regularly told me about the racism inside the department.

Police abusers also often abuse other police officers. I remember a particular police officer, a white man who was young and probably a conservative, but fun-loving and funny. After one impromptu, serious exchange with him and a few other police officers as I was walking into City Hall, I made a comment about how they were always nice to me, making an effort to contrast this treatment with documented abuses by other police officers. This young white officer who always teased and joked, got serious and said quietly, "You should see how they treat us." He meant that those bullying officers also targeted their own. A Puerto Rican and an Irish police officer both decried the protests and confirmed that we sat on opposite sides of the political spectrum. I was struck by how quickly, within a minute or two, their complaints about the outside world not understanding them quickly shifted to the terrible abuse they felt at the hands of their managers inside the department. They seemed unaware that they had much more to say about that than about protesters.

Here is the central, human, and organizational conundrum of policing. It's a stressful job, and also one that can attract abusers who cause real trauma to people both inside and outside the department. It has true racists and sexists, and some very decent people who themselves fall victim to the abusers unless they fall in line, keep their heads down, and don't cause trouble. Some officers, among other things, use stop-and-frisk abuses to fondle women and girls; and others, who have a mean and accusatory demeanor and demand subservience, make it difficult to even walk the streets. This cycle of abuse creates and perpetuates the trauma in communities of color. The nice police officers often cannot protect these communities, so many young people believe that it isn't possible to reform policing. Police departments and unions have themselves to blame for that.

I came to trust many of the officers I got to know, because we came to know each other beyond the labels, stereotypes, and assumptions. I also learned which officers I did not trust. I learned that the NYPD was a bad place to work, especially for those I trusted. There are too many who rise in the police force despite how they behave and too many who don't because they have the wrong relationships or don't toe the line. I witnessed firsthand what some social science research has found. Cronyism, racism, corruption, mismanagement, and lack of true accountability are all too real and deeply a part of the institution and culture.

Policing creates and also reinforces trauma cycles. Black and brown people are traumatized by crimes that could be prevented with much-needed investments in schools, job training, housing, and mental health care. They are also traumatized by police who either believe their abuse is necessary to control crime or are simply abusive. That boomerangs into cycles of traumatic violence for police, too. No one wins. The discussion about "bad apples" misses the whole reality of policing. I left City Hall with an even deeper belief that change had to come from outside the department. The very demonstrations and protests many police officers themselves, all but the most reflective and thoughtful ones, abhorred and took personally were also necessary to counterbalance the political power of police unions who were paying little attention to the workplace complaints I was hearing.

Two years after Daniel Pantaleo killed Eric Garner, I left my position as the mayor's counsel, grateful for all I had been able to contribute and for all I had learned, but also disappointed to have not had an opportunity to play a role in police reform. But the mayor would soon ask me to chair the Civilian Complaint Review Board. That role gave me the opportunity to build a greater connection to community organizations and leaders, particularly in communities where the local precincts had high numbers of police misconduct complaints, and to push for more accountability through state legislation on disclosing police misconduct decisions. Most important, my position finally allowed me to get Daniel Pantaleo dismissed from the police force, thanks to the activism of Mr. Garner's family and advocates. Pantaleo was still collecting a paycheck and a pension, which was a huge problem for accountability. Still, the progress we made could happen only because I had decided to stop working toward agreement and simply move to action. That is the power of organizing and the importance of using power when agreement is not possible. When internal politics stood in the way of the just outcome, outside oversight was necessary for one of the most egregious cases of crooked policing in our country.

CHAPTER 8

GOING NATIONAL

As MY MOM WOULD tell us, the call came in November 1964, just over a year after Dad's jailing. Dad picked up the ringing phone from another room, eventually yelling out, "Wretha? Farmer wants me to move to New York." And she replied, "Okay. Let's do it!" I was not yet a year old, and Danny had just turned two. Syracuse CORE wasn't much older than Danny when James Farmer called Dad and asked him to leave Syracuse and his professional life's work to help lead CORE. Farmer offered Dad, a sophomore in the movement, the number two position at the national headquarters. As associate national director he would be responsible for the day-to-day operations of the national organization.

That version of the story could not be literal fact. Dad had some negotiating to do. Mom's embellished story was not, in its purpose, untrue. She always described their emotional reaction the same way. There was no real question about what they would choose. They would make this leap with little hesitation, as they had done when they married. Hand in hand, babies in tow, they would jump into the uncertain future that was movement work, not as a side activity to their daily lives, but as their entire focus.

There is a story Mom liked to tell about my brother learning to walk, and it always felt like the perfect metaphor for my parents' decision. Danny was a toddler who was not yet toddling. I, on the other hand, was her baby windmill, trying to do everything all at once and always on my own. I pulled myself up and, on wobbling, chubby legs, I took the usual unstable first *Look Mommy! No hands!* step. She cheered with excitement, and I promptly plopped down flat on my cotton-diapered behind.

My brother was seated and playing quietly farther off in the room. He looked up, saw her enthusiasm, and stood up. He walked over as if he had been walking for months, and it was no great feat. It was as if it had not occurred to him to walk until he saw me struggle to take a first step, or saw the joy it would bring our mother. A perfect description of our very distinct personalities—he goes deep and focused and hard on what's before him, and I whirl around like the Tasmanian devil of our favorite cartoon. At least, that was how it felt.

My parents, like my brother, were deep in what they were doing, committed to it. But it hadn't occurred to them to pursue it fully. They saw themselves, to varying degrees, in the background of the movement work in Syracuse. My uncle Al had said that Dad, even as a child, would plead the case for his siblings to his parents using his natural gifts, his brain, his dogged persistence, and his long-honed skills as a charming, determined negotiator. After sitting out the 1964 March on Washington because he believed that local work was critical to movement victory, Dad now stood up and walked into the national role. He believed the local work could encourage the national movement to focus on the ghetto and link the local demands into national demands for better housing and schools and for decent jobs. He felt his new role would be a way to continue making that connection.

My father was also an ambitious man. By ambitious, I mean outcomes more than accolades. In chemistry I assume he pushed to prove himself and wanted to break new ground in his research. When it came to the civil rights movement, his ambition was also for success, but not his own personal success. I don't remember him as an arrogant man. My mother could not tolerate arrogance in men, and I have no memory of him being haughty or self-praising or even anything vaguely self-referential.

Dad believed in Bruce Thomas, and he believed he had to empower regular Black folks to lead themselves. In those Syracuse days, according to Rudy Lombard, "George was never, would never on his own, try and get a position that might be looked upon as prestigious or powerful or influential. You always had to tell him that it was going to do some general good. We always had to tell him that it was good for the movement for him" to take leadership. That was why Dad made Bruce the chairman of the Syracuse chapter. But to accomplish what he could with his talents and to push the strategies he believed in, he needed to be recognized as the Black leader he was.

Dad started a relationship with Farmer early. In 1962, Dad invited Farmer to speak at the university and to see the work of his young chapter. It soon became clear to Farmer that Syracuse could become one of the most substantial Northern chapters, and it was only a year old. Rudy had taken Dad to some of the National Action Committee meetings, and other Northern chapters of CORE copied my father's blueprint for racial justice, which he called "Project 101." His strategic abilities earned him a seat on the National Action Committee in late 1963.

Rudy was Dad's guide, helping him navigate that national table of the NAC. Rudy introduced him to its members and helped him become more acquainted with Southern organizing. Rudy helped Dad because he believed Syracuse was too isolated and Dad had more to offer the organization nationally. Dad felt a natural draw to the Southern chapters Rudy came from and connected him to because he identified with their "militancy." As Dad had come into his own militancy, Rudy and other Southern organizers were becoming more disenchanted with CORE. Ironically, Rudy himself was turning away from integration, something that many young Black activists were starting to do because of the harsh and hateful reaction of white people and the police forces in the face of it. This harsh reaction to demands for basic rights and decency was and is hundreds of years old, so the question of whether to fight for inclusion was a legitimate one. This was equally true in Syracuse.

Dad had not given up on integration, but his view about the importance of confronting the injustices was in sync with the more militant organizers, and he was focused on class and changing society as a whole. In 1964, he wrote, "As Negroes, our most significant contributions to reshaping of values is to profit from our experiences as a persecuted group and by cultivating mores which reject the notion of financial success, societal graces, or the façade of academic degrees as a barometer of a person's worth." Dad wasn't satisfied with legal citizenship for

Black people. He wanted to redefine value, worth, and success beyond signifiers of class position that were also deeply intertwined with racism as a caste system. That was a radical thought in its own right. Worth must no longer be equated with wealth and whiteness. A later chant—preserved on a button I still have from my father's economic justice organizing—was PEOPLE OVER PROPERTY. He meant it. All of it.

Despite his more liberal and optimistic worldview, my dad was not ever comfortable with being considered one of the Black educated elite that Harvard sociologist W. E. B. Du Bois dubbed the "Talented 10th" who would save the masses of the Black poor. Dad was also never patient with the narrowly self-interested desires of a Black middle class. He grew up working-class, with some of the unique investments that came with being a home-owning family. Dad's distaste for educated elitism lived in his gut and he felt it was wrong, even as he fought for and rose to acquire his intellectual standing. He was an educated elite but now his long-standing discomfort with being in the "Talented 10th" had grown, having been drawn to direct action with Black community, he now had more than a belief system about the world that needed to be created. He now had an emotional connection to the anger of ordinary Black folk.

This leap would sharpen the contradictions Dad had to navigate. Being the Black organic chemistry professor was easier with his acculturation to white people from his childhood. Becoming a full-time Black civil rights leader would prove more challenging.

I doubt Mom or Dad anticipated the dramatic shifts this change would bring in their relationship. They were both contending with a movement that was also transforming. CORE was still more militant than other national organizations in the movement. Dr. Martin Luther King, for example, was a radical thinker, but he needed the protections afforded by the NAACP. More radical young Black ministers in the South were not shy about publicly labeling the NAACP as the "establishment"— a bad word on the left. King wanted these young ministers organizing through Black churches in his newly founded Southern Christian Leadership Conference. Roy Wilkins, head of the NAACP and cofounder of the Leadership Conference on Civil and Human Rights (which I would eventually lead), had helped King defeat the harassing tax fraud charges meant to silence his activism. Wilkins asked King not to hire the young, upstart ministers who had been too critical. King acquiesced.

The Student Nonviolent Coordinating Committee operated on the more militant end of the spectrum than CORE. More restless. The young usually are. Dad was not old, but he was in his thirties. To his credit, like Mom, he didn't hesitate to put himself in the position to have experiences that would tap his own radicalism. Neither Wretha Wiley, nor Bruce Thomas, nor Rudy Lombard sowed the seeds of radicalism in George Wiley, but as he talked in African Methodist Episcopal and Black Baptist churches, and as he languished in the city jail, Dad became a militant. He felt he was Black. Knew he was Black. Now he would also own that Blackness differently.

On the national level, Bruce and Rudy could be the guides Mom couldn't be, even though she understood Dad was somewhat naive, as she had been when she met those teenage girls in East Harlem. Mom could no longer partner the way she did in Syracuse. She was the white wife and a mother. She would still go to rallies and marches. She could be a private, personal sounding board for Dad when he came home at night, but she could not be integral to the work. The shift would also seed my mother's resentment, now that Dad was distracted and emotionally unavailable to us. Their partnership took on more traditional gender roles, whereas the demands of the local work had at least allowed them to share household duties. Now she was the homemaker, and he was absent. She was proud of his work, but the distance created by miles of national travel would start to become emotional as well as physical.

Dad always wanted Black people to get to be people, but his engagement in CORE taught him so much more. Dad had helped Bruce see himself as a leader, and Bruce helped Dad take off the rose-colored glasses and see what he had missed. Now Dad was shaping his own ideas more deeply, thanks to his ready activism. In the days to follow, the days when he would grow his afro and don his daishiki, some of his compatriots would wonder if that shift was to communicate what his favorite sports, his white wife, and his Northeastern accent could not. Was it a natural progression to embrace a different cultural connection, or was it a tactic to seek, connect, and navigate the tensions?

The times were changing rapidly around our small, young family. Impatience and anger about the state of inequality and injustice grew, and the Black Power movement was on the rise. This new, unapologetic aggressiveness was often invoked in an almost accusatory way, but it was born from violence perpetrated by the police and the government's accusatory responses to their demands.

It had been a decade since the historic school desegregation ruling by the Supreme Court in *Brown v. Board of Education* and the successful Montgomery Bus Boycott. But the response was retrenchment and more violence. The young were restless, angry, and tired of being beaten with impunity. Poverty was crushing, too, and the victories splashed on the front pages of newspapers and on TV news programs about the Civil Rights Act of 1964 and the Voting Rights Act of 1965 did not soothe that fury and frustration. The new laws would make change, but winning the battle for their passage was not winning the war against racism, and these laws were not accompanied by measurable enforcement or fewer police beatings. I would watch their erosion beginning with my legal career in the late 1980s, thanks to Ronald Reagan and the backlashes his administration represented and supported.

Dad was restless, too, with a newfound sense of urgency. He felt their wins in Syracuse were not big enough. They'd made too little progress and helped too few. He was restless but not reckless. He was not going to give up his career without some sort of plan, even if it was a vague one. If he took the position, Farmer had to commit to support him as his successor as the head of CORE. Farmer readily agreed. Dad also wouldn't yet accept that he'd have no time for chemistry. After his new position was announced, he told the *New York Times* that he might affiliate with a New York City university to continue some of his chemistry research. Delusions of a scientific path aside, his focus remained clear. He would help urban communities, continuing a fight to belong, to survive, and thrive, to have a civil rights movement that produced an end to Black poverty.

This is the central irony of Dad's national CORE experience. His work, demonstrated in his leaving behind a promising chemistry career and his awakening in a more true and shared Black experience, would be unrecognized by the growing Black Power movement. Dad would not be Black enough. The Black Power movement, driven by the youth organizers of the Student Nonviolent Coordinating Committee, was challenging the scions of civil rights. Even King was either unrecognized or snubbed in some Black and poor communities. We forget this today, along with King's radicalism, because he has become much more of a bust on a pedestal than a living, breathing man, buffeted about despite his considerable moral authority and bold vision.

After taking over the daily management of the national office at CORE, my father was already looking for new ideas for the movement. He was convening academics to wrestle with questions of ending Black poverty and bringing meaningful economic and social change to the Black ghetto. As the new associate director, he challenged the organization to elevate the voices of local leaders, as he himself had elevated leaders like Bruce. Farmer, however, felt undermined and betrayed, even while Dad didn't see it or intend it that way. Dad took on advocacy for more direct impact on the priorities of low-income Black communities, as he had in Syracuse. He also pushed for CORE to become more political and fight against Republicans like Barry Goldwater amid Black people's battle in the South to simply register to vote and show up safely to the polls. He believed Black folks could still exert some power, even if they were blocked from voting. That was a huge departure from past assumptions that focused on gaining more influence on policies without becoming more political and directly taking on Republicans. The National Action Committee agreed.

More militancy didn't mean less strategy or research. Mom always talked about how the Brooklyn CORE chapter wanted to stage a general "stall-in" to block traffic coming into the 1964 New York World's Fair. Everyone on the NAC knew it was a bad idea. It would only turn the public against their cause. The strategy was to win support, not lose the sympathy of the public audience, which had been key to the successes so far. The stall-in didn't follow the strategic protocol of protest. First, you had to have a demand and then make it to government officials, in this case New York City. If the government refused to act, direct action would follow. That hadn't happened here. At the same time, everyone also understood why the chapter wanted to disrupt the World's Fair. The absurdity of the World's Fair in a country of such inequality was a poke in the eye to Black people. It would also be an attention-getter and extract a cost for racism and exclusion.

Mom's eyes would glow when she described Dad deftly redirecting protesters away from strategies that would not produce results. He understood you couldn't just say no to people who were angry. He devised a route for the protest that directed the marchers into a parking lot before the stall-in actually stalled inbound traffic to the fair. It minimized attention but allowed the protest to move forward.

Dad was clear that they had to confront Northern racism, even as he aligned with the radical Southern organizers. He wrote, "Though conditions in the South are often more gross and extreme, the deep-seated, hard-core problems of the northern ghetto are much less tractable, much more difficult to define and identify, and thus considerably more frustrating. Racism in the North produces far more emotional tension for the person subjected to it." Dad knew what he was talking about because of his own personal experiences and frustrations with that tension.

His detractors were focused on him being the White Negro. Too intellectual, too professorial. He still dressed like a university professor, had a white wife—specifically a Southern white wife, which, despite her own commitment and work with CORE, just seemed to drive home the wrong message about who Dad was and who he wasn't. He had too many white friends, too. The optics were all wrong.

Farmer, like my father, was a firm believer in integration-ist principles, but Dad considered Farmer too accommodating of the demands of white power brokers. Farmer was not com-pletely happy with Dad, either. He was trying to hold on to some centralized power that might have had some institutional imperatives, like fundraising and marshaling strategy, while Dad was trying to strengthen the field because he believed the local fights had to be empowered locally. This wasn't an uncommon fight in institutional activism. Ella Baker waged a similar battle inside the NAACP to strengthen the field in the 1940s.

Dad wanted to structure the organization in the way that many national advocacy organizations are structured today: strong national and regional offices, a research department, because information and knowledge is part of your power, and a "Friends of CORE" committee to help it fundraise. The result was that he built much of what CORE needed for future strate-gic growth and financial sustainability. It wouldn't be enough.

When Farmer announced he would step down, less than a year after Dad became his number two, Dad had a lot of sup-port to succeed him, and the promise from Farmer himself to support his candidacy. What mattered most was support from the National Action Committee, which meant chapter leaders. Many were in his corner, including many of the Southern chap-ters. What he didn't have was a Black wife and a down-home way about him. And he wouldn't make offers and promises of positions to chapter leaders. He would focus on the fact that he would be a first-rate administrator and a smart organizer. No one disagreed with any of that. But he wasn't Black enough, and while racial justice was at the core of his strategy, that core con-tained economic justice and not cultural performance.

A loud contingency of Black staff and leaders wanted

visible, culturally resonant, Black leadership that spoke Black Power and kicked out white staff, while committing not to take white money. Some of my father's allies asked him, begged him, to just agree to these demands. He could have embraced the rhetoric of anger, while quietly continuing to raise the money the organization needed to do its work. Firing white staff might have been a harder promise to break, but that wasn't even the point. He was a person who believed that how he won was as important as the victory. He would not fire effective people because they were white, even while he understood the reasons for the demand. He refused. His way was to persuade, not to mislead.

Farmer, the integrationist with his accommodating spirit, did not honor his commitment to back Dad and instead backed his opponent. Floyd McKissick, unlike Dad, was from the South. A North Carolinian civil rights attorney, McKissick was also the board chair. McKissick could talk Black and walk Black, and he was willing to cave to the Black staff who demanded unsustainable promises. Dad would lose the election.

A Black woman named Marlene Wilson, from the Columbus, Ohio, chapter, wrote to McKissick after his election about the "underhanded" attack on Dad. She said: "First, everyone knows that CORE is not accepted by the black community and it is not because of any kind of CORE leadership even Farmer has a white wife...The problem is that CORE's members are so busy interpreting and devising slogans about 'the black community' and 'the man in the streets' that they have convinced themselves that they are the experts on the 'ghetto.'" It was a mic drop, in my view. She called out the performative hypocrisy. Dad wasn't pretending to be from the ghetto, and he was determined to participate with its residents as partners to solve the problems they themselves wanted solved.

Ruth Turner, one of the NAC members, led the attack on my father's candidacy while organizing support for McKissick. We later met and had a cordial side-by-side working relationship in the 1990s on civil rights provisions in the Democrats' efforts to reform health care. She was working for the National Medical Association (NMA), the Black doctors' answer to the American Medical Association. I was a young attorney with the NAACP Legal Defense and Educational Fund. It was not the first time I had to turn the other cheek and stay focused on the mission when facing my father's former critics. I worried very briefly that she might distrust me and, therefore, make it more difficult for me to work with the NMA or with other Black organizations. Would I be Black enough for her? I knew that I carried the trauma and fear of a child who was sometimes bullied for having a white mother. It was impossible to feel as confident as Dad always appeared. I didn't have two Black parents and a batch of Black siblings, like he did. I hadn't experienced the direct racism he had.

Ruth never did say or do anything to make me feel attacked. Consciously or not, my white mother was a constant buttress for my Black identity and a builder of my confidence. When Mom learned I was in meetings with Ruth, she just smiled, gazed up at the ceiling, and simply said, "Ah. Ruth Turner." She would, only later, make a matter-of-fact comment about Ruth being a detractor of Dad's. My parents were not grudge holders, and Mom's unconcerned response to Ruth signaled that there wasn't a thing to worry about. Both my Mom and Ruth had moved on from that time in their lives and in the life of the movement, and that freed me, too.

It was not lost on me that CORE, after moving in the direction Turner and McKissick championed, ultimately became a Black-led, right-wing conservative organization shunned by the Black left for its antijustice agenda. The CORE of my young adult years was an example of a slippery slope that resulted in its self-destruction. McKissick would replace Dad with Roy Innis, and in 1968, not two years after McKissick gave in to Black nationalist rhetoric, he was replaced by Innis altogether. After Innis experienced the traumatic murder of his son, he turned into a shill for conservatives, using Black nationalism as an anthem for an unraveling of the very civil rights demands for which he once fought.

I don't pretend to understand Innis's turn against the demands of the vast majority of Black people. It is possible that he was fueled by grief and anger after the loss of his son, as well as by the more fulsome rejection of integrationism and even, in some instances, nonviolent "accommodationism," all taking place by 1968. I do know that Niger Innis, his son, appeared on Fox News stating that his father fought to get more Black people on the police force and denigrating the Black Lives Matter protests against police brutality, while I appeared on MSNBC decrying that same brutality. The generations speak through us, and their decisions live on.

I would not meet James Farmer until after law school. I had just taken the bar exam and some old CORE members, led mostly by Rudy Lombard (whom I had also never met), had planned a reunion in New Orleans. Mom, Danny (now Dan), and I decided to attend.

My excitement to meet Rudy was palpable, but Farmer was a complicated figure in our family history. I was unsure how I would feel, but I anticipated anger and distrust. I also understood that Dad's rejection by CORE made him the man I would be so proud to call my father. I believed and still believe that Dad was a more consequential leader thanks to the trial he underwent at CORE. History had also made clear that Dad would have been the leader who might have preserved CORE as a true civil rights organization. What it had become was an abomination.

I might have been angrier if my parents had been. As a twenty-five-year-old, my pride in my father's principled position at CORE was much stronger than my passive judgment about Farmer's mistake. My mother looked forward to seeing him, and I unconsciously took my emotional cues from her.

When I met the legendary James Farmer I saw before me an elderly man, now blind as the result of a bad beating he suffered at a protest. Even if he had been haughty and defensive about Dad, it would have been impossible to see him as anything other than a fading star of the movement. But he wasn't haughty. His unseeing eyes stared past me, as he stood arm in arm with another former CORE member whom I now cannot picture. He seemed wistful and sincere in his reminiscences as he greeted me. He told me what a great man my father had been. And he meant it. That was all that mattered now.

CHAPTER 9

MOVEMENT, MOTHERS, AND MARRIAGE

ONE NIGHT, MY BROTHER and I were awakened by the ladies. We were very young. I would guess I was five years old. Hearing voices and excited chatter, we snuck out of our beds and tested the waters by sitting at the top of the steps and peering through the spindles of the banister. Usually, my mother would give us a stern look and say, "Back to bed!" Tonight, no one noticed us. We started booty-bumping our way down the stairs until finally, when it seemed no one would shoo us away and we were unnoticed, we joined the circle without parental protest. This was a rare treat after bedtime. We were never excluded from discussions during the day, but sanctioned nighttime conversations were rare and so they held more interest. What was clear to my young ears was that everyone was upset. Humiliated. Angry. I don't recall all the details of what was said, and I'm sure I didn't understand it all then. But what I did glean was that they had been arrested at a demonstration, which was normal, but then abused by the judge before whom they appeared.

The charges for these demonstrations were disorderly conduct, a misdemeanor. The whole point was to overwhelm the system with people so that they were simply released. And everyone understood they were neither a danger nor criminals. Usually, they were brought before a judge who fined them. This particular judge decided to punish them because of his own ideological views. He called on them one by one to humiliate and demean them, the very treatment they were protesting in the welfare system itself. The judge did not comprehend or perhaps care that they were fighting for enough food to put in their children's bellies or to get the roaches out of the dangerously unhealthy homes they were forced to live in.

At a certain point, the adults started calming down and turned to my brother and me for the traditional questions. We were asked what we wanted to be when we grew up. I immediately belted out, "A judge!" This was not a popular answer. I can't say I comprehended the side-eye and quizzical stares completely, but they did ask why. My answer was simple. "Because the judge has the power!" They all burst into laughter.

I didn't understand what was so funny. I meant it. I loved these people sitting around the circle. They were family, even if they weren't blood relatives. Children have a sharp sense of injustice because they have little control over their lives. But as a child, you understand that will change when you grow up. These people were grown-ups, but they did not have the power in that courtroom. I was deeply affected by that vision of the white man, sitting above them, sneering down. I thought that if I was the judge, then I could treat people better.

One of the shows my brother and I watched as kids was a comedy sketch program called *Laugh-In*. It was the *Saturday Night Live* of our young years. Sammy Davis Jr. would make regular appearances as "de Judge." Apparently, the character and sketches came from a Black entertainer I didn't know named Pigmeat Markham, who in 1968 put out an album with a song called "Here Comes the Judge." It was a hit. Pigmeat had originated the skit on the show, but Sammy Davis Jr. became the regular judge. It would open with Sammy Davis Jr. in a black robe and a British-style powdered white wig that hung around his face in stark contrast to his brown skin. He entered singing, a different first line each time he strutted onto the stage for a new skit. One example was "You can testify but you can't win / 'Cuz I'm here ta tell ya you're guilty as sin." He would then break into the line that would send me into giggles of excitement, "Here come de judge. Here come de judge." The skits would then jump to some defendant who would receive absurdly arbitrary and nonsensical treatment.

That comedy sketch seemed to apply in real life as well. In the face of my parents' friends' humiliation, instead of absurdity, I could be de judge who would do right by my heroines. It didn't take long for me to jettison the idea. The next day, my mother explained that to be a judge, I first had to go to something called "law school." It was like she offered me liver. I didn't really know what law school was, but it sounded awful.

My parents were always figuring out the next way to make change. After being ousted from CORE, my dad and his friend Ed Day were still looking for ways to join the races together in a fight for better living conditions. The two men, with no income of their own, had an office with a mimeograph machine gifted them by an antipoverty group backed by the United Auto Workers. These would become the ingredients with which to bake a new organization.

They stumbled upon a little-known legislative fight brewing on the Hill for a higher minimum wage. It would be a big deal for poor Black and brown people. To make the biggest impact, they needed to get domestic workers and farmworkers eligible. The exclusion of this Black and brown workforce was a relic of the Faustian deal made with Southern, segregationist Democrats during the New Deal.

They went to work, pulling data first, as always. Ed had to visit the US Bureau of Labor Statistics, pre-internet. The staffer, Ed said, was ecstatic, because he had been gathering data on wages and workers for years and no one ever took any real interest in it. Armed with information, Dad and Ed identified the relevant offices of the congressional representatives on the committee who would vote on the minimum wage bill. Then Dad and Ed started calling them, sending information and giving them advice about what to demand to expand minimum wage coverage for Black and brown people. After about a month, they were shocked to find they'd had an impact. The bill was better, covering more employers and more employees. They were mobilizing an unorganized base through local leaders to improve policies that would improve the lives of the poor.

It was the beginning of an effort that would later focus on organizing women on welfare. Ed was still based in New York, where he was meeting with two sociologists named Frances Fox Piven and Richard Cloward. There were, according to their research, many people in New York eligible for welfare benefits who did not receive them. Was that happening elsewhere? They put Ed on a small salary with grant money. Ed traveled to six cities, including Los Angeles, Chicago, Philadelphia, and Cleveland, because there was no national database. What he found was that local welfare organizing groups were fighting welfare offices.

Dad and Ed's first formal encounter with some of "the Ladies" humiliated by that awful judge was at a conference hosted by the antipoverty coalition that gave them office space. This conference included Sargent Shriver, who was heading the Office of Economic Opportunity, which was tasked with fighting LBJ's "war on poverty." The women welfare organizers erupted in that conference, particularly Johnnie Tillmon. Shriver, to them, was an ignorant, out-of-touch, condescending bureaucrat who didn't understand their problems. Dad tried to mediate the blowup but was impressed by Tillmon. Ed went to visit her the following week to learn more about her organizing in Watts.

Tillmon had grown up in a Texas sharecropping family. She left the farm at eighteen to get a job as a maid in a white household, where she was forced to eat on the back porch with the dog. Young Johnnie was not tolerating that indignity, so she quit. When her marriage went bad, she quit that, too. She took her six children to Los Angeles, where she got a job in a laundry and became a union organizer. She fell ill, spent a month in the hospital, and lost her job as a result. The laundry provided no health insurance, and her physical condition left her unable to work. As a single mother with children, no way to work, and no other options, she relied on welfare benefits to feed, house, and clothe her family.

At the time, the indignities suffered by women on public assistance, then called Aid to Families with Dependent

Children, included caseworkers searching refrigerators, asking how a TV was purchased, and making unannounced visits to see if a man was in the home. You had to be single. As Johnnie famously said, "You trade in 'a man' for 'the man' except you can't divorce him if he treats you bad! He can divorce you, of course—cut you off—any time he wants to." Johnnie Tillmon would suffer these indignities no longer. She began organizing the other tenants in her public housing development in Watts. These women were homegrown leaders organizing without any money or support. That was part of what made them amazing.

She was skeptical when this blond-haired, blue-eyed white boy showed up in the ghetto asking what she had going on, particularly after the famous uprising about seven months earlier. She wired her congressman, who must have been James Roosevelt, son of FDR, and through him learned Ed was legitimate and not an FBI agent. Dad was also talking to researchers at the University of Chicago who were exploring a guaranteed annual income. They had a conference a week after the meeting. He, Ed, and Professor Richard Cloward, a Columbia University sociologist, helped identify about twenty local welfare rights organizers, secured free registration and free places to stay for them, and got them to the conference. Tillmon was not at that Chicago meeting. She was a formidable person, but according to Ed, Tillmon had one of the smaller welfare rights groups. New York's larger group organized hundreds of people.

As those of us who attend a lot of conferences know, the most valuable time can be that spent connecting with others outside of the formal panels and events. This was true for Dad, Ed, and the Ladies. They had their own casual meeting and talked about their work. The Cleveland organizers shared that they were staging a march from Cleveland to Columbus. A suggestion was made for everyone to have demonstrations on the same day in their respective cities. Much to Dad and Ed's shock, the Ladies asked them to set it all up.

The two men had no formal organization, no money, and no staff, but they had a borrowed office and they had the will to help the joint action happen. They made up a name, the Poverty/Rights Action Center, to help organize the Ladies. The multicity demonstrations were held on June 30, 1966, just twenty-five days later. Dad's marketing skills amounted to a mimeograph machine and a clear message. He had materials from various welfare groups that were sprouting up around the country. According to Mom, he just mimeographed a bunch into a booklet and proclaimed the birth of a movement! His role was strategy, like at Syracuse CORE, except now it would be about connecting local groups to take their work to the Beltway.

At the inception of the National Welfare Rights Organization (NWRO), the founding convention was raucous and the Ladies were angry. They felt the fledgling group, with little money and powered by sheer will, was not doing enough. Eventually they calmed down, and the convention produced a membership structure that was democratic and gave votes to organizations based on size. While small groups like Tillmon's argued one vote per organization would level the playing field, it was decided that scale did matter. The larger groups got a few more votes to create the incentive for organizing and to empower the more impactful organizations, as measured by size of their memberships.

Dad became the executive director of NWRO. That meant he was responsible for fundraising as well as strategy, managing the staff and the relationships with the members. Dad's role meant that wealth and poverty became the sun and moon on my confusing planet of existence. I orbited the sunny wealth of Washington's elite circles and saw the tidal pulls to activism of the poverty imposed on Black people. Instead of getting turned away from the neighborhood pool because I was Black, I went to a neighborhood public pool, too crowded with Black bodies in the crushing heat of a swampy DC summer to accommodate us all. None of us had air-conditioning at home, despite the often ninety-degree conditions with 100 percent humidity. The pool was a place to get cool. You could only splash in the water. It was too crowded to swim.

We also experienced the wealth of Washington's power class. As a little girl, I once attended a party at Sargent Shriver's massive estate. I remember it looked like the one owned by the movie producer in *The Godfather*, who had refused to cast Don Corleone's godson in a movie. This place had grounds sprawling to my eyes, which had spent more time scanning alleys. The estate had seemingly endless lawns, with expansive terraces that gave it the appearance of a royal palace.

Organizing also created tensions around collaboration and credit. It still does. As the traditional civil rights organizations also turned to antipoverty organizing, the tensions grew over who was in charge and how to win. NWRO had begun to consider a "Poor People's" action, and Martin Luther King Jr.'s SCLC was organizing the Poor People's Campaign and needed foot soldiers. Organized Black women on welfare made the perfect recruits. For the women and NWRO, SCLC had been missing in action in their battle for a just welfare system. Who was SCLC to drop in and ask them to lend their feet and faces to its campaign? These women knew how welfare worked, what pending legislation would impact them, and what they wanted from federal lawmakers. King, as the most important public figure and moral voice on racial justice and equality, was also seen as a parachuter by local organizers. He dropped into fights and then departed. King had a big platform to gain attention, and that mattered for battles waged to win public support. That didn't erase the tension between King's SCLC and NWRO.

In my home, I have a photo of my father at a panel table with Dr. King. Between them, cradling her baby grandson, sits Johnnie Tillmon, the chair of NWRO's board. My father is leaning forward, hand raised, palm upward as a gesture of explanation, and looking directly at Dr. King, midsentence. King, elbow on the table, hand and fingers cradling his face, is listening, unreadable. To the uninitiated, the photo is a gentle and banal moment. It looks like my father is catching King up on the status of things. He was actually pushing King to see the importance of their work and, respectfully, trying to tell King that he was coming into a fight he knew nothing about. It was inappropriate to them that King would ask them to be foot soldiers in a strategy they felt they had created. It is an iconic photograph for me, not just because King is in it, but because my father placed Johnnie Tillmon right between them on that stage as if to say, *This is the expert on fighting poverty as someone living it.*

In the end NWRO agreed to work with King's organization because they were on the same side. Through Dad's actions and Mom's advice, I learned the importance of strategy, of knowing when to compromise and when to collaborate. It required both facts and data, but also the truth that comes from the wisdom of experiences of people living the problems.

Even before founding NWRO, Dad had begun to engage in the debate about Black women and poverty. His Syracuse colleague, Daniel Patrick Moynihan, later a US senator, wrote a report in 1965 on "The Negro Family: The Case for National Action," also known as the Moynihan Report. He was then an assistant secretary at the US Department of Labor in the Lyndon Johnson administration, and he exemplified benevolent paternalism at its worst. This report reduced the complexity of Black poverty to the breakdown of the Black family. This became a pillar in the "culture of poverty" argument that enabled the Reagan "welfare queen" trope and the Clinton embrace of "workfare" programs that meant menial labor at below-poverty wages for people who needed more income support, education, job training, and more.

Dad didn't debate the data. Black welfare rates were growing even though unemployment rates overall were falling. Instead, he challenged this report's understanding of what the data represented. It made poverty the result of a failing of marriage, a very personal decision, rather than being determined by policies that created the ghetto and all manner of social problems for Black people. Dad and Moynihan became direct combatants after the latter joined the Richard Nixon administration as the president's urban policy advisor. It was a defining fight for the national welfare rights movement and, for me, an example of the tensions between the big social vision of left organizing and the complexity of governing politics.

Moynihan, building off of the Moynihan Report, convinced Nixon to support a guaranteed basic income. This was important to the movement, too. He called for enough money to help poor families, particularly Black poor families, support themselves, which would help them and their children become increasingly financially independent. It was a good idea in general and consistent with NWRO's demand for a guaranteed minimum welfare benefit. Nixon, however, had NWRO on his enemies list and had been a dog whistle–blowing racist. The devil was both in the Oval Office and, more important, in the details.

Moynihan helped create legislation called the Family Assistance Plan that would do some good things, like allow poor people to marry without losing necessary support, within a certain range of income. This recognized that men in low-wage work also experience poverty. NWRO welcomed these principles. The problem with the Plan was that NWRO didn't believe it would work as promised. Nixon had promised no reduction in benefits, but an analysis of the bill by NWRO lawyers revealed serious concerns about whether the Plan would deliver on those promises. Under the Family Assistance Plan, there would be less in reimbursements for work expenses than under the existing welfare program. There were also other issues, like the right to appeal unfair administrative decisions about benefits. Women had experienced a lot of humiliating and abusive treatment in welfare offices, and the legal ability to challenge the arbitrary, capricious, and unfounded decisions to cut them off was important.

NWRO fought back hard, in rhetoric and in direct action. Dad wanted to improve the bill, but NWRO was blocked from negotiations—which left the recipients themselves, the ones who knew what would and would not hurt them, out of the conversation. NWRO prevented a meeting of elected officials and more centrist groups, like Common Cause, to negotiate provisions of the Plan, which angered Moynihan, the White House, and Capitol Hill. Moynihan to his death would blame and deride NWRO as undermining a major advancement in guaranteed income.

He would even criticize Dad and NWRO, without naming

them explicitly, for the devastating unraveling of welfare support Bill Clinton had marshaled early in his first term. Moynihan complained that the left failed to see that they would win more than they lost in the adoption of the Family Assistance Plan. He wrote, "Symbolic rewards are at least as valuable as real rewards, in ways more so." People who don't go hungry, who don't experience discrimination, and who don't suffer the traumas of what is broken and historically accepted often make this mistake. The Plan didn't even support administrative protections from the abusive authority that living, breathing Black women experienced daily.

It is true that activism is not always strategic. Sometimes there is emotional opposition that has little to do with moving the needle toward justice. Dad experienced that at CORE. When I ran for mayor, I remember having a debate with advocates who wanted me to say that I would "defund" the police. I always defended the right of activists who chose to use the word "defund." I would not use it because it confused people, including the Black and brown communities I hoped to represent, who believed that I would abolish the police department. No mayor would be able to do that in an eight-year period, and many abolitionists understood that. My proposal, which the activists supported, was to freeze hiring new police officers to save $1 billion, which I would then use for things that activists and community members alike wanted. That included mental health care in schools, emergency mental health crisis response groups that would relieve this burden on police—like the police officer who did not know how to handle a mentally ill man with a knife—and other investments in community safety. I used to say, "Call it whatever you want. I call it 'right-sizing' the department, which is massive and often mismanaged." To my great sadness, the words became more important than the policy proposal. I remember a discussion with an organizer who believed that using the word "defund" was important to get to the abolition of policing in the decades to come. I respectfully disagreed for two reasons. It only bred opposition from the very communities who wanted and needed the programs and investments the cost savings would help fund, and not the closing of their neighborhood precinct. I hoped for two terms, or eight years, in office and to do all I could to provide communities with services and supports, and to prevent problems rather than policing them. I was not running on abolition of policing. I was running on major reforms and, like my father before me, would stay true to what I would and would not do. It would have been best, of course, to have a shared language, but my parents taught me not to use the language that fails to speak to the very people we want to organize and serve.

This wasn't happening in the Moynihan fight, which was more akin to a failure of inclusion of the very voices who needed to be heard. I saw this firsthand, too. When I was in City Hall, an advocate I knew from a city rights organization called me and said, "You all are fucking up!" This leader was referring to school-based discipline. I was not assigned to that subject, but instead of declining to take responsibility, I said, "Tell me what we're getting wrong." It turned out that the Department of Education was embarking on a review of school discipline and policing, which included the DOE and the NYPD but not enough of the advocates and other leaders. I called the chancellor's chief of staff and organized a meeting. We crafted a process that included more leaders and was more inclusive. It took more than a year of meetings, but in the end everyone celebrated a better set of policies governing how Black and brown children would be treated. I could take no credit for the substance, but I was able to help create the right environment for it to happen, by helping the DOE avoid the type of mistake Moynihan made.

The Family Assistance Plan loss was a large one, and Dad felt it. It had held real, unfulfilled promise. Luckily, this failure was followed by a victory in aggressive direct action. In 1971, the State of Nevada decided to slash the amount of money in public assistance checks. The cuts were drastic—75 percent of the benefit check. Children were malnourished, and doctors were raising alarm bells. Many of the women who received these benefits worked low-paying jobs in Las Vegas's hospitality industry. The Clarke County Welfare Rights Organization had been formed in 1967, encouraged by the founding of NWRO, and with powerful women leaders already agitating for better working conditions. Ruby Duncan headed the chapter and had come from the cotton-picking South. Duncan made her way to Las Vegas with the boom of service jobs at the casinos. She, too, got sick, lost work, and went on welfare.

Duncan reached out to Tillmon and Dad for support. They planned to hit the governor of Nevada where it hurt—the pocketbooks of the very businesses that the state relied on for revenue, the casinos. Operation Nevada, as it was called, would now have national backing and support. The action would be in the street, and the demonstrations would shut down the touristed corridor and, famously or infamously (depending on your point of view), even shut down Caesar's Palace. A brilliant example of smart disruption, they marched down the Vegas strip with more than two hundred children in tow. They went into a hotel, ordered food for all of them, and then sent the bill to the governor. Like all direct action, the intention was to make the simple and emotional point about the policy demand, through disruptive action that gained the media attention necessary to shame the powers that be, both political groups and private businesses. It worked.

NWRO was about five years old when the women won their fight with Nevada. It had, from its inception, been an organization on a tightrope. Dad was the tightrope walker working to empower women who lived in poverty. He began the organization as the Ladies' partner, but by 1971, they treated him more like a competitor because of the very things that made him effective: fundraising and strategy. His strengths did not negate his weaknesses, and sometimes his strengths created his weaknesses. Dad had the determination of an Olympian. He was not tireless. No one is. But he could work excruciating hours and exhaust his staff. His organizational style made sense to him, and like the mix of tubes, beakers, lights, and the other equipment that scaffolds a chemistry lab, Dad modeled his administration on a logic known only to him.

Even his ability to withstand hours of berating or personal attacks did not always work to his advantage. Having very thick skin meant Dad could slough off onslaughts without rumpling into defensiveness or aggression, but it also meant he could make deeply unpopular decisions. Once, when funds were low, he decided to pay the phone bill over making payroll. The phones were the arteries of this big, sprawling body of work. They connected him and the staff to the tenuous chapters and also donors and decision-makers. Without them, NWRO would be cut off. With them, his extremely low-paid staff could not make their rent. Dad wouldn't get paid, either, but he had Mom bringing home the bacon.

Years later I would handle a payroll problem very differently. We were promised a grant, told to hire against it, and then the foundation staffer who had promised us these six figures couldn't get final approval thanks to some internal politics we were not privy to. It was horribly unfair and taught me not to take people at their word, even if they have the best intentions. I had a second paycheck at home, and I furloughed myself so I could pay my staff through the cash-flow crisis. Even if I didn't have the support at home, paying the mortgage, I would have borrowed money to keep my staff paid.

I explained to staff exactly what our next steps would be, how long I could keep everyone on without layoffs and who might be laid off if we could not make up the income. In short, I leveled with them. I told them I would fight to keep them, but they had three months and should make their own decision about whether to take the risk or use the time to look for another position. I lost a staff member, with whom I have maintained a good relationship, and the others stayed on. I made up the difference in funding.

Eventually the Ladies used their democratic power as a board to fire my father. They would part ways for many complicated reasons. Dad had been their partner-teacher. He helped to train, for example, the members of the Nevada chapter that had become so successful. He empowered them to be armed with facts and to speak their truth, as he had with Bruce Thomas and Anna Mae Williams in Syracuse. His abiding respect and belief in their abilities to lead were sincere. The leaders were Dad's bosses. He had constructed it so. Believed in it. As the organization became more successful and its clout grew, they also wanted more power and more services and support. By Operation Nevada, that acrimony was spilling over internally.

It fell to Dad to explain why an organizer got paid more than they got from their welfare checks, for example. They were doing the work, too. The staff was not too happy with their pay, either. An organizer Dad hired for NWRO in Philadelphia in the early 1970s was offered $150 a month. He responded, "But I can't afford that." Dad, who no doubt was wearing his hole-filled orthotic shoes, looked down at the man's feet and responded, "You look like you're doing all right." In fact, the organizer, who was also Black and from a well-off family, was wearing very nice shoes. That was the end of that. This organizer is a friend to me, and to this day he laughs about this story. Not everyone laughed.

Race, once again, became a factor as well. Dad said he always hired the people he thought could do the job that needed doing, so the staff was made up of Black and white organizers. That was Dad. He was a firm believer in integration, in fighting to transcend racism and poverty, and in respecting and supporting the voices of Black people no matter how little money or education they had. That didn't mean he was always a great manager, and that is a hard thing to say about my dad, who was extraordinary in so many ways.

In 1969, Black staffers were in an outright internal revolt over white staff. One Black staff member charged that Dad had surrounded himself with white people in the policy positions so that Black staff were less able to make an impact. Top aides were more often white. For Dad, this was due to economics. White staff were, no doubt, more able to earn less money. Systemic racism was a big factor. Dad got little sleep and little time with family because he was constantly fundraising and scraping together meager resources to fight. It was bone crushing and there was never enough money. Black staff also complained about Ed Day, who had been a unique, entrepreneurial problem-solver. Mom always said Ed could make impossible things happen. Once

Ed figured out how to get the new NWRO telephone service despite having no money to pay the phone bill for some months. Paying bills was always a problem, and Dad constantly had to hustle, juggle, and make hard choices. All the interpersonal relationships were complicated, too. Ed fell in love with and married one of the Ladies, Catherine Germany, whose daughters were playmates of mine.

I look back on this and know two hard truths. One, race was an issue because the privileges of racism meant white people were more able to get certain things done. Ed was the money man and the guy who you could send to the white telephone company or to the bank. White staff probably had more resources and could afford to live on less. Even Black organizers on staff, two of whom I know even to this day, came from middle class or well-heeled families. Dad didn't fix it. He just focused on moving forward.

I imagine he saw two choices. He could just keep moving at the breakneck pace he had to maintain to keep the work afloat, or he could slow down, promote some staff without the resources to support them, and hope for the best. Or perhaps there was a compromise position that melded these options. I don't know. What I do know is that Dad dropped diplomacy with one of the Black staffers organizing the staff uprising, NWRO's director of publications. Dad said, "John...you are more black-conscious than I am. You put that first and I put that second. I place the highest priority on people who I know can get the work done. Some of those white staff people we are talking about are people who are there until one and two o'clock every damned night of the week because they are doing their work." It was an honest show of anger by an exhausted leader, who was also there with his whole Black self those long hours, too. Dad's blunt honesty worked in that moment, but it was not an answer to the anger of his Black staff.

One thing I have learned, having founded and led both a racial justice organization and a university center, is that money and support are required to live your principles and both are very hard to come by when you are a lefty, grassroots organizing shop. Did he handle his staff well? It sounded to me that he did not. Did he manage to start, maintain, and move work no one thought possible? Yes. What I know for sure is that Dad was committed to racial justice and understood the demand for a Black revolution in the country. I believe his focus on the work over the workplace was a choice he made because he was more worried about attacks by outside forces and money to keep the lights on. What he had done was put women on welfare on the top of the organization as the board, and they would, and did, have a real voice in the organization. Did he solve for systemic racism? No. No he did not. Could he have? I doubt it, but he sure could have considered some ways to improve things for his Black staff. But that is easier to say decades later.

The final nail in Dad's coffin came from his efforts to expand the membership of NWRO, along with coalition partners. That meant unemployed men and the working poor. In the 1970 fight on the Family Assistance Plan, the link between all these groups was clear, but the Ladies believed that would undermine the attention they needed to improve their lives. At their 1971 membership convention, held at Brown University, Dad had included invitees from other national organizations fighting poverty and elected allies, Senator George McGovern and Congressman Ronald Dellums, along with Bella Abzug. NWRO delegates protested that "outsiders" were at their convention. The next year, Dad organized a one-day march in

Washington, with allied groups, to be called the Children's March for Survival. Fifty thousand people came. The news cameras, however, were a no-show. Massive actions have little impact on politicians if the larger public isn't paying attention. Despite Dad's efforts, NWRO's power and impact were in a downward spiral.

At the next board meeting, the disputes over money, policy-making power of the board, and, finally, the fact that Dad had begun an Arkansas organizing project headed by a young white organizer named Wade Rathke without board approval, spilled recklessly into a vote to fire the executive director. A faction of the board had planned it in advance. The vote to dismiss Dad was tied, 5–5. An eleventh board member, Beulah Sanders, who like Johnnie Tillmon was a fixture in my world, would abstain. In a rare display of anger, Dad took a swing at them for not having the guts to fire him. A board member lost it. She leapt at him and began to choke him, and she had to be pulled off. It was over. Technically, they didn't actually fire Dad. The vote was tied but the partnership was irreparably severed.

So was our family. Dad's sacrifices for the movement had come at a personal cost for all of us. His resignation was effective January 1, 1973, the day before my ninth birthday. He would be dead before my tenth. NWRO would shutter two years after his resignation with too little money to operate.

CHAPTER 10

DEATH

OUR PARENTS' BREAKUP WAS a shock. Dad wasn't home much but that didn't cause any fights, at least that I or my brother witnessed. However, the tensions manifested themselves in small ways. My mother was not a complainer, and my father always smiled and engaged when you had his attention. If they fought or had tensions they were experts at hiding the problems from us children. The only time any tension bubbled to the surface was when my brother and I would nag my mother about when Dad would be home. He rarely was.

Sometimes, we would be so heartbroken, so needy, that she would get on the phone with him herself. This would usually happen after several exchanges of our calling when he would say, "Soon." "Soon" never meant "in the near future." I believe he meant it when he said it. I don't know if my mother did. The buffeting of the daily winds of life require more of a united barrier, or they can blow down even strong connections. But as a child, I only knew that my parents were supposed to be together. And I was wrong.

In addition to the house in Appalachia, we had a family vacation spot in Canada. My parents bought a postage stamp of an island, not even two acres in size, on a lake in Ontario that they could camp on. It was a pine-and-birch-tree-covered oasis, with a rocky cliff looking out over a beautiful lake. Friends of theirs bought the larger island next door and built a cabin on it. They let us use it every August. Some of my fondest memories are of going to that cabin.

The way they split poisoned the August vacation, which was the only time of year we had Dad's undivided attention. The cabin was not large but it was warm, cozy, and comfortable. We were used to a four-room, unheated house in West Virginia with an outhouse and no running water. The cabin on Devil Lake had everything. Bathrooms with toilets and a comfortable open-floor-plan kitchen and living room. Like our island, it was covered in pines that left soft fragrant blankets spread about, cushioning our up- and downhill journey from the dock up to the house. It had stoic and striking birches with their papery skins that peeled white and gray as if to say this island was safe. There were loons, floating low in the shining lake at sundown, and the gentle, trilling tease of a loon called us to attention as it turned to a gentle and soothing wail.

Dad would take us fishing in the little outboard motor-boat, or we'd fish from the dock, learning how to attach the worms and drop the rod. Fish were easy to catch, so no skill was required. But we learned to skin the scales, slice the belly, and remove the gut. Mostly we threw the fish back, feeling sorry for them. It was more about being on the water or the dock on the idyllic lake where few boats passed and one could see no populated shoreline. The visible side of the lake shore was protected land, which shielded us from any prying eyes. Sometimes we would motor over to our little island to jump from the treed cliff into the inviting water below. It was scary but exhilarating.

Mom would mostly use these trips to read uninterrupted, her favorite pastime. She would bring books for us to read or to read to us after dinner. Before dinner, Dan and I would go toad hunting. The toads on the island were tiny. Their small bodies blended into the browns and grays around them, but they were active at dusk. When caught, they would pee in our hands to get us to drop them, which we found hysterical. Dan was always my best and easiest playmate on these trips, and on most days. Willing, gentle, accommodating, and up for anything.

Mom would make dinner every night, but the real treat came after dinner. Mom was health conscious, so we were denied sweets growing up, unless it was Halloween or our birthdays. But in a cabin on an island on Devil Lake, she made us "heavenly delights." Heavenly delights were ice cream sundaes. In retrospect, they weren't all that amazing. We only had vanilla ice cream that I can recall, no fancy flavors. But she might make them banana split–style and then pour a maple walnut sauce over them. The true magic was the maraschino cherry on top. Mom always knew how to make something special even more magical. We would eat them, and Mom would read to us from the book she brought for these evenings. I remember her reading Robin Hood to us and even now, as I type these words, I can feel myself in that room, hearing her voice lilting through the lines, my father perched at the sink with yellow rubber gloves doing the dishes.

It was in that cabin that he taught me the proper way to wash dishes. The water had to be very hot. As hot as could be tolerated. You had to use a big pan filled with soapy water. Rinsing was important, and you had to do it a lot. Dad was a chemist, so he knew these things.

These trips were otherworldly slices of heaven because there were no phone booths, no meetings, no marches or rallies. There were no interruptions or real ways to interrupt. Nor did Mom need to collapse into her tired need for solitude after a day at the office. We didn't even have family dinners, and so these Devil Lake nights were pure bliss, as were the days.

But this August would break the magic spell and leave us in a dark daze. My parents had decided to call it quits, but rather than disrupt our family vacation, we went as usual. They told us at the lake house. I think it was toward the end of the trip, but I can't be sure. I only remember that it was daytime when they summoned my brother and me to the cabin and explained that they would no longer be living together, that they still loved each other and they loved us, but they were separating. Mom, as I recall, did all the talking in her usual, calm, in-control and kindly, direct way. Dad was not the explainer in the family unless it was about his car or some other practical matter. I don't even remember Dad's face during all this. I'm sure it was quiet and unreadable.

But he was the dad who, when he wasn't traveling, came into our room at night and sang us a good night song or two. Or three, if we begged hard enough. His favorite, "Que Sera, Sera," seemed a cruel joke now. When Dad wasn't home, which was often, Mom sang to us herself. Her reliability made it easy to take her for granted. Dad, on the other hand, was now moving out of our house. It was hard to accept. We asked the usual "why" questions that earned us a somewhat more detailed version of "Sometimes people who love each other just grow apart." We were used to families that didn't have fathers. Most of the women who were the organizers, the leaders of the welfare rights movement, were single. Ed Day had a nice wife we liked, and she had come with all of them from Syracuse to New York to DC. She and Ed got divorced, and he married one of the leaders. But this was very different. This was us.

We went off for a walk together after being released from this conversation, which had felt like being struck by lightning. Looking back, I can almost imagine us looking like a scene from *The Little Rascals*, one of our ritual weekend shows. The characters often played with fireworks or engaged in some science experiment that would blow up in their faces. The inevitable explosion would leave their hair standing straight up on end and faces darkened with soot that exaggerated the illuminated whites of their wide eyes and O-shaped mouths. Only this was far from funny. Nothing prepared us for this vacation gone wrong. We had no clue, no inkling, that they were unhappy. I wracked my brains—we both did—for the evidence we had missed.

The worst thing that I could remember happening was Mom, who never really exhibited anger, getting mad at Dad because I had taken a dollar to buy candy I was not allowed to have. I think I must have recruited Dan into my scheme because he was in trouble, too. Mom was apparently tired of being the sole disciplinarian. She gritted her teeth together and said "George" in that way that I only heard directed at me when I was in trouble. Mom could grin so widely, but she could also frown deeply. She never raised her voice, but she could snatch you suddenly by the nape of the neck with her tone. But she didn't have to rely on her tone, since she was demanding that he spank us.

Mom was the spanker, although we weren't spanked very often. Spankings stopped altogether, when Danny and I were still very young, after she discovered the sainted Dr. Spock. This punishment predated him. Dad very reluctantly put me over one of his knees and Dan over the other. We hung there as if we had been perched on massively tall tree limbs, and Dad very half-heartedly brought his hands down on our backsides as if he were playing the bongos. I remember screaming and crying as if I was being tortured by a dictator's special, secret spy unit trained to extract secrets from the rebellion. After that, I learned to search the sofa for change that fell out of his pocket instead of taking the more precious dollar bill. After all, I could buy Mary Janes or Jolly Ranchers for a penny.

But this memory was too far in the past to explain their breakup. Dan thought maybe we had incurred some bad luck. He made a reference to a tree log he had stepped over and maybe shouldn't have. None of it mattered anyway. There was no joy left in what remained of that trip, and it would be the last of those August island getaways. It would end everything as we knew it.

When we got home, it was late at night. Even though Mom had explained that Dad would be moving out, it hadn't formed a permanent home in my brain. But when we got home in the darkness, we watched Dad collect two prepacked suitcases as he said goodbye. It was a smack in the face. I was broken all over again. We begged him to stay with our moans of "why" and "for how long." Mom explained that he wouldn't be far away and that we could go and see him, and he would come and see us, but I just remember being confused and disoriented. He walked through the door and then right back out.

I had a hard relationship with my mother already, by which I mean I was very hard on her. She would observe that I was "contrary." And I unconsciously blamed her for much of my pain because it was impossible to blame Dad. His love could be doubted, not hers. Mom worked hard to make sure Danny and I did not feel responsible for their breakup. She succeeded. I blamed her. The visual of her holding the door while Dad walked out with a suitcase in each hand made it easy. She was making him leave. Like most children, I didn't know what I didn't know. I only knew what I saw.

Dad moved to a house he rented with others, which was walking distance to his office and to us. But the meetings were no longer at our house. We saw these activities less, but we saw my father more. Now he made more effort to make his time with us about us. We went on drives and to the movies and to the playground more.

My parents' separation was made permanent in a completely unpredictable way. We had a period as a broken family but with more fatherhood. It was a gift of many months made more so by what was to come. But I did not always fully participate because I was angry and expressing it with a kind of oblivious obstinanance. It was not necessarily new, but now new pains were prompting it.

We were used to being in the car with him and, weather permitting, when a pay phone came into view, he would pull over. If this happened, it meant the top to the convertible was down and we were supposed to be doing something fun. My brother and I would moan, "Daaaaad!" He would swear he wouldn't be long. We sat bored in the back seat of the sports car that was like an amusement park ride for us, only the roller coaster had been stopped for an interminable amount of time. Used to this, we would periodically raise our bored heads and whine, "Daaaaad…come on, let's gooooo!" Or "How much loooooongeeeeer?"

On this trip, things felt different. We were on an adventure; Dad was going to pick up a cabin cruiser he was buying, and we were going to cruise from the Chesapeake Bay back to DC. We drove to the Chesapeake Bay with the roof down. The wind was blowing in our faces, and we were excited and happy.

We weren't exactly boat people. Up until that day, my brother and I had known only our little outboard motorboat, which putt-putted us from the mainland to our little rock of an island. My parents' friends' cabin was so close that, if you didn't mind leeches, you could wade between the two. My brother and I didn't like leeches, so we usually took the outboard motorboat over if we wanted to "visit" our island. It was basically a dinghy.

Dad would give us each a turn steering the little motorboat whenever we went to or from the island.

Once we spent the night on a yacht owned by wealthy donors to my father's organization, so he could fundraise and we could understand what wealth looked like on the water. I remember the wife loved my brother and practically purred with auntlike adoration over him. Her voice would rise a few registers when she addressed him, and her eyes would turn into swimming pools of glistening attention. Back then, when we were in elementary school, Danny was a little smaller than me. I could be mistaken for the older sibling. He had a mass of silky brown curls, which fell on his forehead and around his ears in large, gentle rings. It often prompted women to stop my mother on the street and ask if she got his hair permed. I had a nappy afro and dirty knees that my mother asked me repeatedly to try not to scrape up and scar any more than they already were, as she laughed at my tomboy antics.

Our personalities in front of adults matched our size and appearance. I was abrasive and brash, demanding and outspoken. Danny was calm, patient, self-contained, and therefore, in the eyes of many adults, "good." He *was* good. Good as gold. And I was a brat. I will never know if the wife didn't like me because of that, or if she didn't like me because I was a brown girl who didn't fit the part. I only knew that this woman did not seem to like me and adored Danny in a way that made me shrivel inside.

The room on the massive yacht designated for us had bunk beds. They were exotic, and of course, we both wanted the top bunk and fought over it. Dan could be relied upon to always give in to my angry insistence. He could hold his own but preferred not to spend a lot of time fighting or dealing with my very long, dark periods of punishment for not getting my way.

I remember this wealthy host came into our little cabin with the bunk beds to say good night...to Danny. If she was trying to hide that she thought my brother adorable and me a monster, she did so very poorly. I should not have had the top bunk. That was clear. She shot her scowl at me as she praised him for being so sweet. He *was* sweet. Or, at least, accommodating. I remember not regretting the fight for the top bunk because I was a child and I wanted it. But I also remember it being very clear that this white lady was nothing like my mom. This woman didn't want me to be fierce or to fight. She wanted me to be docile and quiet, like Danny. But even if I was, I doubt she would have liked me. I somehow understood that, and it made me hate myself more.

The cabin cruiser Dad bought now was not a dinghy, nor was it anything like that yacht. It was neither large nor impressive, but to us it was amazing. It had a small cabin with two cots, one on each side of the bow, the forward berth for boaters, but I didn't know that. It had a small kitchen, or galley. Very small. My dad and brother each slept on one of the cots, and I had the kitchen table to sleep on. I didn't mind. I felt like an adventurer.

That night would be our first time sleeping on the boat, and we had nowhere to go until the following day. But it was a beautiful afternoon, and Dad took us out into it. That was when he gave us our first lessons on driving the little cabin cruiser. It was easier than driving a car. Or at least I thought so, having never driven one. It had something similar to an automatic gear shift, but the only options were slow, medium, fast, and reverse. The rest was all just steering. Easy. He showed us how to drop anchor, and then we just jumped off the boat for a swim.

My brother and I experienced this evening very differently. It was a peaceful dusk. The sky was gently turning from pale blue to streaks of pinks and yellows as the sun set. We went for a swim in the water, warmed by the August sun. I remember it as the three of us laughing and splashing about. It felt simple and easy and fun to be together. Dad dove down and came back up with a mussel he broke open and ate raw, which brought shouts of utter, joyful disgust embedded with peals of laughter from my brother and me. It was one of the best days I can remember with Dad. That was a bit ironic because my brother, having been in summer school to support his learning, had not had the same lessons I had. He dove in the water and thought he would drown. For him, it was a scary event and one that would foreshadow what was to come. But for me, who couldn't believe Dan could drown and didn't understand how much fear he felt, it was bliss.

The following morning was gray and the waters choppy, but Dad still planned for us to make our way back up the throat of the Chesapeake to the Potomac River. The nice man at the slip, who I had assumed was the owner of the boat, too, told Dad we should wait until the next day. I remember clearly that they were talking about it. Danny and I were too busy being excited about the boat and the water and the trip to pay close attention, but I still see them, both tall, next to the little dock. Dad wasn't worried and nicely dismissed the man's concern. It still didn't seem to be anything like a storm. Dad was so confident, as he always was, that it was impossible not to be infected by it.

Danny and I were taking turns driving. It was so choppy that Dad had to shimmy his way from the stern of the boat to its bow on a very narrow walkway. He kept his body pressed to the little cabin, and he held a handrail running along the top of it as he sidestepped on the plank. The spray of the waves that angrily slapped the sides of the little cabin cruiser seemed relentless. Dad had to get to the windshield and wipe off the spray so that Dan or I, whoever was driving, could see other boats or buoys to be avoided.

Instead of being afraid of the forceful waves and the dark gray sky, it all lulled me to sleep. I had gone below to escape the weather and, if I'm honest, boredom more than anything else. I ended up in a cat-curl nap on my table bed. I was awakened by the sound of a splash accompanied by my father's and brother's laughter. There was a long, narrow window above my head. I sat up and instinctively looked out the small window over the table.

It was the shore-facing starboard, or the right side of the boat. I couldn't see anything funny, but it seemed fairly obvious what was happening. I didn't want to miss the fun, so I didn't bother to look out the window on the opposite side, or port.

I climbed the short ladder to the deck and saw what I expected. Dad had fallen into the roiling waters of the Chesapeake Bay. He swam like a fish. When we were little, Dad would give us rides on his back in the pool. The Chesapeake, however, was no pool, and it was disturbed that day. Threatening gray clouds had driven off the sun, and the waters rolled menacingly in response. The waves were carrying him farther from us.

Danny's skinny, small, ten-year-old, pre-growth-spurt frame managed the wheel. He was fifteen months older than me but still shorter, so neither of us could see everything over the boat's dashboard. I glanced to see his profile, eyes trained on the waters before him, concentrating as he navigated dangerous waves. His mouth curled up as he looked ahead, laughing in the staccato half-laugh, half-exclamatory way he had. Usually, my brother's laugh sounded like a beatbox counter to my father's, which comfortingly reminded me of keys jingling in his pocket. Dad had his usual grin as he bobbed out there, confident of his body, his ability, and the boat. None would save him.

Danny explained what I could see plainly. Dad had fallen off the boat. I remember seeing his torn life preserver, two pieces that seemed to be carried in opposite directions. Dad was confident but not reckless. He insisted that we all have life preservers on at all times, except when we were sleeping, moored in the slip the night before. Apparently, his large six-feet-plus, two-hundred-pound frame was too much for the rusted screws on the railing. It had given way, and he had fallen backward into the waiting waves. I had a passing curiosity about how the life preserver split apart, but the thought flew by like a seagull. Swift and seen but soon forgotten.

Danny circled Dad, but we were both afraid to drive up beside him because we might accidentally hit him as we battled the waves. I don't know how long that went on, but we were no longer laughing. Dad asked us to hurry in a matter-of-fact tone. As an adult I would realize my father was probably working on controlled calm. But to a child it was an attention-getter, and the cold fingers of concern began to creep up my legs. I only half noticed; a strange kind of one-eyed self-awareness gave me a false sense of seeing myself, but it was a distorted view.

At my big brother's direction, I went to a pile of rope heaped in the back corner of the boat on the port side. The same side beyond which my father's head bobbed almost like a human buoy, only buoys are unsinkable. Dad had a weight on him out there in the troubled waters. The rope happened to be near the ladder we had been climbing the night before when swimming was a joy. I imagined Dad climbing up this rope from the water, smiling at the humor of his fall. I couldn't loosen the thicker, snaked coils, so I started throwing a skinny rope against strong winds. My long, thin arms and the thin rope were no match for the winds encircling us like a perturbed flock of seagulls.

Dad started yelling with more urgency, "Hurry!" The cold fingers of that creeping concern were becoming something else, something that began to squeeze my stomach. I was deeply aware of the thicker ropes lying in impossibly heavy, knotted coils. I tried again to pull at them but I could not begin to figure out how to pull the right one in the right direction. I was terrified of taking too much time on a lost cause, so I went back to my thin reed of hope. My brother was now yelling at me, too, but I couldn't hear the words. I think he was telling me to get Dad the rope. He couldn't see the heap of knots at my small feet. I have no idea how long this went on. Twenty minutes? Less? My mind didn't care about measuring time when it had to figure out physical movements and emotional survival simultaneously.

Dad was getting tired. The angry wind had blown aside his grin. He was no longer confident. "Hurry. Hurry." My dad was scared. Desperate. It was a sound I had never heard from him before. The icy fingers were now a cold-blooded snake enveloping my body up to my neck to choke the breath from me. His fear did not freeze my limbs, but it solidified something deep and unnamable inside me. I have spent time forcing myself to break the ice of that frozen lake to face the dark beneath. My father's strength was leaving him. The water was winning against it. What did that mean for mine? What did it mean about anything I had believed about life and living? It was unfathomable. Something deep within me shuttered, a feeling that even now lives inside me as an ever-present echo.

Danny and I agreed that he should risk pulling the boat alongside Dad so he could climb in. As my brother drove the boat away from our father to turn and pull back up beside him, I turned around. Perhaps it was because Dad was no longer yelling for us to hurry. Perhaps it was just coincidence. I can't remember. But when I did, I saw him. I saw his head drop under the waves. His face seemed calm to me. Or maybe I willed that image, or I simply mistook its meaning. It looked like a simple head dip. I thought he would reemerge. My eyes searched blindly. I yelled to my brother. "Dad's head is gone." Children are literal. I was literal. He had been a floating head and now the head was gone. It wasn't our dad that was gone. This disembodied thing that only resembled what I knew my father to be when it was confident and laughing was gone.

We circled. We circled. We circled. Nothing. The cold snake that had grown from a creeping cold and icy fingers had melted into me. I was now numb. How quickly laughter had become quiet, concerned concentration and then frantic fear. Now, I just felt nothing but an intense focus on survival. The snake had made my brain reptilian. Getting back to shore as two young children alone on the Chesapeake Bay was its own emergency. Dad was not here to help us. Even at nine years old, survival was a very conscious act. I was clear. The reptile in me proclaimed that I was not going to die.

Danny seemed clear, too. We were close, although as the younger sister of the preternaturally calm, sweet and talented, miniature older brother, I was always conscious that I sought him out, observed his reactions and feelings, and generally trailed him. He was patient with me, which was not at all the same. I loved him so much I would take anything I could get. But in this moment, we were a team. We didn't even need to talk much. We agreed. Point the boat to shore and just drive as close as we dared, drop anchor, and swim the rest of the way to get help. We could see the beach off to the starboard side. It strikes me still that our boat stood between Dad and the shore for much of the ordeal. The beach wasn't crowded but some people were swimming and others sunning themselves, oblivious to the drama unfolding out of their earshot and vision. There were houses dotting the beach too. We would get help.

Without really thinking *Dad is gone*, its truth splashed against the outer edges of my mind, like the waves slapping our boat. I would not allow them to jostle me about. I had a singular sense of purpose driven by fear. Mom was in West Virginia, at our four-room weekend shack. We called it "the Farm" even though it was never a working farm. It had once had cows grazing on the Shenandoah Blue Ridge Mountain it sat atop. It still had "cow plop," as we called it.

The blue ridges rippled majestically on three sides at the topmost point of the land the previous owner had cleared for his cows. A sea of mountains as blue as any dark body of water and that appeared as infinite as any ocean. Mom always loved the mountains; in the relatively short years of their marriage, Mom and Dad had an escape from the city. I was so small, but I remember Mom asking Dad if we could have that property. That shack with no running water. He said yes and Mom, in her usual exuberance, unfurled her sails of a broad smile and clasped hands with my brother and me. Dad joined with his full-faced, gleeful, almost mischievous grin, and we jumped around in a circle, holding hands and celebrating. It was odd to imagine her there, alone. A place that was always peopled with us and friends. Even more odd for its mystical distance to a now-menacing challenge. Somehow, we had to get to her. Get home. Nineteenth Street. 1736 Nineteenth Street. Home.

I experienced my dad's death with a different and new kind of duality: I was very clear that we had lost him and that his cries would never stop echoing in my head. I also thought only about myself and my brother and our survival. It didn't yet occur to me that we weren't supposed to be here, on this boat, on angry waters that swallowed my dad in punishment for demanding to play during the Bay's temper tantrum. Get to Mommy. That was the clearest, loudest bell ringing in my head.

We got the boat as close to shore as we dared. We knew we weren't supposed to run the boat aground, and somehow that serious lesson had a grasp on our minds at a moment when it probably would have been more rational not to care. Danny was still driving, so my job was to drop the anchor. I yanked and pulled frantically to get the contraption that held it in place at the bow of the boat to release its grip and, as was usual in my relationship with my far superior brother, told him I couldn't do it. He easily released it and dropped it in the water.

With all the seriousness we felt in the weight of the moment, we paused, looked at the water, regarded the distance to shore. We were pretty close. Not so close to the swimmers that we had been in any danger of hitting them with the boat, but close enough to make out faces and see their curious confusion at the sight of two little kids, in life preservers, one taller and Black and the other a curly-headed white kid, wobbly kneed and about to jump.

We clasped hands. It was raw instinct. We were not a hand-clasping pair of siblings, but we loved each other, and we were in this thing together. That required no discussion. We jumped in that water together and laughed out loud as it struck us. The dangerous and arduous swim in lapping waves we had imagined was a dramatist's fantasy.

The moment of humor didn't last. We immediately started trudging against the current to get to shore. We were yelling now. I think. I was certainly yelling in my head. Now, so many years later, I can't say if the sound was emerging from my mouth. What is irrefutable is that these white people, shocked and awed, were not coming to help. I remember being stunned. Why were they just staring at us? Why weren't they coming toward us? Asking us questions?

We climbed the beach and began asking the sunbathers for help. They looked at us as if we were speaking a foreign language. The beach was not all cloudy but had real, albeit dimmed sunshine. The waves were not menacing here. It was a stark contrast to what I felt out on that boat. Two separate worlds bounded by proximity, like much of what I witnessed my whole childhood: only those in peril could see what the others refused to, even when it was plain and before their eyes.

We quickly decided to run to the houses. We rang a bell. No one answered. We rang another, and I think at the third house a middle-aged white man with receding hair answered. He was surprised to see us but did not slam the door. I was nervous and felt like these white people were not our white people. They were those other white people that I knew existed but rarely met. But this white man was looking at us with concerned confusion. I remember us telling him our dad had just drowned. Dan does not think we used those words and, in any event, years later he said he didn't believe he was drowned at that point. Just lost. Either way, we pointed out to the water. He was the antidote to the venom of disdain and detachment from the *this is not my problem* people. I felt more than knew that without my presence, my brother might have gotten more immediate help and concern.

This man, whose name I cannot remember but whose kind concern I will never forget, immediately ushered us into his home and called the police. He asked us questions kindly and in a way that told us we had found a grown-up. We could now let go of the wheel of that boat and be children again. When the squad car came, I can only remember one officer because he was also kind. He was young. Maybe a rookie. But he would become my companion for the day and into the evening.

As the story unfolded, and calls were made to the Coast Guard or Maryland Marine Police, there was still in our young minds some shred of possibility that they would find Daddy alive. It was not rational, but it hung as a small ray of sunlight piercing through ominous clouds. We knew it couldn't beat back the clouds, but we clung to it anyway, not fully believing. Danny seemed to be experiencing the emotions of the day now that we could relinquish self-preservation, although he described years later feeling numb and buttoned up. I consciously refused to be anything but rational and in possession of all my faculties. There was a checklist forming with this young police officer. Find a way to reach someone who could find a way to reach our mother. Find where Dad had bought the boat the day before and his car. The little red Austin Healey convertible he loved so much, with the little rumbly seats only we could fit in and which we loved riding in. Find our way home.

This was my first real experience with a police officer who was not an "Officer Friendly" but a friendly officer. And this experience was not with a "pig," but a young and sensitive (at least in this set of circumstances) police officer. I don't remember if he had a partner with him. He drove us in his squad car to the precinct, which was not large. Every officer there was white. They sat us in wooden chairs at their desks, from which our young legs dangled. They offered us sodas and asked us questions, and they made calls. We had been trained to remember our home number and address, of course. And we knew all of our parents' friends and had family-not-family who lived with us. Still, there was no answering machine, and we didn't know the phone numbers of the friends. I recall the officer I was with looking through DC phone books. At some point, they reached someone, Pam or Harriet? They were both single women, smart, professional lefties who lived with us but were not in Dad's work. They were family, though. Some group of them were going to try and reach Mom, by calling a neighbor who had a phone up there so she could come to collect Danny and me.

Danny, at some point, had begun to cry some. The full emotional weight of Dad's death, and what we had just witnessed and navigated, settled so heavily on him that it bowed his head and shook his shoulders. I remember feeling embarrassed and made deeply uncomfortable by it. I almost never saw my brother cry, and I knew it meant something was wrong with me because I had no tears. I also remember thinking that I was fine. That Dad was gone, and I couldn't change that. We had to find his car. We had to get to Mom. There were things to get done, and I could help. I was not judging Danny; I was bolstering myself. And probably, some part of me relished being the helpful child for a change. It's a hard admission. Danny was so much better than me. He was a better person. A better artist. A better tennis player. He could build things and fix things. He was patient and kind. I was…ordinary and uninteresting, volatile and unreasonably demanding at times. Now I could do something helpful. I could hold it together.

Danny stayed at the precinct, and I went with the young police officer in search of Daddy's car. It was something important to do to help. I needed that so badly; I needed to know I could be something despite Dad's death. I also needed that officer's kindness. He let me believe I was helping. I had no idea how to get to the little marina with the small shingled, one-room building on a pier that didn't hold many boats. I don't think I even remembered the name. We drove around, stopping at various places because I thought I recognized the road. But the officer could ask about little marinas nearby, and we eventually found it.

The man at the marina, the man who we had met only the

day before, another white man, was shattered when he heard the news. He grabbed and hugged me and cried. He had warned Dad the day before not to take the boat out. He was devastated to be proven right. I was oddly moved that he cared so much. It was all so strange to me, such a contrast to the disinterest I had felt from so many white adults. I wanted to make him feel better but didn't know how. I wanted him to know we were okay, and it would be okay. Looking back on it, I realize how detached I was from my own emotions to stand in that dark, wood-veneer-paneled room, with the crying white man, a rare sight for me, and wish him comfort, despite the devastating loss being mine.

I was the one who would never see my daddy again. Never hold his hand again. Never sit on his lap again. Never giggle and scream and complain about mushy kisses again. I would never be able to make up for being an angry daughter, an ungrateful one. I would never be able to be good for him; I would never find a way to be what I had felt so ashamed I wasn't. And all I could think was, *I'm doing really well because I am okay, and I am not crying and I am helping. It's not my fault. It's not my fault. It's not my fault.*

CHAPTER 11

LIFE

THERE WAS A POINT after I told Danny that Dad was gone that reality dawned on me. Daddy had disappeared. He was under the water, and he wasn't coming back up. Danny said it was my fault. I'm not sure those were his actual words, but it was what I heard. What I heard as an accusation hit me like a swarm of angry bees. My bewilderment became a silent protestation. Responses swirled in my head, not daring to seek my mouth. Danny was never one to explode. He was the boy-man who managed himself always. Now he was in pain, and confusion bubbled up but had not yet burst out. I should have gotten a rope to Dad, he said.

As my mind battled through that attack, I was numb, the stinging on my face my only sensation. I swatted the bees with the image of that heap of knotted rope. Like when I was bullied, my brain was my companion, cataloging the events, explaining that I had done nothing wrong. How could I have untangled that mound? I pushed the thickening mass forming in my throat, as if that mound of fibers had found its way into my mouth. Danny was upset and I somehow understood that.

I felt Danny had lost something I wished I had. Together, he and my father could attack a project with a silent synchronicity and joyful patience I couldn't fathom. Reattaching Dad's muffler to the guts of his car, they would work with little speech, occasionally consulting, thoroughly in the moment with each other. They reveled in figuring out how to fix an appliance on the fritz. They always tried to engage me and make me feel a part of it, but I had no interest in their projects, which made me feel doubly alone.

They also both loved tennis. Tennis was Dad's favorite sport. My brother continued to play through his adult life. I hated every minute of the free, ghetto tennis lessons I had at the courts at the community center. They were in the afternoons, and I endured them through the full test of the midday sun in a city built on a swamp with 100 percent humidity. It was a torture chamber, and I felt punished by being forced to be there. Danny silently bore the heat, uncomplaining and committed to mastering the game. I crumpled, staggered, and barely raised my racket.

Like much of DC, the back of Dad's house was bordered by an alley, which was where he parked his little red sports car with its Campbell's-soup-can fixes and patches of rust. Behind the alley was a grassy field and a fenced-in court, and just beyond that a small playground. That was something we didn't have on Nineteenth Street. The court was neither a full tennis court nor a basketball court that I can recall, and the playground had little play equipment, but the wall that separated it from the court was a good place to practice hitting a tennis ball. Dad had bought my brother and me a matched set of tennis racquets. He rarely took us to play there. We usually just ran out of the house to play by ourselves at the playground.

At some point, Dad decided to spend some time with Dan and me separately. Mom probably suggested it. On one sunny, beautiful day, Dad took me to that back court wall to hit some tennis balls. This was Dad's sport. It was an activity Danny concentrated on. I didn't hate tennis, but I hated being less good at it. I had to be instantly good, or I was instantly angry.

This particular day, Dad repeatedly hit the ball gently to the wall for me to return back to him. I kept missing. My play deteriorated from poor to dismally bad. I responded, as I always did when I felt ugly and dumb and alone, by getting angry and mean. Normally, Dad would ignore my explosions, but it was rare for us to be alone. He became unusually frustrated. He said, "You're not supposed to miss the ball with a tennis racquet!"

His outburst seemed to confirm my ineptitude and outsider status with the men in my family, and my humiliation was complete.

Dad had never criticized me before. He was the rock in the river. The white water just washed over him. He would usually laugh or smile to defuse any situation, or he would just keep moving as if my outburst hadn't happened, not ignoring it, just staying nerveless and serene in the face of it. But this time it was as if he'd spanked me in public. I felt he was finally conveying his true feelings about me. I raised my shield of anger and threw my tennis racquet to the ground. My eyebrows were now a single row of cloud cover, as I stormed off the court and back to the house. This argument is all that I remember of that day, leaving me not one happy memory from the rare slice of solo time with him.

At some point I stopped going to Dad's as often. It wasn't that I didn't want to see him, but I felt no tug to go. Danny would try to encourage me to come with him. Neither Mom nor Dad would make me go. Danny called with Dad when he got over there. "Come. Just come," they would say. I would simply say "I don't feel like it," which was the plain truth. I just didn't. It was a kind of malaise, although I didn't recognize it at the time. Instead, I would watch the Saturday Matinee movies on TV. There was always a Laurel and Hardy comedy, a Bela Lugosi horror, and maybe an Alfred Hitchcock as part of the triple feature. I would lay on the floor in my room, watching by myself on a little black-and-white TV while Mom recuperated from her week.

What memories did I miss out on making? Each one became so precious and guarded, even the fights, because there was always the truth of Dad's love at the end of them. I would have fewer memories than Danny because I couldn't manage my own self-loathing. As I got older, I better understood what Dad was going through with the demise of NWRO: the periodic and painful repudiation of his own Blackness, despite the sacrifices he made because of his conviction that Black people deserved better. Dad was lonely, his marriage ending, his middle age upon him, and his exhaustion deep, and I didn't feel like it.

When Danny said that I should have thrown the rope to Dad successfully, it reminded me of my incompetence, never matching Dad's or Danny's cleverness. His words cut, although I know he never intended to hurt me. But they left a little sliver of doubt that periodically forced my thoughts back to that impossible pile of ropes over the coming weeks. Maybe Danny could have gotten farther than me in untying them, but in time? I didn't believe he could. Or if I had gotten those ropes detangled, I don't believe any would have reached Dad in that wind. If sufficiently thick ones lay hidden at the bottom of the pile, they were likely so heavy that their weight would have pulled them beneath the waves before reaching him. I just knew it.

Also gnawing at me was a different reason we could blame ourselves. We didn't try pulling the boat closer to him sooner. We circled too long. He was crying out for us to hurry, his cries were terrifying because he was so strong, so in control, and the one who took care of everything. Dad was desperate, and it's hard to remember those cries even all these years later. Maybe we could have reversed the boat to him so he could swim to the small ladder off the stern? Maybe. I had a bottomless well of that "maybe."

The police officers at the precinct, or maybe they were state troopers, made up cots for Danny and me to sleep on and brought us toothbrushes. Some of them were oddly paternal in the most incongruous of ways, given the relationship my family had with the police. They got us dinner, made us shower and brush our teeth before making sure we lay down, and covered us up with blankets. I had no sense of time from that bleary, hyperconscious, dream walk of a day. It was dark. Very dark. We knew our people were coming. We knew that they had reached Mom, and she was making her way from West Virginia back to DC. We just didn't know the timing, and it didn't matter. All that mattered was that it was happening. That we no longer had to hold the wheel and steer the boat. We had Dad's car. Mom knew. We had survived.

Three friends retrieved us, all of whom were very close

to our family. It seemed Dan sobbed the entire car ride home, his head on a lap, but of which adult, I can't recall. He doesn't remember crying a lot, and maybe my memory exaggerates the feeling that he was more expressive and I was more frozen. I sat, stoic, remembering myself a silent witness to his pain. My heart broke for him. Not for me. For him. I was in control. I was okay. I understood Dad was gone and nothing I could do would bring him back. I was handling this. I was strong. I could be strong for both of us.

We weren't home long before Mom reached us. We were in our pajamas, in our own beds in our shared bedroom. The room had this horrible plastic fiber rug that was like cheap Astroturf. It was just like my mother to buy something indestructible for us to play on. It had blue and green fibers that made it look like a cheap, fake sea in between our twin beds. We had not yet fallen asleep when Mom ran into our bedroom. She gathered us up and sobbed. My mother, Wretha Whittle Wiley, sobbing. That was too much for me. I had never seen her tears before. Never. She was always an active witness. Always in control. Always okay. I was emulating her, wasn't I? Strong and in control? And here she was with tears so powerful, they overcame my dam, and mine flowed, too. We all three sobbed, distraught, bereft, inconsolable, and simply together. One heaving mass.

I don't remember us speaking that night, though we must have. We were all talked out anyway. That night, there was nothing more to say. Dad was gone. It was unfathomable, but it was also undeniable. He was swallowed whole by the Chesapeake, leaving no evidence of his death. We didn't know if we'd ever have any, though a few days later they recovered something I knew only as proof of an event. The body was not my dad.

"Remains" is a more accurate word. We would never see them. I am grateful that we never overheard a description of what three days in saltwater does to "remains." I was only told there would be a closed casket because saltwater does things that people don't need to see. I preferred to not add to the horror of his screams, so I didn't push to see him. Dad was life itself, so the strange casket was merely a symbol. It was what we lost that mattered, not what remained.

With the lights out and Danny and me in our parallel beds, in a house with my mom and other adults with whom we felt safe, we could finally sleep. In the dark quiet of the secure and familiar, my memories of the day burst the emotional dam I had hastily constructed. I would never get to hug Dad again, never get mushy kisses or rides on his back. I would never again have his lap to sit in. The man who was too absent, too stellar, too funny, too distant, too incomprehensible, too important, too singular, was now gone. I cried softly but with abandon that night. I don't know how long I cried, but it was enough to drown out his loss. I still sometimes cry softly in seemingly random moments when everyone else is asleep.

My emotional survival I owe completely to Mom. She anticipated and dispelled the dark, roiling sea of questions that so many avoid examining after a traumatic death, and especially with children. The very next morning, she began asking us questions. What happened? She was gentle and direct and unblinking. She wanted us not just to tell her but to tell ourselves, to confront and face what had happened not just to Dad but to us. She believed the trauma should not be allowed to fester as a taboo topic. I was excavating a cave to hide it in, and she was determined to force it out of the dark places. We talked about it all the time. And not just Dad's death but Dad's life, our memories with him. She encouraged us, often starting sentences with "Remember when your father..." It would be many years later, after my mother's own death when talking to a long-lost housemate who was dear to us, that I would learn that she'd asked her friends to get us talking about it, too. It was a strategy that she consciously deployed to help my brother and me survive this trauma. It worked.

Mom went so far as to take us to the Maryland Coast Guard meeting to hear their report of Dad's death. Like fire departments, they investigate tragedies to identify how to help others stay safe. It didn't occur to me that it was not a Coast Guard requirement that we be present but her choice. She came with her two young kids, the gawky nine-year-old and the serene, serious ten-year-old, each grasping a hand. She wanted us to know that there was nothing we could have done to save our father, that if we had pulled up beside him in the boat and he had tried to climb in, it would have capsized on us, and she would possibly have lost us all. She wanted us to hear it from the Coast Guard so that it would be irrefutable.

It went a bit further than that. No one outright blamed Dad for his own death, but no one shied away from the fact that the decision to take the boat out that day, a decision Dad made despite being advised to wait a day for the weather to calm, a decision he made with his two little kids and no other present adult, was a tragically bad one. Mom, I would later learn, was not only deeply saddened but also angry that he had been so reckless with our lives and his own. Later in life, Mom told me that he had predicted he would die young. The very boldness with which he had lived his life, that produced so much achievement and impact, would also end it. Dad was not only dead, but he was dead because he was imperfect. Survival demands seeing.

The next day and in the days that followed Dad's death, the phone seemed to ring off the hook. Family, friends, and leaders were calling to express condolences and hear the story of his death. I heard my mother and our other housemates on the phone constantly answering questions and recounting the story. Reporters were calling, too, searching for something much more thrilling than a drowning. Was it murder? Was he assassinated? To their disappointment, I imagine, he only died a tragic death at forty-two years old. It was still a story. "Dr. George Wiley Feared Drowned" was the *New York Times* headline. It was strange to sense the disappointment that he was not martyred, like Dr. King, or, like Malcolm X, murdered by members of his own tribe because of internal power plays.

I remember feeling, once again, uniquely superior to my otherwise perfect big brother that first day dawn broke without Dad breathing somewhere on the planet. We were in the kitchen eating breakfast with Mom. The day was turning for us in a sort of slow motion, but then the phone rang. Mom greeted someone I can't recall. She confirmed that, yes, George was dead and began the first of many recountings. She was sullen but emotionally fixed on the transaction. Not rote, but not carving any pieces of her emotional self off to be served up to feed someone else's emotional need. She was a conservationist now, saving herself from the needs of others and steeling herself for all that must be managed, including her own complicated emotions about the death of her not-quite-yet-ex-husband, the father of her still young children and an icon and father figure to many others.

Danny had been calm that morning until Mom started recounting the horrors of the day before. He ran out of the kitchen crying. I was again numb, clear-headed, and rational.

And I also felt a tug of uncertainty about whether something was wrong with me. Danny's behavior made more sense and so I ran out of the kitchen after him, copying him, but without the tears or heartfelt emotion. I followed him at a distance to be near him and with him but also feeling outside of his experience, like a camera recording the action without being a part of it. He ignored me, deep in his despair, lying on his bed and crying hard. I sat in witness, knowing I had nothing to offer him and wondering if I would cry anywhere other than my bed at night when I thought about Dad's key-jingling laugh.

I would remain that child. Nurture her, reinforce her, tell her she was doing great and that she was mature and could handle all of this. I actually told myself these things alone in bed at night. I would kick myself for being such a horrible, selfish daughter who took my dad for granted. I would tell myself I couldn't have saved him and that I was handling it all so well. As strange as it sounds, I believe to this day that all of this had truth in it. I had survived the event of his death and the sorrow of it. I would live with it. I could live with it.

There was something about Dad's face in that last glance I had when I turned and saw him disappear. Resignation, perhaps. Acceptance. Did I just attach these adjectives as a kind of emotional buoy I could cling to so that I wouldn't drown in his cries? I even wondered if he just descended into the foamy water to save us when he realized he was beyond saving. These are heartrending thoughts, but the contradictions in my emotions have always been a balancing act, like standing on a boat being buffeted by rough seas without toppling over the edge.

Family therapy came next. I actively refused to cooperate, resenting the whole process. The three of us went to some older, pompous white man, with a beard and mustache, who seemed to look down his nose at us as he leaned back in his large chair behind a desk. I remember intensely disliking him. Mom did all the talking and I tuned it all out. Dan was back to his usual stoic, calm self and appeared attentive, but I don't remember him talking, either. Eventually, Mom gave up.

It only got worse, by my estimation. Mom sent me to individual therapy. Just me, not Danny. I had been congratulating myself on my exceptional emotional adjustment. After all, I was not the one crying all the time. I recognized that I was lucky to have Dad in my life, even if it was only for nine and a half years. I missed him, but I understood and was grateful for my good fortune. What else did that woman want from me? To be a heaving mound of flesh? Her decision fueled my sense of familial problem-child status, and I was both hurt and resentful, which only made me more obstinate.

I did like my new white male therapist. Unlike his predecessor, he didn't have an arrogant air about him. He was much younger, with a close-cut mousy-brown beard and mustache that was typical of the 1970s. He seemed kind and was easygoing. He sat in a less ostentatious chair in a brighter office, and with only a coffee table between us. Sometimes I went to our sessions, but I often pretended to get lost on my way to his downtown office after school. I would just walk around for an hour in the general vicinity of his office and then head home. I don't know how many times I "got lost," but far too many to be credible. Once I asked Mom why I had to go to therapy and complained of its uselessness. Without giving me much information, a rare thing for the woman who gave me a biological answer to the question *Where do babies come from?*, she simply said that it was useful.

My disengagement meant that I remember little of our

sessions except one, during which I asked why he had placed his chair with its back to the door. It seemed to me that made him vulnerable to attack. To me, there was nothing strange about making sure people didn't pull up behind you unnoticed.

Once, after the bell rang at Adams Elementary, signaling our release from captivity, the halls and stairways of the three-story brick building had chatting, laughing, screaming hordes of us racing to the exits. I usually ran with the students stampeding to the gaping mouth of the front doors.

For some reason, on this day, I decided to run out of the side door. Fewer students went that way because it was less direct. You had to go to the far end of the hallway and down a set of stairs to the side of the building, then run around to the front. I thought it might be faster to avoid the crowds. I was wearing a dress, which was common school attire for me. My grandmother made my dresses, and they were often different colors of plaid, with an empire-level tie to the back and a white collar. The style varied less than the fabrics, as I recall, but I loved them.

I burst through the door, and suddenly, two older boys I didn't know grabbed me. They pushed me to the railing that faced the neighborhood beyond. They held me from behind, reached under my dress, and tried to pull down my panties. I was probably seven or eight. They could not have been older than ten. I managed to get a hand on the front of my underwear and clutched my panties in a tight ball. They were strong and I was frantic and terrified. One of them rasped, "We just want your panties, girl!" I couldn't see, but I think the side door opened and they ran off.

I was trembling. The attack left me feeling much more vulnerable in a building where I already faced the threat of being beaten up periodically. I felt humiliated and completely terrorized. I ran all the way home, shaking. I told no one what had happened. I was too ashamed. I somehow felt to blame for exiting the wrong door. I had been stupid, reckless even, to put myself in that vulnerable situation.

Danny and I both walked home from school, and we were released about the same time. His special, safe, small school was not more than six blocks from my massive and sometimes monstrous public one. I begged him to come walk me home from school the next day, but he declined. I interpreted his "No way!" as *Are you crazy? I'm not going over to that dangerous school! You're on your own!* And that was how I felt. To be fair, he didn't know why I was so desperate. I also didn't blame him for not wanting to put himself at risk. He had no reason to even know I was at risk, and I was probably misinterpreting his refusal.

Danny had protected me. After our parents split, a group of boys looking to feel better about themselves found us on the playground behind Dad's group house. We were an obvious target, and they started throwing bricks in our direction. These boys were much bigger than Danny, but he screamed for me to run. It was a short way back to Dad's house, and I understood what Dan was going to do, without discussion. He distracted them and got them to chase him in the opposite direction. That put him at risk of being beaten up or, worse, pummeled with flying bricks. He had to run out and around the whole block to get back to the safety of Dad's house.

As opposed to Danny's experience at school, I was learning to keep my back against the wall in a school that made me feel constantly off-balance and sometimes endangered. Mom was always open about his brain damage from birth and his need to learn differently. Every student in his school was "special" and needed a special school. Danny yearned for normalcy and was certainly unlikely to see himself as the lucky one, and he was right about that. I should have felt like the lucky one, but I didn't. I just felt less important. I wanted Danny to have what he had. I just wanted to have it, too.

Before Dad died, Mom would sometimes remark to me, "You're fine." She was sharing her honest assessment of my competence and ability. She meant for me to feel better, more supported. She wanted me to feel that I had what it took to get through hard times. The implicit message was that Danny was the one she worried about. I was angry when I heard "just fine," but also when I heard "I'm off duty." Those days I sat drowning myself in the Saturday Matinee movies, alone, while she recuperated, or the nights I needed her after a hard day of bullying, were Mom's "off duty" times. When she was available, I threw my anger and frustration in her lap, like an emotion-emitting hand grenade.

Sometimes others would receive the back hand of my outrage. The most memorable example was a day I tried to learn to whistle. Our babysitter at the time was a skinny, white hippie with long hair and a short-cut beard named Rick. I always thought of him as Jesus' fraternal twin due to his striking resemblance to the light-up Jesus portrait that Nana and Papa had plugged into the wall. One day when we were not out treasure hunting in our neighbors' garbage bins, Rick was teaching Danny to whistle. I had walked in on this and promptly demanded to learn, too. Rick began demonstrating, showing me how to push my lips out and into an O shape and softly blow. I could blow but not softly, and I got increasingly frustrated as my more amazing brother began to whistle. This escalated into more aggressive blowing. I became angrier and angrier, as if Rick were somehow to blame. My squall grew into a tempest, and Rick tried to calm me with a bear hug, which made my tantrum worse. Rick and Danny found a way to melt away.

In an unusual eye of my storm, I proceeded to turn—gently, so as not to break anything—all the sitting room furniture upside down. I placed the metal, canvas-covered butterfly chairs, the coffee table, and whatever else I could upside down, but in their proper place. Mom wasn't obsessive, but she was an orderly woman who insisted on a clean house with everything in its place. I had found the way to walk right up to the line of bad behavior that wouldn't result in punishment. It was one of my more elegant efforts to get her attention. As usual, I succeeded in deepening her exhaustion while failing to break down the wall of her patience. I was simply told to turn the furniture right side up and not disorder the ordered again.

It was clear that I needed help and outlets for my anger, fear, and grief, but I don't recall addressing these topics in therapy. Maybe we did, without my direct awareness. Despite her unexplained position that I needed therapy, eventually my mother allowed me to drop it. I was relieved but not triumphant. What bothered me more than going to therapy was her view that I needed it and my brother did not.

After my father's death, Mom made major changes in her life for Danny and me. She quit her job as a management consultant to hang out her own shingle and be at home when her traumatized children returned from school each afternoon. It was a gutsy move for a woman in the early 1970s to believe she could attract business on her own. She was working, specifically, on developing and implementing affirmative action policies, mostly for governmental entities, including the Rochester,

New York, police department. She had also been deepening her own activism through third-party politics, helping to draft the People's Party platform for Dr. Spock's 1972 run for president, which would include a maximum wage and legal abortion.

This showed that Mom would not be the public widow who organized her life around preserving Dad's memory. This had nothing to do with their separation. She had spent their entire relationship working with and supporting him, though he was no saint and she was no servant. Mom, when asked, always expressed love for Dad and pride in their marriage as a true partnership. It seemed to me a one-way partnership, outside of what I learned about the Syracuse CORE days, but it mattered that she valued their relationship. She would also not seek recognition for her role in the movement, or in supporting the work to promote his legacy. Dad was no martyr in death. She would not try to make him one. She made it clear that her identity was not tied to his while illustrating how this commitment was not a rejection of him or their marriage. Mom also wanted us to walk in our own sunlight and not in his shadow. She wanted us to remember him and be proud of his work, but not believe falsely in his perfection or feel pressured by his legacy.

Around this time my life improved in another way. Before Dad died, and despite navigating what was, for her, the painful demise of her marriage, Mom had begun the arduous process of finding me a suitable private school. Her political support for public education and desire for me to experience it had not faltered, but she would not sacrifice my education, either. She had me tested in second grade to determine my grade-level attainment. I don't know how Mom did it, but she miraculously convinced the Georgetown Day School to accept me at my age-appropriate grade, despite the fact that I would not enter the fourth grade with the same level of knowledge as my new classmates.

Everything was changing radically for me at a time when the country was also historically unstable. The Watergate scandal was underway. The welfare rights movement was dying. The civil rights movement had been transformed from activism to activities by the short-lived war on poverty that created community service delivery programs. It would help usher in the election of a little-known Southern Baptist governor from Georgia two years after Richard Nixon's resignation. My first year I had to allow an extra hour to get to school because the streets were choked with cars waiting to fuel rattling gas tanks. At the time, there was an oil embargo by the Arab-dominated Organization of Petroleum Exporting Countries, a punishment for the US government's support of Israel in the Yom Kippur War. American exceptionalism was shattered by the realization that our boatlike vehicles were dependent on the foreign governments of brown people.

I would also travel at the beginning of math class to a hallway math tutorial, necessary to catch me up to the rest of the class. It was a huge relief not to fear bullying, even while it was deeply unnerving to sit in the hallway at the little metal desk with the attached right-handed table, with my kind, older, white math tutor. Inside the classroom, my white and Black classmates were doing short division and whatever came next, while I was drilled on the times tables. It was necessary and humiliating. But the humiliation was not meted out by my classmates. It was an internal shame, and I would never overcome the sense that I was a math failure, even as I challenged myself in college with the unnecessary torture of calculus, just to try and prove to myself that I was not a dolt.

Georgetown Day was mildly mixed, and mostly upper-middle-class. It's bright, cinder block corridors and classrooms were filled with the children of doctors, lawyers, and political elites, but they were not all white. My classmates included artist Sam Gilliam's daughter and Congressman Walter Fauntroy's son. More than three-quarters of the city's population was Black, and that included a sizable Black middle class and upper middle class. That was on display at my new school. I had friends who were not only Black, but to them I was not an enigma. Georgetown Day was not perfect and came with its own challenges. Many of the Black students didn't live near me. They either lived in the Black middle-class neighborhoods in the Northeast or Southeast parts of Washington, or in the Maryland suburbs. With the familiar public buses, I could spend a weekend night at their homes, here and there, but the time it took for us to get to each other on public transit lowered my social time with them out of school.

A girl in my class—I'll call her Gail—was popular, and we were friends, but I was not in her inner circle. I was accepted and invited over sometimes, but it never felt completely comfortable. She would regularly be one of the mix of Black and white classmates whom Mom would religiously invite to my "birthday slumber party," which would inevitably make me sad and lonely. We all got along, but these were two different friend groups mingled into one. Often my Black friends could not stay as long or, in some instances, come at all. My oldest daughter, at that middle school age, divided her peer group into "friends" and "associates." Friends were confidants and trusted. Associates were people to hang out and have fun with, but they weren't as trusted. Gail and this group were associates. They were not bad or mean girls, but they really were not my girls. I was a tolerated distant planet in their social solar system, and Gail and her best friend, whom I'll call Beth, seemed to me to be the suns.

On one occasion, Gail invited me to come to her house after school, and because she lived on the bus line I could take to get home later, I was happy to go. She and my other classmates knew that my father had drowned. He was well-known in DC, and his death was newsworthy, so their parents, who ranged from civil servants to politicians or prominent attorneys, would obviously have talked about him at home. We were waiting for the bus to her house. It was quiet and I was excited to be going to her house, a rare occurrence for a lonely kid. Gail asked the question everyone found the courage to ask when alone with me: *What happened to your dad?* I recounted all of it. It was like pushing a button on one of those dolls with prerecorded common statements, so it felt like you were having a conversation with them, even though they said the same things over and over. I was that doll. When I had finished, her lips curled upward in a kind of disgust, as if she had just caught a whiff of something putrid, and she said with biting judgment, "How can you just tell it like that!" I was supposed to cry. I was supposed to be traumatized in a way she could see.

I didn't understand. I was supposed to be able to tell the story. Mom had trained me, at least inadvertently, to tell the story. I was secure in its facts and resigned to my loss, and I saved my tears for my bed, when I had them. Gail had judged me defective, almost monstrous, and it felt like a different kind of bullying from public school. There would be no threats of physical blows, only psychic ones. I collapsed into myself, unanswering and calm, frozen in pain, feigning nonchalance. I trailed her to her house and remember sitting with her, feeling like a powerless fraud. I just wanted to go home and didn't know how to leave.

Later, I confided this story to Mom. She used it to teach me to find compassion in the face of pain. She told me Gail had a hard time at home and was angry about it. The message was *It's not you. It's her.* Mom was never one to share others' details, but I did know Gail's parents had split up, and she didn't like her mother. It didn't make me hurt less, and I never quite fit in or felt close to Gail or some others at GDS.

Like all middle school experiences, many friendships felt unreliable. Even with the Black girls there were periods of being "turned out" when the popular one would decide that one of us—sometimes me, sometimes another—was annoying. Private school's "in group–out group" dynamic seemed both more mean and more frivolous. I felt simultaneously off-balance and more widely accepted.

The proof was in an incident that was both empowering and humiliating. There was one very popular kid I'll call Dave, who was Vietnamese and adopted. He was small, gracefully athletic, and insecurely cool. There were really no other Asians or Latinos in our Black-white paradigm. Coming from public school, Dave's bravado was completely transparent and somewhat humorous to me. The posturing projected nothing but softness in search of a kind of proactive protection that was completely unnecessary in a school where the worst thing that happened to a kid was largely mind games and hurt feelings. I was undeniably ignorant about what traumas might have created Dave's behavior.

I knew the Vietnam War was bad and wrong and had even been in a group called Children Against the War led by this kid named Jamie Raskin, who would later become a

US congressman and a key part of the Donald Trump impeachment trial team. We would meet in his living room, and he would stand on a chair and give long, impassioned speeches about the evils of the Vietnam War, while the rest of us eight-year-olds wriggled. One kid, whose name I have forgotten, would hide behind furniture and shoot spitballs into my afro. He was ejected from the group before our march past the White House, which consisted of about five kids accompanied by a motorcade of police officers who were not amused that the massive antiwar rally they had prepared for was just a handful of unruly children; meanwhile, our activist parents cheered our little march from the sidewalk so as not to distract from the core message of "children" being against the war. All this gave me a sense of my own righteousness. I was a Wiley. I was enlightened and even a child activist!

I found Dave to be a compelling personality based on his beauty and his bravado. Unlike the one, working-class Vietnamese immigrant classmate I had at Adams or my accentless neighbor who also had been adopted from Vietnam, Dave was different. His mild but distinct hint of mispronunciation declared him a nonnative speaker, and he wore his silky, black hair long. The effort he put into his image as the tough kid seemed palpably practiced and exhausting to me, but it seemed to work magic on four or five white boys in the class, who floated around him as if proximity to him might make them equally interesting. If Dave sat on the desktop, a single foot on the chair and forearm perched notably on his thigh, they sat on the desktops and raised a foot to the chair. I found this mimicry a bizarre ritual. The Black boys in my class, of whom there were only about three, seemed to ignore all this.

One day, our teacher was out of the classroom for some

reason, so the desktop sitting had begun. Dave and I were not friends, but there was no tension between us. I didn't have any tension with anyone in my new oasis of calm upper-middle-class comfort. I was also about twice his size, the tallest in the class except for one of the Black boys, who was about my height. This particular day, somehow things shifted unexpectedly. I think Dave said something and I scoffed at it. We got into some silly back-and-forth. In my view it was a teasing kind of word-based swordplay. You had to be able to cut someone down to size if they threw any words your way.

Something in Dave's face showed he was not bothered by anything I said, but it did threaten his image. He had to do something. I was laughing at this point. He lifted his arm, pointed a practiced, nonchalant finger in my direction, and said to his minions, "Get her." They were momentarily stunned, and I stood bemused, waiting to see what they would do. I knew they wouldn't hit me and that they had no stomach for an attack. A couple of them awoke from the frozen stupor and each grabbed one of my arms, which prompted another couple to begin to move toward me as I started to fling the first two off. I had height advantage, and I was unafraid. And it felt so good. All I knew was that in this school I was the hard rock. They were uncommitted, so while they tried half-heartedly to gain control of me, I became more aggressive. The teacher walked in at a point when tensions were clear but nothing else was. The boys, relieved that they could back down, dropped away. Still, I remember dropping the ugly words at Dave without thought, to have the last word: "Flat face!"

In that moment, I was being literal, and I meant it to insult his beauty because he was beautiful. In my old school this would have been a mild insult, and its racial nature was lost on me. I was shocked to see the tears that welled in his eyes as he walked off. He disappeared around a partial wall that separated our desks from the coat hooks. I followed him back there—to do what, I didn't know. I saw the tears streaming down his face. I had punched the part of him that had been hurt before. I felt ashamed immediately but didn't know what to do or say. I hadn't inherited righteousness, and activism alone doesn't bring it. I had been taught as a Wiley to create the world we want. I knew I was wrong and that I should've known better. I had to admit it to myself, even if my shame would not allow me to tell my mom about it. I prayed she wouldn't find out, and, as far as I know, she didn't.

I now lived a strange existence of being both powerful and not abusing that power. Wileys knew how to fight, but it had to be right. Wileys always looked to use their power to negotiate, and compassion always mattered. A compassionless fight was not going to create the future we wanted. In-your-face, direct action didn't mean defacing, defaming, or dehumanizing. I had to be a Wiley. I needed to be a Wiley. Dad wasn't here anymore, but I was.

Georgetown Day was more comfortable for me, but I didn't completely fit in. I knew in some semiconscious way that my parents never really fit in, either, even as they were accepted in their relative environments. I also saw that the movement created a way for them to fit in somewhere, with others who shared a deep, if often complicated, bond. Movements create a community of those who otherwise may not have one. I felt I fit in even less so in my new life without Dad, even as we adopted the same modes as "normal" people outside of movement activism.

When I was in fifth grade, we would leave our group home on Nineteenth Street, pushed out like our neighbors—only we would move uptown, literally and figuratively. Cleveland Park was only a mile away, but it was a world apart. We were just a few doors down from my former nursery school. All the homes were big Victorians, with yards and driveways. The recession was in full swing, and Mom had convinced Harriet to go in on the house with her for a very good price. Now we lived in an upper-middle-class white neighborhood, where only one other Black person resided. Lou Stovall, the artist, lived around the corner with his white wife. Peter and Marian Edelman would move in not too long after us, adding another interracial family to the mix. That didn't change that two white women were living in a house together with a white boy and a Black girl.

Leaving our redbrick row house was hard, but also a bit exciting. There would no longer be the swirl of different residents like the students from the then newly formed Antioch Law School, which is now closed but lives on as the University of the District of Columbia Law School, where I serve as the Joseph Rauh Professor. It was created by the same benefactors who helped found the Legal Aid Society, and its mission was to produce public service lawyers who would represent and defend the rights of minorities and poor people. Other inhabitants included an excellent National Public Radio reporter, students, and other progressive young adults. Two of them, one who was Puerto Rican and white and one who was Black, taught Danny to ride a unicycle, and the three of them would ride in summer parades. Mom had a long dining table, and housemates took turns cooking dinner. That year of Mom's separation from Dad and the year following his death, she sat at the head of this long table, presiding over political and social conversations. Danny and I sat by and listened. For us, these meals became our family dinners, without biological connection. They were fun and engaging, and I loved these nights.

Moving uptown meant that those dinners spent with smart and politically active adults sitting around a long table each day came to an end. Our lives became much more conventional, much more white, and, for me, much more emotionally disconnected. But it also meant that the conditions were set for me to move beyond my anger. When I look back on all the trauma and transitions, I understand how important it was to feed my and my brother's abilities to shape our own lives and be emotionally healthy. My mother was creating something new for us. Not only would she be home during the day, but family dinners would now be a small, nuclear affair every night.

As much as my life improved, we lost the engagement and interesting exposure to young activists and professionals in our group home, the activism of Dad's world, and the possessed feeling that I had in my neighborhood. The neighborhood of Northern DuPont Circle was mine and I belonged in it somehow, despite the contradictions. Cleveland Park was alienating and lonely in its safe, tree-lined parade of large homes with wraparound porches and sprawling lawns with long driveways. No more back alleys. Although everyone in our old house was white after Dad moved out, now everyone in our family was white, too, except me. I walked the streets a stranger in my own neighborhood for years. To this day, when I return to DC, it is the house in DuPont Circle I walk past wistfully.

In Cleveland Park I stood out like a sore thumb, and kids on our block never came around to ask me to play with them. My relationship with my mother only got more tumultuous after Dad's death. Some of this was, no doubt, my entering the middle school years. It was made more difficult by Dad's death and her dating. Mom started dating one white man after another. This in and of itself didn't bother me. Dad was dating, too, before he died. There was his lefty Black lawyer girlfriend, and one or two others. We always liked Dad's girlfriends, probably because I didn't really understand that they were his girlfriends. I would later learn that some of them predated Mom and Dad's split. We were so used to having adults around who were not family that it didn't seem strange.

Mom first dated a Jewish man, who I later learned had been her divorce lawyer. He was funny and outgoing, with a big personality. He had a daughter and son that were Danny's and my ages respectively, and we liked them. They would come for weekends to our shack in West Virginia. Because I liked this boyfriend, I fought with him in the most defiant and unnecessary ways. I recall him directing me to do something. While I can no longer remember the particulars, I do remember that I refused, choosing to defy any authority he might have thought he wielded over me, just because he was dating my mother. He demanded and I got angrier, and the next thing I knew, I was shouting. I was in a full tantrum. He grabbed me in a bear hug from behind in an effort to calm me down, which instead drove me wildly over the edge. I kicked, bit, and screamed, and we ended up rolling around the floor. He finally gave up and let go. I'll never forget his daughter, who was my friend, looking at me in sad confusion. Later, she would gently ask me why I acted like that. I was struck with deep shame and embarrassment. I honestly didn't know.

Then came Nick Johnson, who had written a book called *How to Talk Back to Your Television Set* and had served for several years, until 1973, as a commissioner of the Federal

Communications Commission. Nick was arrogant and, to me, unlikable, which made him wholly irrelevant. I never fought with him.

After Nick came Donald Bruce Hanson, who was just called Bruce, and would become my stepfather. He was the only one whom I got along with. (Although if the lawyer had come after Nick, I would have gotten along with him, too.) Bruce had never been married and had no kids, which was a disappointment, since there was something exciting about inheriting siblings. I loved Danny, but he could be distant and was increasingly spending hours in his room quietly working hard at his studies or cartooning, the formal start to his artistic abilities. His concentration could not be shattered. I was a bit lonely and often bored.

Bruce was tall, friendly, and unassuming. An "old friend"— which apparently meant "former boyfriend"—Bruce had met Mom at Union Theological Seminary. A white Anglo-Saxon Protestant like Mom, Bruce would become an ordained minister in the progressive United Church of Christ, and an associate pastor at the historic, abolitionist First Church in DC. He would take a leave to join the National Council of Churches Racial Justice Committee. Bob Moses, the unflinching and creative civil rights organizer in Mississippi who devised Freedom Summer, asked Bruce to create the training program for the white, Northern college students who would travel down to Mississippi to help register Black people to vote.

Bruce would spend that summer of 1964 in Mississippi with Moses and with John "Jack" Pratt, who was a civil rights lawyer sent to help get people out of jail for the audacity of demanding their constitutional rights. When he came back into my mother's life, Bruce was at the Center for Community

Change, a nonprofit supporting farmworker organizing and economic development organizations and would later support other forms of organizing. In other words, Bruce made sense, despite his much more straitlaced and preppy ways. He wore Lacoste and L.L.Bean, but we forgave him for that.

When Bruce moved in, the four of us had family dinners every night. Danny and I began to ask when they would get married. I was eleven when they did. At their wedding, I was the maid of honor and Danny the ring bearer. I thought it was great, until we got home from the family honeymoon.

From my perspective, Bruce changed. The easygoing man had become a more frustrated adult. At dinner, he began to tell Danny not to fidget with his napkin holder and ask me not to eat my broccoli with my fingers. I loved to eat my broccoli with my fingers. I would pick the "tree" up at the base of the trunk with the pincers of my forefinger and thumb, throw my head back and lower it into my mouth, like my mouth was a garbage compactor. Apparently, his stepchildren's table manners had been annoying him for a year, and the marriage certificate became his license to correct us.

These were small things made large by the sudden shift. The camel's back broke for me when Bruce complained about my towel not being hung properly in the bathroom. It was a legitimate complaint, but I told myself I hated him and began to act as if he was invisible. Nonexistent. He would say hello when I entered the kitchen in the morning, and I would walk past him as if I heard nothing and no one was standing there. I maintained this silent tantrum for about two months. I am sure it hurt and confused him. Nothing in particular broke my silence. It was just hard to maintain.

There were other small tensions. Even though we lived in a

big house in a nice neighborhood, Mom and Bruce did not earn big salaries, so we were on a tight budget, with one car. Beyond trips to the shack on the mountaintop—which we were becoming too old to want to visit—we did not take vacations that entailed anything other than a drive in the station wagon. We weren't poor by any stretch, but my mother always laughed as she reminded us that we "lived beyond our means." The reason my mother could afford private school, in part, was the Social Security survivor's benefits she got as a result of my father's death. I knew that because she never shied from explaining her frugality. But it was a tough pill to swallow in the midst of our new surroundings and the wealth they entailed.

My acting out at home had yet to bleed into school. That would change in middle school with a teacher I'll call Kate. She was the first teacher at GDS I neither liked nor respected. Middle school was awful for all the reasons it usually is awful. Puberty, mean girl–mean boy dynamics, cliques, and psychic torture around becoming whomever we were unsure we were becoming, all mixed with that transition to the teenage testing of adulthood. Kate was a bland and unimaginative teacher. To this day, I do not remember what we studied or learned. I only remember Kate as unhappy and terse, with little ability to control her classroom and constant lectures about "responsibility." For the entire year, I was respectful despite my disdain, and generally focused on trying to find some kind of satisfying social life and maintaining my boring B grade averages.

Then came the end of the year and the annual class trip. The big end-of-year event was field day, which entailed the entire lower school competing in organized events at the park, like the fifty-yard dash, along with boxed lunches provided by the school, which was a joy all by itself. I had spent my entire childhood limited to tuna fish and peanut butter and jelly sand-wiches. When Bruce came into our lives, he would buy deli meat for himself, but that was not ours. The food budget was Mom's dominion and she ruled it with an iron fist.

Not too long before that momentous event, we got a break from the classroom with some social time in the park. The weather was sunny and very warm, and the flowers were bloom-ing. It was the kind of day when being in school was deeply painful. We could feel the freedom and heat of summer that was about to be ours. The park we were in was large with rolling hills. My friend Donna and I were on top of one when the day took an unexpected turn. Donna was my preschool best friend, and we had been reunited at GDS. I don't recall how the fight started, but an exchange of insults had begun between Donna and another classmate I'll call Will. He had straight white-blond hair in a 1970s bowl cut that often fell in his face so, like many of the boys, he was constantly shaking his head to get the hair out of his eyes. Until then, he had been a perfectly fine nonen-tity in my classroom life that year.

What had started as normal middle school back-and-forth somehow transitioned to a larger fight. Donna had said some-thing that struck some unknown nerve in Will. It quickly esca-lated into Will becoming a wild-eyed, screaming, crazy person. We had been standing near a large tree. Frantically, he reached into it, managed to break off a green switch, and started lashing Donna with it. She was on the ground, head between her knees, crying. It was shocking. I, having been taught not to fight and to call a teacher, and now in a school where that seemed logical, yelled for Kate. After trying to get her attention, I had to run several yards closer so she might hear me.

To my rising anger, I could see Kate, arms crossed, slowly

walking up the hill. Everything in her body language and pinch-lipped scowl communicated annoyance at being disturbed. When she got to the top of the hill, Will had stopped the whipping—regaining some control, I suspect, because Donna's cries finally pierced his rage. But Donna was still crumpled on the ground sobbing, and a few small droplets of blood had appeared through her lightweight summer shirt. They weren't serious injuries, small welts with a few punctures, but the blood was clear evidence that something very wrong had happened. Will still held the switch but stood stark still.

Kate shrugged blandly, and said, "There's nothing I can do." She slowly turned on her heel, arms still crossed, and began to stroll back down the hill. The rage in me built swiftly and unequivocally. This woman who had lectured us all year about "responsibility" was shirking hers. I was so angry I slapped my left hand into the inside of my right elbow, propelled the right arm up into a ninety-degree angle, and without hesitation, flipped my hand so the back of it faced Kate's hunched back, shot up my middle finger, and yelled in a decisive and unwavering voice, "Well fuck you then!" She turned immediately, jaw dropped, eyes wide, and in shock. I held my stance to ensure the full effect. I was not hiding. I wanted her to see and feel my complete and utter derision. She proved me right a second time by failing to walk back up that hill and confront me. I was braced for discipline, but Kate couldn't even woman up enough to face a disrespectful middle schooler.

Donna stopped crying, Will stomped off, and the day ended as they all did, in the usual ritual of getting back on the bus to go home. When I got back, my mother called me into her home office, a small room near the kitchen off the hallway that connected the front entryway to the back of the house. It was where I could find her every day when I came home from school. On this particular afternoon, she didn't just greet me, she asked me what happened at school. That meant she had gotten a call. I told her, with utterly self-righteous satisfaction, exactly what had happened. I was not ashamed in the slightest. Kate earned my disrespect and I made sure Mom knew it.

My mother, in her usual rational, unflappable way, told me she could understand why I was upset and that I had a right to be, but that it was not an appropriate way to express my anger. She told me I had to apologize. But private school had proven that there was no reward for compliance, so I told Mom that I wasn't sorry and would not lie. It was then Mom informed me that I had been suspended. It was a first for me. I was surprised but made an almost instantaneous calculation. There was less than a week or two left of school. We were finished with work and projects. They couldn't hold me back, so screw them.

Hearing my defiance, Mom pulled her trump card. I wouldn't be allowed to attend field day. She knew, I suspect, that if she had thrown all the implications of the suspension at me at once, I would have doubled down. She let me walk through this step by step, and by this third go-around, she had me. Field day was fun. We waited for field day all year. I always ran the fifty-yard dash and always hoped to win. I couldn't miss field day.

But I would not lose completely. I couldn't feel defeated by sniveling and contemptuous Kate. I negotiated. I would apologize for saying, "Fuck you." That felt fair. I would not be sorry for my disrespect, just the curse words themselves. My mother nodded her approval. I gave my narrow and very specific apology to Kate the next day. She was either too lacking in the subtlety of mind necessary to realize it was not an apology for challenging her, or she knew she wouldn't get more. Either way, I went to field day and never got over the fact that Donna had been beaten but that, as far as I knew, Will went unpunished.

This disappointment would make me a constant discipline problem, for a mix of complicated reasons. I felt the failure of adults was a deep and intolerable injustice, and as a Wiley I felt empowered to act upon my indignation. I wasn't being bullied anymore and was less afraid. I was also rebelling and acting out my survivors guilt. I had survived and Dad hadn't. I had escaped fear and Charlene hadn't. I had left the classmates who were angry about my class privileges, and here I was fully enmeshed with the upper middle class of Black-and-white DC. Seventh grade became a year I was regularly thrown out of class and constantly in danger of suspension. My mother was frequently called in for meetings with teachers and then administrators because I would tolerate none of their inadequacies.

My mother, unbeknownst to me, was applying to my brother's high school, the Field School, to free us from GDS. I hadn't considered a different high school but was thrilled to join Danny. His previous school had no grades, and so he and I found ourselves in the same grade when he switched to Field. Field was so small. We both joined the same massive thirty-student class for ninth grade in a house near Embassy Row. I was now fourteen, fully grown to my full five-foot-nine-inch self, and still miserably sporting an afro that my mother refused to allow me to straighten. This would be the year I broke her down.

At fourteen I had one last major conflagration that seemed to burn out all the anger in me. When the flames died and the smoke cleared, I could see my mother and my relationship with her in a new light. Like many of the fights I started with Mom, I don't remember the origin. It usually began with something innocuous. Maybe she asked me to do something I didn't want to do, or she wouldn't agree to let me do something. This time we were in the kitchen, the two of us standing at the stove in our long, deep kitchen that had a dark-burgundy-colored wall-to-wall rug inherited from the previous owners, and she was cooking. The words began, with her reasonable and matter-of-fact and me emotional. When I was displeased, I would start verbally poking at her. She must have been tired, but I don't know what her day had been like. Unlike me, who never suffered in silence, Mom was stoic and found the positive amid the difficult. Today I was starting to get a rise. I had hopped up onto the counter and sat facing her profile, essentially taunting her.

She told me sternly to leave the kitchen after I called her a bitch. I saw my chance here. I arrogantly said, "No!" It made her angry in a way that would have been completely normal and understandable to an outsider. But Wretha Wiley Hanson had biblical patience. Now her register had climbed an octave, and she was visibly angry and shaking and yelling at me to leave. She grabbed my arm to pull me down off the counter, presumably to push me toward the narrow back staircase, which at one time in history must have been reserved for servants. I was off the counter, and we were shouting.

The words are a jumbled blur. All I know is in that moment of us facing off in the kitchen (she was still several inches taller than I was then), terror struck me like a bolt of lightning. I was never afraid of my mother. It was as if a curtain had been drawn back from my eyes and I could suddenly see so vividly that this was my fault. She did nothing to incite this, but I had finally achieved what I had failed to do for years. I had pushed my mother over the edge. All those tantrums, all those fights, the time I turned the furniture over in the sitting room, I was trying to get a strong emotional reaction from her. To get her attention, not her calmness, to make her see me and focus on me with intensity. Not with a banal "You're fine."

I was terrified at the results. I started crying and screaming, not in anger but in fear. I ran into the formal dining room. I began to dash around the dark wood table, Mom chasing after me, no longer in anger, but with a confused and questioning "Maya?" She was bewildered, not angry. Just as I had never seen her level of reaction, she had never seen me melt into hysterical fear, especially in the absence of any rational reason for this abrupt mood swing. I was screaming, "She's going to kill me!" and she was baffled and trying to calm me.

In usual fashion, Danny was shut up in his bedroom upstairs. Bruce was in the first-floor den that passed as his man cave, which held his recliner, the television, and his pipe. It was his room and we generally stayed out of it. And in this moment, he stayed put, newspaper opened in full and covering the entire upper half of his body. I ran out of the dining room and to the den, diving headfirst behind Bruce's recliner and begging him to protect me from Mom. Bruce, having been a conflict-avoidant bachelor for forty years, simply continued to read his newspaper as if nothing at all was happening.

By this point, the scene was so absurd that Mom, hands on both hips, began to laugh out loud. Through my tears I began to laugh, too. From that moment on, everything changed. I couldn't see it before. Now I could. I could see that I was responsible for my own misery at home. She just loved me and was patient and there for me. From that point on, there was no more fighting, no more hard times, and no more tension.

My mother and I remained close, very close, for the rest of her life. My brother was also a big part of my life, thanks, in part, to our being in a small high school together. He reminds me that we used to fight a lot, but I was just constantly trying to be in his world, getting his attention and, therefore, getting on his nerves. By high school, I was, hopefully, a better sister and we were definitely closer. But our closeness didn't make home life happy, nor was it sad. It was just lonely. I tolerated Bruce, my stepfather, while watching his and Mom's unhappy marriage. They didn't fight, but now I was old enough to feel the distance between a husband and wife. They melted into a slump in their bedroom at night to disappear into the television. Danny sat in his room struggling through his learning disability to master his homework. There was nothing to keep me in that house or in that neighborhood, which never felt like mine. I was sick and tired of being the Black girl in the white family in the white neighborhood. It was numbing to stand apart, and I missed the way we felt a part of something larger when Dad was alive and there was a movement.

I began to wonder what I would have been like, what my life would have been like, if Dad had lived. Sometimes I'd imagine a big, explosive reckoning with him, like the one I had with Mom. Often in that alternate life, I saw my growing self holding on to my anger and defiance. I was struggling to find some sense of self-worth and some place for myself that wasn't defined by or in opposition to Dad. It was hard to shake the horrible thought that it took my dad's devastating death to shake me hard enough to search for myself.

By tenth grade, I had a second family. A Black family I escaped to every weekend. I met Gina (not her real name) through mutual friends. She was tall, light-skinned, outgoing, and, unlike me, wore Calvin Klein jeans daily and carried a Louis Vuitton purse. She became one of my best friends.

Gina's father was a dentist. He sat on the board of a Black savings and loan bank and on the board of the DC Urban League chapter, and was prominent in DC Black life. The family lived on "the Gold Coast." Riding the spine of upper Sixteenth Street and bordering Bethesda and Silver Spring, Maryland, it was the enclave of the Black professional class. My mother just called it "Boogie," which was how she pronounced "bougie," and it wasn't a compliment. But she never interfered.

For me, the draw was not Gina's mother's Cadillac Seville, or their large home, the location, or the bougie-ness. What drew me to Gina's family was a nuclear Black family and the end to my loneliness. The first time I visited their house, her mother, also named Gina, immediately got my name wrong and it became a joke. She started calling me Myrna and it stuck. Gina, the daughter, began calling me "Myrn" for short. Her father also seemingly adopted me immediately. Day-Day, as we called him, was tall and quiet, and seemed to rarely smile. His personality was the opposite of my "Smiley Wiley" father's, but there was something in his appearance that reminded me of Dad. They were a comparable height and build, and there was something similar about their mouths and the shapes of their faces. I felt immediately at home that first visit, and for more than a year, I was there every single weekend. It became so routine there was never a discussion of "if." If I was not at Gina's by a certain time on Friday, I might get a *where are you* call from Gina's mother.

Many years later, Mom and I would discuss this time. She would explain, as she teared up, that she knew I needed something she couldn't give me, and she knew that Gina's family was providing it. What no one could give me was a direction. Strangely, Reaganomics put a mean hand on my back and pushed me, inadvertently, to study psychology. President

Reagan, new to office, was quickly unraveling as many social programs as he could, from job training programs to the survivors benefits we received. He was also railing against the "evil empire" that was the Soviet Union and pushing his seemingly insane "Star Wars" program, which would deploy missiles in space to shoot down any nuclear attacks the evil empire might launch against us, thanks to his constant provocation.

It was a terrifying time because that seemed a real possibility. Gina had burst into tears when Reagan was declared the victor in the 1980 election. She believed—as I and many of my classmates also feared—that Reagan would start a nuclear war, which couldn't be contained within a sovereign border. Danny had to register for the draft.

Our family's eligibility for survivors benefits fell on Reagan's chopping block. My maternal grandmother, Wretha the elder, had socked away some college money for all four of her grandkids, not just the blond-haired, blue-eyed ones. It would cover tuition for one semester, a real help, but hardly enough. Mom would be incurring debt with two children starting college the same year and with a now-shaky consulting business, as Reagan had also gutted the affirmative action programs she was being hired to help implement. Mom, with the support of Elizabeth Ely, the founder and head of Field, worked out a way for us to enroll in college senior year so that we would qualify for the phasing out of survivors benefits, rather than suffer the abrupt loss. Mom explained that Danny and I would take two classes at night at Northern Virginia Community College, and we would also take a certain number of courses at Field School so that we could still earn credits for our high school diploma while retaining some benefits.

Danny had saved up from his summer job busing tables

at a neighborhood steak house and had bought a 1968 Dodge Dart. Our father's son, he decided to take a mechanics course so he could rebuild the eight-cylinder engine. It would also get us to and from Northern Virginia Community College, or NOVA Coco, as we called it back then. I would take accounting in an effort to gain some practical skills and Introduction to Psychology, because it piqued my interest. I failed accounting, but truly enjoyed psychology. The professor encouraged me in the subject, and I was at the top of her class as a high school student. It was a strange, new sensation to see the possibility of being really good at something.

It helped me recognize that people opened up to me, and I was a good listener who could empathize, having also been a trauma survivor. This last part was not a conscious thought. I was a trauma survivor and had been in therapy, but I didn't consider it useful for myself. I just knew I had some skills that were applicable, and that I liked and wanted to work with people. I also thought I could do something good in the world. I wanted to understand people, what motivated them, made them racist or not racist. Perhaps I could help support some of the social and psychological underpinnings of what activists needed to persuade people. Ever decisive, I declared that I wanted to major in psychology in college. Mom approved. Now, maybe, I could find my way to being a true Wiley.

CHAPTER 12

COLLEGE TO CAREER

I HAD BEEN CUTTING my teeth on racism in the elite Ivy Leagues. Dartmouth didn't just have Republicans, it had the strain of beyond shocking emerging conservatism. Dinesh D'Souza, the felonious former congressman who had been an academic star of the Reagan-era right wing, was a senior and the editor in chief of the notorious and unaffiliated *Dartmouth Review* newspaper. A *60 Minutes* exposé revealed the paper to be funded by conservative alumni intent on dismissing all of the isms and crashing through the walls of propriety the civil rights movement had built. His girlfriend, Laura Ingraham, was a sophomore and also worked for the *Dartmouth Review*. They had horrible views even back then, though I couldn't yet imagine the roles they would play in the Fox News era of Donald Trump.

My first encounter with the paper was at the very beginning of my first semester. It was an intentional tool to try to influence the political views of the next generation. The alumni support meant that the *Dartmouth Review* was free, and a courier deposited the filth at every dorm room door. I remember picking that first paper up and seeing an article on the front page was entitled "I Bes a Black Student at Dartmouth." It was Al Jolson in blackface, and it rocked me to the core.

Every Sunday night, when a young man would come with the paper, I would demand that he keep it. He never said what I hoped: that it was just a job, and he needed the money. If he had, I would have treated him differently. Instead, he would defiantly drop it at my feet as I recited that this room refused delivery and not to bring it back. The ritual was both futile and frustrating, but it felt necessary to me, even as I couldn't imagine other strategies of nonviolent resistance. To this day I regret I didn't organize other dorm members to link arms and block entry.

Later I would move into the Afro-Am building, or just the Am, as we called it. Its official name was the Malik El-Shabazz Center, a small redbrick building with offices on the first floor, and a multipurpose lower level comprised of a kitchen and a TV room, and was home to the Saturday night dance parties, DJ'd by a student. We would all gather there after stopping by the frats for the first few hours in large groups to partake of the free alcohol, before returning to the Am's alcohol-free zone. The upper two floors had single dorm rooms, females on the second floor, males on the third. More important, the couriers from the *Dartmouth Review* would not dare to enter the building, with its entryway adorned with a painting of Malik El-Shabaaz, Malcolm X himself. I would very happily allow that visage to shield me like an umbrella in the rain. I would stay in the Am almost my whole Dartmouth career, taking advantage of all the opportunities to engage in Black campus life, from gospel choir to the Black Underground Theater Arts Association, to cofounding the Dartmouth chapter of Delta Sigma Theta Sorority, a Black sorority founded in 1913.

My protest against the *Dartmouth Review* took form again when I joined Black students in futile meetings with the dean to demand that the campus sue the off-campus paper to remove the Dartmouth name, since it was not a campus publication. The Republican administration, presided over by an alumni businessman who we believed failed into his job by bankrupting the company he ran, took no action.

We were entering adulthood at a time when the US racial justice movement had turned its attention to apartheid South Africa. I suggested we lead our own letter-writing campaign to press Dartmouth to divest itself from anything that helped support apartheid South Africa. As a college with a long and strong fraternity tradition, three-quarters of campus students were in a Greek house, and a huge part of student organizational life was based in these groups. That meant, more than student government, organizing Dartmouth students meant organizing fraternities and sororities. Fraternities had weekly "meetings," which in most fraternity houses meant excuses for members-only keg parties. That led to a frightening evening descending into fraternity basements on meeting night, which would better be described as "drunken debauchery night." It wouldn't take long for me and my friend to decide it was dangerous to assume that fraternities were actually holding business meetings.

My coping mechanisms, refuge in the supportive arms of Black faculty and friends, and a few happy accidents led me to have a significant and transformative experience at Dartmouth, despite all the challenges of racist conservatism on a preppy jock campus. It helped to explode preconceived stereotypes I held, burst me out of my rational but relatively passionless career path onto the right one, and helped me to grapple with who my father was and who he wasn't.

At Dartmouth I learned to listen to and take in others' experiences and stories. I had many lessons, and the most notable ones were with white men very different from any I had known before: a Marine Corps captain and a conservative psychology professor. I met the Marine Corps captain when I volunteered to be the liaison at Dartmouth's career services office for recruiters looking to recruit Black students. I was introduced to Captain Mylee, a Marine recruiter. Being from an antiwar, movement family, I asked him point-blank why Black students should join the racist Marine Corps. I'll never forget the conversation. Mylee didn't blink. He didn't argue. He told me his story.

He was from the rural south—Tennessee, I think—and said outright that he grew up a racist. He had believed Black people were inferior and, in his town, the Ku Klux Klan were heroes. He'd had few opportunities or options for his future, so he joined the Marines and was stationed in Zaire, now the Democratic Republic of the Congo. He said with glistening eyes that met mine directly that the Marine Corps had changed him. The exposure not only to Black Marines, but also to the people of the Congo, opened his eyes and his heart. He saw his own ignorance and hate compared to the intelligence and resilience of Black Congolese he met. He met and married his wife there.

Never in a million years had I expected such a powerful personal story. It didn't change my view of the military, but it exposed me to my own stereotyping of others and gave me hope that there really was a possibility of defeating prejudice even in a racist.

Instead of leading me to a PhD program, college psychology served instead to reinforce my path to law school. A conservative professor who taught a course called Law and Psychology was a big part of that realization. Rogers Elliott was a barrel-bellied, tall white conservative with a PhD in psychology and a law degree. His class covered things like cross-racial eyewitness testimony and whether we could consider "ebonics"—the language of descendants of African slaves—a dialect of English and affirmative action. Professor Elliott and I fought about everything. I challenged him in class, and he challenged me back, and he loved it. He became a huge influence on my decision to become a lawyer, but also exploded my view that a white conservative would never help a lefty Black student like me. Professor Elliott was someone who demonstrated to me that not all opponents are enemies. He even insisted he would write one of my letters of recommendation to law school, even though I didn't ask him.

His course also showed me that I could be a Wiley as Maya Wiley. I could argue, advocate, and take action on issues and for people I cared about, as a lawyer. I was naturally argumentative, and now the strong-willed, irreverent, and angry me could channel my survivors guilt and my sense of purpose in my own shoes, which seemed to align with my parents' footsteps but set me on my own path.

I also got meaningful support from the Black faculty. There was a professor we simply called by his first name, Ray, who taught Social Movements and had written a book on the subject. He was one of the few people on campus who knew who Dad was and what he had done. He helped me get a job in the sociology department office as an assistant to the secretaries, answering the phone and filing papers. He also convinced me to do an independent study with him on my father's work. Until this point, I had not focused on the details of the work that had been spilling around me. Dad's work was so intimately entwined with my childhood that it never occurred to me that I could study it. It also felt sad and a bit dangerous. I still believed I was not living up to being a Wiley, or George Wiley's daughter. Studying just how much I was failing seemed scary.

I still agreed and requested interview notes from many of Dad's closest supporters and two of his captains in the movement from the archives at the University of Wisconsin, Madison. Both of these captains were still living, but calling on them seemed much too personal. One afternoon, I was in my Am dorm room. It was one of the large corner rooms, and I had a little refrigerator in it and a cot-like twin-size bed that I had pushed into the corner, as most students did, to maximize the space. I was lying on my bed, as I always did when doing homework, paging through an interview with Ed Day.

I thought I would be simply reading about George Wiley and his passion for equality, but the words knocked the breath from my lungs like a punch. Ed explained that Dad's extramarital affairs were the reason Mom left him. One of them was with the mother of a family we were close with and whose children were regular weekend companions for me and Danny. This family regularly came to West Virginia with us.

Irrationally I felt I had been an accomplice to Dad's cheating. And I was angry at myself for all those years I had blamed and mistreated Mom because of their separation. Instead of apologizing, I called her to complain that she hadn't told me.

I had run to the hallway pay phone, not having the money to spring for my own private line. I called Mom religiously every Sunday, but it wasn't Sunday. She picked up the phone, happy to hear my voice. I gushed with "Dad cheated on you? How could you not tell me!" She lost the easiness in her voice, dropping her voice and calming it. She said simply, "It was not your business. It had nothing to do with you."

I felt like a small handmade boat with a makeshift sail in a storm. I was tossed by the waves of these revelations, which shattered my sense of who my parents had been together. Mom, of course, was like the captain of a rescue ship, striding the same waves, calm and confident in her ability to ride them, giving me clear and unchallengeable direction. "Your father and I had a good marriage for years. He loved you. We just grew apart. I am proud of our marriage. It ended." That's it. That's life. It goes on and we go on. Mom always drilled into us that Dad was wonderful and imperfect and we should see him as a human being. Now I finally did.

Over time, she shared a bit more information. She was no longer able to be in the movement work with him, and he was lonely in it. Their partnership had been strong, but it had also been built on activism. When that was gone, they grew apart. Dad had asked Mom for an open marriage, and Mom tried for a year before telling him it could not work. She believed he needed someone who could be in the work with him. He had fallen in love with Gloria Steinem. Gloria did not reciprocate, which was also mentioned in passing in a biography I couldn't bring myself to finish. She was a stranger to me, though she would endorse my run for New York City mayor, a request I made with only momentarily mixed feelings. I knew that no one could hold a candle to my mom, and Dad should have known that.

Eventually, I was done with Dartmouth. I had not only survived, but I had found a new sense of myself as me, beyond being George Wiley's daughter. I would be that proudly, however; I was a Wiley, who knew what I needed to do. I had to work at the storied NAACP Legal Defense Fund, affectionately called the LDF by insiders, founded by Thurgood Marshall, who argued *Brown v. Board of Education.* I knew that to get a job there I would have to go to a top law school because the jobs there were highly competitive. With encouragement from Dartmouth's Career & Employment Services office, Yale would be my target and Georgetown, in the top twenty, would be my boundary. I would be selective and make informed judgments about how to get where I wanted to go. I was no longer drifting. I had a direction.

After Dartmouth, I transitioned to Columbia Law School without the culture shock I experienced entering Dartmouth. When a white student asked to know my LSAT score, possibly to consider whether to invite me to join a study group, I could call up the resilience I had learned at Dartmouth. That made it easy to simply shrug these incidents off. I had nothing to prove to them and cared more about the support we could give each other as Black students. A few other Black first-years and I formed our own study group. That didn't mean I was immune to insensitivities that came with the Ivy territory or that I had mastered my rebellious temper in the face of any indignities. I was confident enough, like my dad, to take risks, but I didn't have his humor in my hard moments, or his ability to descend into charming persuasion.

In first-year property class, as we were covering the inheritance aspects of property law, Professor Curtis Berger, who I liked, asked about the legal right to refuse to allow a white daughter to inherit property if she married a Black man. The question felt like a two-by-four to the face, and I imagined my Black classmates going numb or sliding down in their seats. For me this was no hypothetical. It was personal. It wasn't just about inheriting but also the emotional disavowal Mom faced without flinching. I could face this, too, as could any of my Black classmates. White students don't ever have to endure the opposite hypothetical. I felt attacked, and without taking a single breath or formulating my thoughts, I shot my hand up in the air, a slight improvement on my seventh-grade self, but just barely.

"Yes, Ms. Wiley?" came Professor Berger's unsuspecting response. I sat near the front in his class, as did my closest friends, three other Black first-years. It was second semester and we had come a long way since hiding in the back of the class in the fall. Professor Berger was a very short man, but he towered above us on the dark platform raised like a stage. There were almost three hundred of us in the amphitheater-style lecture hall. There was a wooden banister, reminiscent of a courthouse bench, and the professor had a dais to stand behind. In the lower rows, you had to look up, which I did.

I was sharp-eyed and humorless. I asked, "Well, what if it was 'You inherit unless you marry a Jew'?" I meant the question to be shocking and act as a mirror to the underlying bias and insensitivity of his original framing. He stumbled only for an instant, recovering quickly, and staying on track. If there was a collective gasp in the classroom, I didn't hear it. My ears were filled with my own white-hot rage. I believe he just took a more legally dispassionate argument from a white student. My friends were stock-still. As I emerged at the end of the class, standing outside the lecture room, still fuming and with my classmates chattering around me, Professor Berger entered the hall, walked straight over to me, and said incredulously, "Maya?!" I simply replied, "Professor Berger!" We stared at each other momentarily, him with confusion and me with firmness that held no rancor and no remorse. I was not proud of myself. I liked Professor Berger, but I did need him to understand that my question was no more offensive than his. This was not how a Wiley would handle the situation, but at that stage of my life I didn't care. I was exhausted from the innocent offensiveness of the Ivy League.

In the semesters that followed, I jumped into the Black Law Students Association and became its president my second year, joined the *Columbia Human Rights Law Review*, and spent a summer in the Philippines as an intern investigating human rights violations. I had been trying to find a way to South Africa since I was an undergrad, seeing it as the site of the most important activism we had in the United States at that time. Organizing and protesting around apartheid occurred, and was galvanizing and real, yet it hadn't reached the level of the civil rights movement or anti–Vietnam War organizing. My human rights summer fellowship to South Africa was not to be. The apartheid government had imposed martial law and would deny visas to students coming to intern at South Africa's Legal Resources Center, where I was supposed to work.

Instead, I was sent to the Philippines. I was completely ignorant about Asia as a whole and the Philippines in particular. The Filipino Legal Assistance Group, simply called FLAG, was the premier legal rights institution in the country. It was not long after the peaceful People Power revolution had driven dictator Ferdinand Marcos and his wife, Imelda, from power. Filipinos had elected Corazon Aquino president, and the fragile country was reckoning with its violent past, continuing communist insurgency, Muslim insurgencies in the South, and a rightly distrusted military. It also faced the emergence of organized, armed, and terrifying vigilante groups that were an informal and violent arm of the military, according to human rights workers.

The head of FLAG had been named the nation's human rights commissioner and had fallen out of favor with the organization and the other human rights groups by reportedly failing to sanction the military and the vigilantes who were aggressively violating human rights. When we showed up at the FLAG offices, the then-current head—the daughter of a murdered human rights icon—declared we were unwelcome. We were left reeling with no real internship and no contacts. I managed to connect with a human rights reporter who worked with a group called the Ecumenical Movement for Justice and Peace. He invited me and the other students to go on a fact-finding mission regarding allegations of military abuses on the island of Ilo-Ilo. My relationship with this group took me to the heart of the conflict, Davao City in Mindanao, the southern part of the country.

I would end up the guest of liberation-theology nuns. Their convent was in a neighborhood overrun with vigilantes who had decapitated a person they claimed to be a communist guerrilla. The nuns helped me find a room with Filipino students active in the human rights movement, and I went on a mission up into the mountains with families displaced by a massacre who wanted to bury murdered loved ones. We were supposed to have an army escort. That alone was a bit disconcerting, but it was active territory for fighting between the New People's Army and government forces. Despite the formal letter we had from the government, the military refused to accompany us, as they had started shelling up in the mountains. The group, including myself and another student, decided to go anyway. We were a caravan of trucks with coffins and carrying survivors, as well as human rights workers.

It was hot under the summer sun, and the drive was beautiful but horrifying. We could hear the shelling off in the distance. When we arrived at the little village of thatched huts, we saw the remnants of strafing, when shooters spray a building with gunfire to indiscriminately kill as many people inside the dwelling as possible. It was a heinous massacre technique. They had killed the elderly and children alike. It is difficult to describe what it felt like to be in the midst of such beauty and danger with those traumatized by this massacre, abandoned by their government and its military, who were now left to exhume the bodies of their family members and carry them back to Davao.

In that moment, I was not special or uniquely strong, and I certainly was not heroic. I simply felt moved. As hard as it was to watch my father die, at least I hadn't watched him be murdered so wantonly and callously. I certainly was not without strong emotion, but I also went to that blank, dark space of trauma. That space where the brain is working, but the emotions shut down so you can carry on. The journalist began getting ill, so I took over documenting the bodies being exhumed with my camera. The other student, Mike, a lighthearted partier from the Pacific Northwest, was so upset that these survivors had to dig up their own relatives that he jumped into the dirt and began digging with them. I couldn't have done that in a million years. I could, however, bear witness. I watched a young woman uncover her grandmother. When men retrieved the body of a toddler, I had to briefly turn my back, struck by her similarity to a dirty rag doll.

After filling the coffins and loading them into two trucks, we had to ride back down the mountain while sitting on top of them. The smell of death remains unforgettable. Our bandanas were ineffective barriers to it. We started chain-smoking because it dulled the olfactory nerves. Even more terrifying than the shelling we heard off in the distance on the way back were the drunken soldiers with semiautomatic rifles slung on their backs or loosely hanging from their hands. There was no sense of safety with the Marcos military still intact. Mike and I understood that our primary purpose on this trip was to shield these human rights workers and survivors with our US passports. We were quickly introduced to the drunken soldiers who gazed mockingly up at us with bloodshot eyes. I remember thinking, *I sure am glad Mike is white.* Despite my height, my skin color, and the longtime presence of military bases populated with Black soldiers, people often asked if I was Filipina. My passport alone would not be enough, but I felt sure Mike's pale skin and blue eyes would be. The soldiers let us pass.

There was no real government reckoning with the murders of the villagers or recompense to the survivors, during the time I was there. Witnessing this and understanding the incredible toll of colonialism was the most humbling experience to date. I didn't know how to feel except relatively useless. I didn't even know what to do with the photos I had taken. I kept them. I still have them. It feels like a betrayal to throw them away as much as it does to show them. I returned to New York feeling as though I had taken so much more than I had given from people who had too much stolen from them. I hadn't completely understood how the fight for justice in a place like the Philippines could teach me as much as a country like South Africa. But my learning was emotional, which I have come to value as being equal to the intellectual. I understood in a way that only the fragile lives of the unprotected can teach—that the law, which I had gone to law school to meaningfully impact, could amount to nothing in the face of unchecked power. My generation had been reaping the benefits of the crop of laws planted by my parents' generation. In the Philippines, I felt the strength of the people written off as powerless, the same strength Dad must have seen in the Ladies on welfare. I believed in their power, but all adults seem powerful to young children. Belief is significantly less meaningful than firsthand experience of that resilient power.

I could also view my own trauma through a prism of tremendous luck and privilege and accidents of birth. My dad was not murdered. I didn't have to bury him quickly and flee for my life. I didn't have to return under shelling and dig at the dirt with my bare hands to recover an unspeakably broken and bloodied body. I was so very lucky by comparison, so very protected. There is a fortitude that comes from surviving deeply difficult and even traumatic events, of being able to stand up in some way. And everything matters. Every little act of compassion, of outrage with action, of relationships and reflection. It all matters even when we don't know what it will produce. That is true faith, and it felt like my parents' religion.

I would enter my second year in 1987 at Columbia as the civil rights fight of the decade ramped up. The AIDS crisis was in full swing. ACT UP was the kind of activism that reminded me of something long past. It was electric and absolutely unabashed. My entire third year in law school was spent fighting AIDS discrimination and organizing a daylong sit-in when Columbia announced it would fire one of the only openly gay faculty members and end its AIDS legal clinic. A legal clinic is a practical course in which law students take on outside legal work under the guidance of law professors licensed to practice law. It is a kind of apprenticeship that allows hands-on experience.

Jack Greenberg, vice dean of the law school, was Thurgood Marshall's successor at the LDF. Jack was one of the reasons I chose Columbia. His wife, Debbie Greenberg, ran the clinical program, but this particular offering was organized by Mark Barnes, a Canadian lawyer who was one of the only faculty members who was not closeted. We, the students, loved Mark. He was a true activist lawyer. Smart, committed, aggressive in his advised tactics and strategies.

We were not yet members of the New York Bar, which is to say, we were unlicensed to practice law. The federal and state laws at that time did not protect LGBTQ people from discrimination and did not recognize AIDS discrimination. But the New York City Human Rights Commission, which had enforcement authority over the city's human rights laws, had an administrative court. Mark had founded the clinic in partnership with the commission so that students could be assigned clients who wanted help with the complaints they filed.

I was assigned a clinic partner who came from a family that by my standards was wealthy. His father was a very successful lawyer. Our client was Joe Laraia, an Italian American man who lived with his boyfriend in a ground-floor apartment in Riverdale. Joe was HIV positive with a dangerously low T cell count. He was also the superintendent for the apartment building he lived in, so his housing was linked to his job. He had worked there for years, and he felt it was home and that the other tenants were like family. They had been kind to him over the years, and he was not closeted. Joe did not hide his HIV status from the building residents or co-op board, and they, in turn, wanted him out.

Joe was relying on two inexperienced, third-year law students to save his home and livelihood. It was by far the most intense of all my clinic cases, and it took over my life. I was struck by his vulnerability and by my need to protect him. But I was also moved by the guilt his partner felt about Joe's HIV status. He had not been positive himself and refused to use a condom. When he shared this, I was shocked to silence. Although we shared different forms of survivors guilt, I was completely ill-equipped to discuss the choices they were making. Nor was it my role.

Our case with Joe became all-consuming. The stress alone was clearly endangering his health. We were getting regular updates from his boyfriend on his T cell count and waited, holding our breath, hoping it would not fall below 200. We got a temporary restraining order against the building management to prevent Joe's eviction. With Mark's advice, we engaged in organizing tactics in the building, like writing a letter to residents that we slipped under their apartment doors in an effort to get support for Joe. It was both amazing and completely stressful. The learning curve was immense, and I literally felt responsible for Joe's life.

Eventually, we were able to negotiate a settlement for Joe that prolonged his stay in his apartment and gave him a little money for a new start. Joe was so grateful. He still faced an uncertain future; in his fifties and HIV positive, he would need to figure out how to get a job and health insurance, and survive. To me, it was not enough. It felt both satisfying to give him some relief and disturbing to have lost. He was genuinely grateful despite my feeling of failure. He gave me a crystal as a thank-you, and I cherished it more than any piece of jewelry I had ever received.

In the midst of the fight for Joe's life and livelihood, I had my own medical challenge. I had my first-ever surgery. A white male doctor insisted I had to be pregnant because I had an "enlarged uterus." I told him that the Angel Gabriel had not appeared unto me, and so that was simply not possible. I was no virgin, but I didn't have a boyfriend at the time and had been busy fighting for Joe Laraia. He didn't believe me.

I had an ultrasound, during which I thought the technician was going to have a coronary. She had this *Oh my God* look on her face and kept passing the jellied hand wand of the ultrasound machine as she stared, neck stuck forward like a chicken. She wouldn't tell me what she was seeing. I would later learn from a gleeful white female doctor that I had an ovarian cyst the size of a grapefruit that was completely covering my uterus. I'd had no symptoms. Amazed, she expressed how lucky I was that it hadn't burst, which could have been life-threatening. Her exuberance was not for my good luck but for her research. She would be able to slice me open and remove it, and it would become part of some research paper she was writing. I don't think she or the white male doctor intended their horrible bedside manner. And yet they were completely blind to their stereotypes and insensitivities. I thought of my mother and her labor that almost took my brother's life.

The doctor said they wouldn't know until they removed the massive growth whether she could save my ovary. I had not yet used my ovaries, and I had every desire to do so. There was no recognition that I was a human being, a young woman who hoped to have children someday. Campus health care was awful for this lack of human compassion, and yet I also knew that I was lucky I had the student health insurance that enabled me to get the diagnosis and the surgery I needed.

I would not agree to immediate surgery. I could miss classes, but I couldn't stop attending to Joe's needs. I would have the surgery immediately after Christmas and try to min imize my time out of pocket. My clinic partner had decided to take a cruise with his family, which made me livid. He even had the lack of compassion and self-awareness to tell me that I was insensitive because I didn't realize how much he needed the cruise. My primary demand was that he be there for Joe, because I would be in a hospital bed. He went on the cruise anyway. It was the end of a friendship and I no longer saw him as a partner in the clinic.

Mark, the amazing faculty member who founded the clinic, and just a great guy, was there for me and for Joe. He promised that he would handle anything that came up. I was so grateful for him. Mom found someone to cover for her at work so she could come up to New York, spend the night with me before the surgery, and check me in. But she had to go back after the surgery. One of my best friends, Bobbie, who was six years my senior and much more grown up, but a year behind me in law school, committed to taking care of me at her apartment after I was released. I spent three days at Bobbie's, then pushed my body to be back in classes and the clinic when the spring semester started a day later. Joe's employer did nothing terrible to him over the holidays, I would not have cancer or lose my ovary, and I would be back in the saddle as planned.

Somewhere in the midst of all this came the announcement. The clinical program, for no reason we could fathom, had decided to end the AIDS clinic at the end of my last semester. Mark would be out of a job, too. We were outraged. It was the first legal clinic addressing AIDS discrimination in the country. We had all become deeply committed to our clients, and it was the best education I could imagine, as well as the most urgently necessary. We clinic students demanded a meeting with the heads of the program to protest. We were condescendingly told that clinical education was meant to teach skills but was not committed to causes. I couldn't believe my ears.

We began to organize out of the clinic offices on an upper floor of the law school. We used the phones there to make calls and used the law school's own resources, including the copy machine, to post flyers against it. We decided to stage a sit-in. I was absolutely convinced that the only protesters sitting in on the first floor of the law school, refusing to go to classes and chanting, would be the dozen or so students of the clinic itself. I didn't have any faith in the Wall Street–bound, oxford cloth crowd that populated much of the law school. It didn't deter me.

The following morning, as the clinic students milled around the main hallway near the law school entrance, students poured in from the classrooms and, to my utter and complete shock, began to sit down. By the end of that bell, we guessed we had up to two hundred students sitting and chanting as we stepped over legs, giving speeches in between chants of "One, two, three, four, do not shut the clinic door." The *New York Times* showed up. We were protesting on the anniversary of the 1968 protests over Columbia University taking over a park in Harlem as well as the lack of faculty diversity and the war in Vietnam. Back then a thousand students were arrested after taking over multiple buildings on campus. The reporter wanted to know if we were inspired by that day, as if our own fight to serve clients and fight AIDS discrimination was not of sufficient interest to him.

I was somehow tagged as the leader of the group. I was aware that the clinic students were consistently looking to me for the next moves, but I was very much pressed into that service. As the day progressed, my role became more apparent, and I found myself a bit stunned and wondering what to do next. What would Mom and Dad do next? I talked to the *Times*.

The reporter wanted to know whether we chose the date out of inspiration from those antiwar organizers. We hadn't, but I knew I should say yes, so I did. The coverage would put more pressure on the dean's office. I'd learned from my parents that protesting meant little if you didn't generate enough public attention in support of your cause. The city's gay community, the community of Stonewall, was the epicenter of ACT UP organizing, so there was a good chance they could use Columbia to bring more attention to the issue of AIDS discrimination, although we had no direct connection to the movement. It only later occurred to me that we should have reached out to them.

After that interview, the students grew restless, and I knew we had to translate the support we had built into some kind of action. When people asked me what to do, I neither hesitated nor thought it through. We would march to the dean's office and sit there until we got a meeting with Dean Barbara Black. I led the students willing to follow. The dean's office could not accommodate a hundred students, but we had a large enough group pile in and populate the outer offices, with me leading the charge. Jack Greenberg, my mentor and the person I needed to help me get a job at the LDF, stepped out and told us we had been heard and could now leave and get back to our books.

He stood outside the dean's door and I stood on the opposite side of the room. The other students were sitting on the floor, for the most part. I stated that we would not leave until we met with the dean. He turned on his heel and disappeared. I was sure that campus security was being called, and I was worried that I might be responsible for ruining the law careers of some of my dear friends and some strangers, too. But here we were. Here I was. I might also be throwing away my chance to work at the LDF. All I could think of was Joe. I was okay with losing an opportunity, and I steeled myself for what would come next, secure in the fact that Mom would not be disappointed in me, even if it derailed me.

To Jack's tremendous credit, he returned a few minutes later not with a goon squad but with an acceptance of our demand. "The dean will meet with your representatives now!"

We didn't really have any representatives. We weren't that organized. But it was pretty obvious the group should be made up of those of us actually in the clinic, who had organized the sit-in. I and about five others went in to speak with Dean Black, a legal historian, the first woman to lead the law school and frankly, someone who seemed deeply out of touch. We made our case. The clinic established the law school as a leader. We needed an education relevant to the world, that made change in it. And Mark, an adored excellent faculty member and an openly gay man, was a necessary voice in the clinic's work. The dean agreed to investigate further and create a working group to discuss the clinical program and to diversify the faculty.

It was enough of a concession to disperse the students and start a process. It would not save the AIDS clinic. It would not save Mark's job. It would not make me feel like we had prevailed or like I had done enough. It would, however, make me hungrier for more impact. It made me realize I could not back down from leading if offered the opportunity, just as I would not necessarily seek it out. We had succeeded in something. We got Columbia law students engaged in something beyond themselves. We began a process that ultimately would help the law school create a social justice program. We cannot say we were more than a seed, but the seed grew and reseeded and spread. That was something.

I was now on a path that was completely mine, on a mission I shared with my parents. I was becoming a lawyer at the end of Reagan's reign. He would leave office after appointing four justices to the Supreme Court and almost four hundred judges to the federal bench, the most of any president. As law students we watched Reagan nominate Robert Bork, a bloodred conservative who fired the Watergate special prosecutor, and who, as an academic, was a father of the "original intent" theory of Constitutional interpretation. For me, that meant allowing the words chosen by slaveholding founders and their times to shackle the future to the past, often ignoring the new future the country fought a Civil War over. To Bork, it was a dead document that could not breathe life into a different, racially inclusive future. To Bork, even "one person, one vote" was a radical departure, and certainly a woman's right to choose an abortion was not fundamental to him. As law students, we wrote letters demanding Bork's confirmation be voted down, and later we'd be blamed for being the "liberals" who politicized judicial nominations. Bork was Borked, but shortly afterward Clarence Thomas was confirmed, despite Anita Hill's testimony about her sexual harassment; Thomas effectively played the race card he claimed to abhor. The predator claimed to be the victim.

These were bleak times to be entering the legal profession as a civil rights lawyer, particularly one who seemed to cry out for the activism of my parents' generation. I wanted to be a movement lawyer, despite not working in movement times. Mom would remind me that the work didn't stop. Movements come when masses of people in different places around the country get fed up with something. I thought I could still be a tool in the toolbox for the people fighting between the movement times.

CHAPTER 13

CIVIL RIGHTS

I KNEW A CLERKSHIP with a federal trial judge would help me learn more about litigating and beef up my résumé, but I got so much more than I hoped for. I must have applied to at least twenty judges. The only interview came from Judge James T. Giles, a District Court judge in Philadelphia, the Eastern District of Pennsylvania. I didn't know much about him and had applied because he was Black and appointed by President Jimmy Carter, which seemed like reason enough. He was also fairly young, having been appointed a decade before at the age of thirty-six.

Judge Giles was a quiet, gracious, and principled man who relished resolving cases, loved trials, and was extremely generous with his time teaching his law clerks. The clerks worked in the chambers library, which, in addition to rows of tall bookshelves, held my desk and the desk of my coclerk. Stacks of reports of every federal case with a written opinion stood behind us in a uniform, washed-out clay color, and each report had a red band across its thick spine. The judge's own large, impressive office was separated from our stacks by a reception-style, open, airy room, where his secretary, Chris, sat behind a desk; it served as the waiting room for lawyers who came for chamber settlement negotiations. Chris was surrounded by the file cabinets that stood between our library office and the central entry room, which she protectively presided over. The judge's office was expansive with large windows, a large wooden desk, and plush guest chairs that we clerks rarely sat in because the judge was so unaffected by his powerful position that he would often just wander back to our desks. He had a round table in his office that he had specially made. He explained that you had to force people to look at each other, not just at you.

The judge, as we always called him, would periodically emerge from his massive office, walk past Chris to the filing cabinets, and, with his sleeves rolled up, begin rummaging. A hard worker, if he had any downtime he would look for cases to try and settle. A brilliant mediator, he'd announce a swift trial date to bring in the lawyers, then masterfully work them on the facts to see if he could broker a deal. This particular day, though, he emerged from the file cabinets with a slender folder and dropped it casually on my desk. I looked up, wonderingly. He simply said, "Just put that back after you've had a chance to read it." Then he turned his back and casually walked back to his office.

I opened the folder, curious about the case inside. But it wasn't a case. It was my application for the clerkship. I realized he was allowing me to read the otherwise confidential letters of reference I received. The first was from my First Amendment professor, Kent Greenawalt. He was a close friend of my stepfather, but he showed no favoritism. He was very scrupulous that way, like Bruce himself. I really enjoyed the class and was an active and challenging participant, enjoying the back-and-forth, particularly on hate speech.

I remember going to Professor Greenawalt's office to ask him if he would write a recommendation letter for me. He had agreed and asked for my transcript. He would later remark, in passing, "I was surprised that a student as smart as you does not have higher grades." I was simultaneously embarrassed, hurt, and flattered. His letter was no surprise. He praised my intellect, while remarking very positively on how I pushed him on whether hate speech should be protected speech, and underscoring that my grades were not a reflection of my abilities.

Then there was the letter from Professor Berger. I pored over it while sitting at a desk in auspicious judicial chambers, surrounded by books the vast majority of Black people would never touch but would always be controlled by. He wrote, "She is bright without being brilliant." It was a staggering blow. It was akin to saying, "I had to write this letter to inform you that Maya Wiley is unremarkable." Judge Giles and I never discussed these letters he shared. It seemed to me a clear message: *Don't trust Professor Berger again. I hired you because you were a student who both deserved and needed the opportunity.* That is, at least, the way Judge Giles made me feel. I felt the pain of that blow but also the adrenaline rush to prove Berger wrong. It was my oath to myself that I would not let my judge regret hiring me. I feared his regret more than Professor Berger's judgment.

The judge never stopped teaching. One day, straight-faced as always, he walked into the library, having shed his robe with sleeves rolled up, pen and draft opinion I had written in hand. He pulled my guest chair around from the far side of my desk to sit beside me. Without introduction he began running the pen through phrases and whole sentences, pointing out anything unnecessary, the split infinitives and whatever else needed pointing out. He shared unforgettable wisdom and anecdotes I still use today.

I knew the criminal justice system wasn't fair. He taught me, in a practical and legal way, why the federal sentencing guidelines were particularly devastating to Black women, through a bone-crushing case he had. We had a case where a Black mother was charged and convicted of being a "mule." That meant she had carried drugs, in this case in the trunk of her car, for her drug-dealer boyfriend. There was no evidence that she was selling the drugs, but that didn't matter. They were in her car, so she transported them. Like many prosecutions, those higher up in a drug operation could flip on others and potentially reduce their own sentences. Judge Giles, like so many judges, hated the sentencing guidelines because prosecutors had more power than judges to determine the lengths of sentences, by the number and severity of the charges they brought. It was sobering to see this powerful and principled man, who was a balanced jurist but also a Black man who had some sense of the context for these cases. He was powerless to ensure that this young woman's sentence would be reasonable.

I revered him to the point of protection. While I was clerking, Iraq's Saddam Hussein, whose brutal and dictatorial rule did not make him an enemy of the United States thanks to the country's oil, invaded neighboring Kuwait. Antiwar protests broke out around the country, and from our windowed chambers, I watched the demonstrators march and chant on Market

Street. I felt pulled to go out there and march, but I didn't want to do anything that would undermine the credibility Judge Giles had so rightly earned. I never asked my law father. I just decided that our choices had consequences and I had made mine. Activism was not in the cards while I worked for a neutral arbiter of legal disputes.

I would go back to my passion after the clerkship, and that meant vying for a job at the LDF. Even with the AIDS clinic protest at Columbia, Jack and Debbie Greenberg did not abandon me. Jack made sure that Julius Chambers, head of the LDF, met with me during my clerkship. The man was so busy that I had to go out to LaGuardia Airport to meet with him before he boarded a flight. He agreed we should stay in touch and see what might be possible after my clerkship. When the time came, the LDF didn't have the funds to hire me, although Julius told me they would look for money. I had applied to a fellowship there that would focus on access to health care. I really didn't care what I did so long as it was at my dream job and dealt with race and poverty. I would not get the fellowship, though I would be encouraged to reapply to do something different. In the meantime, I needed a job.

Cathy Albisa, one of my close law school friends, shared an apartment with me in South Philadelphia. She commuted over the Ben Franklin Bridge to her federal clerkship with a judge in Camden, New Jersey. Cathy, a whip-smart, sarcastic Cubana from Miami, was one of the few law students who also focused on social justice work. Her clerkship was a year long and mine was two, so she was on the hunt for her next job while I had another year to look. She found the Karpatkin Fellowship at the ACLU's National Legal Office and had encouraged me to apply in case I couldn't get a job at the LDF. She would get a different fellowship in the Women's Rights Unit, once helmed by Justice Ruth Bader Ginsburg, to do reproductive freedom litigation. I would later win the Karpatkin Fellowship.

It was named for Marvin Karpatkin, a prominent civil liberties attorney who had represented conscientious objectors among other important clients. He had died just a few years after my dad, and also in his forties, of a heart attack. I didn't think I would work at the ACLU, and I worried I'd be forced to represent the Ku Klux Klan and neo-Nazis. The ACLU had represented neo-Nazis marching in a heavily Jewish community in Skokie, Illinois, more than a decade earlier, and it still was not known widely for racial justice litigation as much as free speech cases. When I went for the interview with the national legal director, I had not even researched him.

john powell spelled his name defiantly in lowercase. The ACLU national legal director had a large corner office. When I walked in, I was stunned to be greeted by Black Jesus. A handsome man, he was basketball-player-tall and slender, with a long, gentle nose that spread at the nostrils, giving it the appearance of being a downward arrow. Hanging coarsely beneath his unseen chin, a salt-and-pepper, V-shaped beard added to the directional pull of his nose, curling slightly around the corners of his lips. The top of his head was balding, and he had one clouded and wayward eye, which added to his striking and unforgettable appearance. He was wearing Birkenstock sandals on his feet, which necessitated socks because it was the fall or early winter—I would later learn that he was almost a year-round Birkenstock wearer. john had the calm, wrinkle-free countenance of a very wise man. Like Judge Giles, john was a placid lake, not revealing what, if anything, was roiling underneath the surface.

His office was large, with a big wooden desk and filled with piles of books. I settled into a sofa that rested against the wall. He folded himself into a chair opposite me, his long, spidery legs practiced in bending to accommodate chairs a bit too low for him. I remained stunned. This lawyer, the highest ranking in the ACLU, looked so counter to the white civil libertarian I had imagined based on my dated perceptions. But I was still wary about the job, and I focused on the Ku Klux Klansmen and neo-Nazis I had no intention of representing. john was working to change this, but I didn't know that, having been singularly focused on the LDF.

After the requisite introduction and question about my interests, I came out swinging. I straightened a bit, looked him directly in his good eye, and declared that I wanted to work on the cases that would help dismantle poverty for Black people. I had no specialty in mind, and I didn't know exactly what kind of cases to expect, but that was why I went to law school. I was sure this would bring the interview to a conclusion and I could be on my way.

john's eyes lit up visibly. He probed, and I talked about Dad and my upbringing. The conversation was getting interesting in a way I had not anticipated. john discussed a docket of cases that he had led the national office to file, most of which addressed the connection between race and poverty.

Education equity cases, in particular, were a focal point.

Ronald Reagan had filled the federal bench with conservative judges who were hostile to civil rights. We were watching them erect barriers to cities creating affirmative action programs, and soon after they would chip away at Title VI, the civil rights statute central to much of our work, that made it unlawful for any entity that received federal funds to discriminate based on race. This meant implementing a strategy focused on bringing cases in state court, not federal, which was a marked departure from the civil rights strategy of the 1950s and 1960s, where states couldn't be trusted and the federal government was more likely to enforce rights. I was hooked and knew that I wanted the job, and john knew he wanted me.

After two years in a federal clerkship, conducting myself with a rigor that my love for Judge Giles commanded, the ACLU was a very different and decidedly undisciplined experience. There were few attorneys of color there. I was lucky to have Cathy in the Women's Rights Project, while I sat a few floors higher in the building in the National Legal Department. I also had Victor Bolden, now a federal judge in Connecticut, who was in my unit; Jackie Berrien, who would later become President Barack Obama's chair of the Equal Employment Opportunity Commission; and, briefly, my dear friend Teresa Yates, who would join the Worker's Rights Project but later move to South Africa.

This was the period in education reform work when Black educators and thought leaders, rightly angry at the failure of underfunded and segregated public schools, were forming Black immersion academies focused mostly on the crises of Black boys. New York City was fertile ground for the immersion movement. Our New York City chapter was adamantly opposed. john and I, however, agreed that this was much more nuanced and complicated than the pro-versus-con discussion allowed for. He tasked me with developing a memo to lay out a more complex analysis than he and I had discussed. It was intellectually exhilarating, but also personal for me—I understood the anger and fear that prompted demands for something different. While I wasn't conscious of the integration fights my parents fought in

Syracuse, I certainly understood what they had. Black parents had real reasons to question waiting for meaningful and fair integration strategies because their kids didn't have decades to gain the education they deserved. We focused on educational quality and outcomes, along with the intent and the possibility of school integration. He had me deliver the paper as a speech at the national convention, which was a great honor for me as the lowest rung on the ladder of experience and authority.

The first actual case I worked on had me paired with Victor. We were assigned to find plaintiffs and help develop the legal theory for a quality education lawsuit in Louisiana. It was the civil rights community's answer to Reagan judges. If we couldn't win in the federal courts, we would look at state constitutions. Louisiana, as in Alabama, where there was a companion lawsuit, had a provision that guaranteed a quality education, but the state had abysmal public schools. Their segregation academies, the private all-white schools set up to avoid integration, were not better, but that didn't stop them from keeping white children enrolled. Mostly white public schools existed and, unless they were in wealthy communities, suffered from inadequate funding as well. Victor and I would spend much time driving around the state looking at the schools and interviewing parents and school administrators.

It was my first big case project, and it felt personal in two ways. I knew what it was like to be in school with overcrowded classrooms, no real math instruction, and no science program. I knew what it was like to avoid the bathrooms, and in Louisiana we learned they might not even have toilet paper. Textbooks could be so out-of-date as to be just flat-out wrong, as well as offensive. I also felt I was melding the life lessons and work of my parents. I was my father driving around the segregated

South, working with Victor to serve not only Black parents in New Orleans and Baton Rouge but white parents and educators in Shreveport. Mom commented to me that Shreveport was basically Texas, by which she meant Southern Baptist racism in a culture that was very familiar to her.

I remember the Southern Baptist school principal in Shreveport who was shocked that ACLU attorneys, whom he clearly did not like, were there to try to get more resources for his school. He didn't add *Black ACLU attorneys*, but I believed he was thinking it. I told him that my mother grew up in the Southern Baptist church. It was my way of acknowledging that I understood him without agreeing with him. The church had not yet apologized for supporting racial segregation and slavery. That didn't happen until the mid-1990s. I knew he was trying to imagine my mother, whom he presumed was Black, as a member of his segregated church. I would not set him straight.

We would struggle, Victor and I, to find a legal theory that would allow us to bring race together with class to fight racial discrimination in the education system, and fight for more public school resources overall under the state constitution. Our supervising attorney did not give us a clear charge. He was a nice guy who was also a distant and irrelevant mirage of a manager. He wasn't based in the New York office and never went with us to Louisiana, although he went separately on some occasions.

Victor and I, however, felt this case more personally. Our goal was for our work to benefit all students while correcting the hundreds of years of refusing to fund Black students' education, and the insistence on undermining *Brown v. Board*. But school integration cases didn't come with resources for Black schools, and these institutions typically needed more resources for everything: improving the physical buildings, attracting certified teachers, providing resources to support professionals like social workers and counselors, developing arts education, and more. The list was endless, but neither state nor federal law recognized the simple fact that improving these students' outcomes wasn't just about bodies in a building. It was about building up the bodies and minds with the required resources. This often meant that to be equal, Black schools needed more money, not the same amount of money.

Louisiana has a long history of underfunding public education, and it showed in its educational outcomes. Louisiana, like other Southern states, also diverted limited funds to private schools after desegregation orders. White people suffered in a bad public system, too, but race and politics still played out in questions of taxes and voucher programs. As with many states, there was not a lot of community- or state-level organizing and advocacy infrastructure in Louisiana, and Black people were catching hell. The school's antipoverty clinic was run by Bill Quigley, our local collaborating attorney and an amazing and lovely law professor at Loyola Law School. Students worked on all kinds of cases, from public benefits to housing. For me this was a mirror of the kind of lawyers that NWRO sought out.

One day we were having a meeting with Bill at Loyola Law School to discuss organizing plaintiffs and identifying other people to meet with in the state. His phone rang. He picked up and calmly but with deep concentration began to ask questions. He turned to his computer and started pounding keys as he spoke. Victor and I knew the look of a lawyer jumping to action. When Bill hung up the phone, he quickly explained that a woman was being evicted from her public housing apartment. He was pounding out a temporary restraining order to stop her eviction.

We hopped in the car with him and rushed to the down-town public housing development, an outwardly attractive col-lection of buildings to my New York City eyes. The apartment complex was a neat patchwork of two brick buildings sitting amid grassy lawns with meandering walkways between build-ings and trees. This was a far cry from the skyscraper density and institutional appearance of many projects in New York. Bill explained as we rushed that the downtown public housing projects were on very valuable land and, thanks to decades of neglect, were also in bad shape. We were seeing firsthand the fight to keep people in seriously inadequate housing because they would have nowhere else to go. The elderly woman we were now meeting in her apartment, a silent witness to the traumas produced by a hard-hearted society, had been paying her rent. She was being evicted because the housing authority wasn't repairing her apartment. Whether intentional or not, the impact was the same. Disinvestment was driving evictions, and the evicted had nowhere to go. The only beneficiaries would be private real estate developers.

I knew from Dad's work through NWRO how difficult it was to organize people who must struggle all day every day just to get by. Dad also believed this kind of antipoverty organizing would help unite people who shared the same needs—a decent welfare check—into a multiracial force. In Louisiana, I encoun-tered the igneous rock that is racism in America, so deeply embedded as to be foundational, and yet people could stand on top of it without seeing it.

It was the year David Duke, the grand wizard of the Ku Klux Klan, was running for governor against Edwin Edwards, an erstwhile and corrupt member of Congress who had been convicted of racketeering. The choices were so dismal that we frequently saw funny bumper stickers in New Orleans that read, "Vote for the Crook. It's Important." It was terrifying to witness the popularity of the white supremacist and neo-Nazi. Duke eventually won hundreds of thousands of votes in the 1991 race.

I remember sitting in my New Orleans hotel room one night watching the evening news. Duke had been promising to force women on welfare to go on birth control, spreading the myth that women and girls just had babies to collect a meager check. The Reagan welfare-queen stereotype was thriving. A local television news reporter went to a welfare line where most of the women were white, something commonly misunderstood about the largest number of recipients. I can still hear the reporter ask a white woman in that line why she was supporting David Duke for governor. She, a welfare recipient herself, agreed with Duke's stereotype about women on welfare being lazy. She meant Black women. She was so clouded with racism, she couldn't see herself as part of the caricature.

Victor and I would not figure out how to get more funding for these schools and the case would not proceed, despite the year's worth of hard work we put into the case development. I would one day speak to Bill's students about the need to have movement organizing and about how lawyers had to support that organizing. I wasn't seeing that opportunity at the ACLU, but I was grateful for john, Victor, Cathy, and so many others I learned with and from. But it was a volatile place where some fought for traditional civil liberties and others pushed for racial justice.

I left on my own terms, but I learned years later that someone high up in the ACLU wanted me gone, despite my being one of the lowest-level litigators in the hierarchy. It seemed to boil down to the fact that I caused trouble internally as part of a group of young lawyers who stormed a national board meeting to demand higher pay. I wasn't even on salary as a fellow, so I was mostly showing up in solidarity.

I assume my disfavor may also have been due to my response to the brutal beating of Rodney King. On March 3, 1991, in Los Angeles, four officers beat King viciously with batons, hitting him about fifty-six times as more than a dozen people watched passively. This type of brutality was as old as policing, but bystanders capturing it on video was newer. It was one of those moments that created a clear call for action. I and a few of my colleagues organized an open meeting for the New York office, which included all the national programs and the New York City chapter. We printed and posted flyers all through the building. Only Black and Latina lawyers (there were two Latinas, including Cathy), a couple of white colleagues, and the Black support staff attended.

It was shocking to us. It felt as if our white colleagues and more senior attorneys didn't care. The next day, I bumped into one of the supervisors in the department. I asked why this supervisor didn't attend the meeting. This wasn't planned. I was angry about the lack of engagement, but I didn't know just how angry. The response was something to the effect that this supervisor did the work every day, as if to say their attendance was unnecessary. My own anger and helplessness turned into outrage. How could this person be so aloof and have no compassionate emotional response to the pain we more junior attorneys and staff, I and other Black staff, were feeling? I know I was disrespectful, but I have no recollection of the angry words that immediately poured from my mouth.

Her response reminded me so much of my middle school teacher. Squeezing her thin lips together, arms tightly crossed in a self-protective pout, the supervisor turned and walked away. I don't remember anyone but john talking to me about this, and I don't remember him lecturing me. That wasn't his way. My mother, mind you, would have helped to organize the meeting, and if supervisors didn't attend it she would have agreed with my outrage, but she also would have used the opportunity to call me to more appropriate behavior. Despite my earning disfavor, john not only protected me from termination, he offered me a permanent staff position. I turned it down. I wanted to continue to work with john but had no desire to stay at the ACLU.

When the time finally came for me to join the LDF, it was like going home after a year abroad. I felt like I had an instant family. Julius Chambers was the quiet, busy, and absent father. Elaine Jones, his number two, was the strategist leading the DC office, and she was a bit like that revered auntie you saw every year at Christmas. Bill Lan Lee, who headed the Los Angeles office, was the unruly older brother who was driven by a desire to make good on the promises of the moment we were in. He was the more jocular of the three, although he was serious about the mission, and the West Coast work seemed more activist.

I joined the Poverty and Justice Unit, which was made up of me and three other young lawyers experimenting with everything from litigation to stem Black land loss to environmental justice. Now the health care attorney, I was handed a lawsuit against two merging hospitals. One of them was St. Luke's, where I'd had my ovarian cystectomy. The LDF wasn't trying to stop the merger, but rather the transfer of the maternal and neonatal intensive care unit (NICU) beds from the St. Luke's

Hospital location to the Roosevelt Hospital location at Columbus Circle. I would learn that powerful, well-heeled lawyers experienced hospitals differently than I did. They hadn't had a brother who nearly died at birth or been gleefully told by a doctor that they needed an operation.

During my first few months on the job, Julius announced that he was leaving. Elaine Jones would become the first woman to head the organization. The opportunity to be in the organization under a Black woman was invigorating. Elaine would become my first woman mentor. She was completely unlike the past heads of LDF. Not interested in building her record of Supreme Court arguments, she was a strategist through and through. She was also a generous leader who sought to empower others. She would bolster my sense of myself as a leader.

I was focused on my hospital case first and foremost, which made me feel like I was finally coming closer to being a movement lawyer. We had to show that Black and Latina patients would not likely get services at the Columbus Circle location. Demonstrating the realities of the incredible shackles of poverty to those who never had to forgo a meal is always difficult.

Like my parents before me, I knew facts mattered. You had to make your case and have a plan to push it, so we worked with an academic at Hunter College in the groundbreaking field of Geographic Information Systems. New York was the rare state that collected data about hospital patients, which enabled researchers to show that every time a Harlem hospital had closed—and there had been several closings—patients would disperse a certain distance and in certain directions. It was clear that they would go to the two remaining hospitals in Harlem, which were closer and more accessible than Columbus Circle.

Some of that was due to the public transportation cost and the time of travel. Many had more than one child and no formal childcare. We also knew that the mostly white doctors preferred affluent, insured white patients to low-income Black and brown patients. Mount Sinai had infamously planned a Medicaid ward separate from its private pay area, and the racial implications were obvious.

My colleagues had already filed the complaint. My job involved working as cocounsel with the Puerto Rican Legal Defense Fund, now called Latino Justice, and the Legal Aid Society. The community was mobilized and had been taking direct action to stop the movement of the maternal and NICU beds.

Ben Jealous, who would be the NAACP president and a Maryland gubernatorial candidate, was an eighteen-year-old Columbia University student working at LDF as an intern. His job was responding to the mail from inmates, but I pulled him out of the mail room because he was an organizer of the financial aid protests erupting at Columbia. When I ran for mayor, Ben endorsed me with a humbling, emotional Twitter thread in which he recounted me pulling him out of mail room obscurity. I let his considerable talent loose on organizing activism in Harlem to prevent those beds from being moved. When Ben became the president of the NAACP in 2008, I was so proud. I give myself little credit for his meteoric rise. He was a star at eighteen, and I just saw the bright glare.

Ben and I went to visit one of our named plaintiffs, Yvonne Mussington, at her apartment on 125th Street. She had six children, and her husband did itinerant construction work. Their home was small and had peeling paint. Some of her children had lead poisoning. We had a private law firm helping us with the case pro bono. The attorney assigned to the case was a straitlaced white attorney who had defended paint companies in lead paint litigation. He studiously avoided the obvious contradictions; he had the greatest and utmost concern and empathy for Yvonne and her family because he had gotten to know her. But I noted how he remarked that she was somehow "different" from the plaintiffs in the lead paint cases he defended. She was "deserving." They were not.

When we visited, Ms. Mussington was cooking dinner, and it was hardly enough for two adults, let alone a family of eight. Her husband came home in the middle of the visit, covered with construction dust and clearly exhausted. Poverty is a trauma. Hunger is a trauma. Still, she did what I have seen time and time again among people who don't have enough. She acted with pride and generosity. She offered us dinner. We politely declined and soon left, having finished the interview we were there to conduct, and to give the family their privacy and dignity as they shared something that would be much less than a meal. I left feeling that I was in the right place, fighting the good fight and also deeply worried that, like my experience in the Philippines, little would change in her family's life simply because we were there and fighting in court. It would not reverse the lead poisoning or put food on her small table with its hungry mouths.

I spent two years fighting for health care access at the LDF, for people who often couldn't get enough food to eat or money to pay their rent. It was at a time when Joe Biden and others were pushing to expand the crackdown on crime with the infamous Omnibus Crime Bill, while the Clintons and others were parroting the words of some social scientists who labeled young Black kids "superpredators." At the same time women's rights groups were pushing to pass the Violence Against Women Act, which was an important piece of legislation, but would be attached to the Omnibus Crime Bill. It was also a time when Black women wanted to challenge the Hyde Amendment so that Medicaid would pay for abortions, but women's groups, largely white-led, would not fight for it because they felt it was a losing battle.

While we were litigating the St. Luke's case in 1993, Bill Clinton promised to transform the American health care system to make it affordable for everyone, which would include meaningful health care services for more welfare recipients, and to stop closing hospitals. Harlem and other communities of color had been bleeding hospital beds for years because of the cost of unreimbursed emergency and other health care costs. The hospitals were running from poverty to ensure profits.

For me, Clinton handed a victory to "welfare queen" Republicans, those who judged people for conditions imposed upon them. It was a victory they would not have won on their own. Clinton campaigned on "changing welfare as we know it," a betrayal of a set of principles that Dad, antipoverty lawyers, like-minded academic social workers, and, most important, Black women, had fought to establish through the Johnson, Nixon, and Carter administrations. None of the work had been a complete victory, but the principles of the struggle were sharper and clearer, and had repeated policy attempts that would continue to be a foundation for a new social contract.

It did create more welfare organizing like Dad had led. The other upside, ostensibly, was expanding health insurance coverage and primary care, which would be a huge benefit to the poor, particularly the working poor. My seething frustration about what was happening to welfare recipients bathed me with purpose to try to at least make the health care opportunity real. We could actually make lasting change through policy. This was always what litigation was meant to do. It was a hammer in the hands of carpenters for building a stronger and better house of justice and opportunity. I went to Elaine as one of the newest lawyers on the team and with only a few short years of post–law school experience under my belt, and I told her I wanted to do something about health care for Black people. To do so we had to be in DC influencing the health care reform agenda being led by Hillary Clinton and five hundred experts behind closed doors, one of whom was a friend a year behind me in law school and member of the AIDS discrimination clinic.

Elaine was a powerful lobbyist and leader, but was also accessible. To sit with Elaine was to feel like you were in a backyard on a hot day, sipping lemonade and plotting something that could catch fire. She had a clear Southern way of saying "Now…" at the start of her sentences. She would raise a pointed finger tipped by a painted nail. Her left eye would narrow into a squint as her right stayed wide, and her lips would curl up mischievously with the ideas racing through her brilliant brain.

I had to say very little for her to see my vision for our next steps. She was a Hill strategist and knew exactly why Congress and the White House mattered. We could sue a hospital and maybe win, or we could influence legislation and change the nation's health care system and primary care services. My goal was to get the LDF's DC office, our lobbying shop, on the case and feed it with my suggestions about what should be in the package from New York.

Elaine met me in DC, where she was still based, and told me we were going to the NAACP Washington bureau. She explained little else. We walked over to the NAACP's lobbying arm. Much to the confusion of many, the LDF was no longer affiliated with the NAACP. As two completely separate and wholly independent organizations, the history and connection still bred collaboration along with periodic competition. But Wade Henderson, the head of the DC bureau, and Elaine were allies and friends. In DC, they were the Black leaders making sure that the civil rights coalition's work produced racial justice gains for Black people. Ed Hailes was Wade's number two in a small but mighty shop; they could call on the organization's other chapters across the country.

When we walked into the office's conference room and sat down across the table, Elaine turned to me without ceremony and said, "Tell them what you told me." I was a bit stunned. I had expected Elaine to deliver my message and that I would answer questions. To be clear, Elaine had introduced the topic, and I have no doubt she talked to Wade in advance. She never told me that I would do the selling, though.

I was not one to be shy or quiet. I spoke simply and said what I believed. Wade answered equally simply with an "Okay, we're in." I was left thinking, *That's it?* I couldn't believe how easy it was. Health care was not a top-of-mind civil rights issue, despite its central importance. Schools, jobs, criminal justice, and housing were much more prominent. The next step was to take the proposal to the Leadership Conference on Civil and Human Rights, the national alliance that formed the lobbying coalition for the civil rights movement. Founded in 1950 by Roy Wilkins, head of the NAACP; A. Philip Randolph, head of the Brotherhood of Sleeping Car Porters; and Arnold Aronson, head of what is now known as the Jewish Council for Public Affairs, it had expanded to include most of the major unions, the women's rights community, disability rights groups, and more. This had to be a coalitional effort, and at the time I had no idea I would later become its president and chief executive officer.

As Elaine and I left the office, she said, "You'll work with Wade and Eddie." I was stunned again. I was a litigator, and an inexperienced one, at that. I had no lobbying experience, nor did I see myself that way. And I lived in New York. Lobbying meant DC. But it wasn't a request. It was an order, and one I would obey because I had, in effect, asked for it unwittingly. Elaine had listened, had gotten directly engaged, and had moved my idea into action. Now it was on me to help deliver. I understood that she was demonstrating faith and trust in me. She was also investing in me. She told me she would be there when I needed her and that she would assign a more senior leader in the DC office to help guide me in relationship politics and understanding the coalitional dynamics. I suspect she also knew that Wade would nurture me, too, and he did.

The result was that I got to live with my mom four days a week for part of two congressional sessions. I would take the train down on Sunday or Monday and stay until Thursday, when I usually headed back to my Fort Greene, Brooklyn, apartment.

It was 1993. In 1984, Mom had made a major career shift. I was a college sophomore, visiting my boyfriend in Oakland over spring break, when during a call with my mother she announced that she was buying the Franz Bader Gallery. I was speechless. I made her repeat herself, and as she did so, I repeated the words in turn to my boyfriend in disbelief.

When I was growing up, the Franz Bader Gallery seemed to be the only "serious" gallery in a town that was dominated by the Smithsonian's vast array of free museums. Art life in the vastly Black city was minimal, and Franz Bader, a German Jew who made it out before the unspeakable gas chambers were established in Nazi Germany, was a local icon for establishing a DC gallery. Sometimes we would go with Mom as a kind of family outing. After Reagan's anti–affirmative action policies had completely gutted her consulting business, she had begun to show ceramics at our house, by appointment only. It was initially just a sideline pleasure, but her business became increasingly brisk and took over the house. Beautiful hand-thrown dishware, vases, serving bowls, and platters sat all over the first-floor dining room and living room.

As a high school student, I found the strangers and the constant ringing of the doorbell a bit annoying. But her small business flourished, and at one point she even found a partner to add handmade wearables to the collections. By then, Franz Bader, elderly and retiring, had reached out to ask her if she wanted to buy the gallery. Mom, being Mom, said yes with little thought. She not only became the proprietor of the city's most prestigious art gallery, but also gave it a purpose. Bader had made much of his income selling Canadian Inuit soapstone sculpture. My mother made it a true contemporary sculpture gallery, along with some paintings, and would only show artists who were raised in DC or who lived and worked in DC.

Now that I was living at home for most of every week, I became her helper at gallery openings. It was a lot of fun for me to see Mom in that role and to be able to meet the artists whose work would be rotated every six weeks. Eddie Hailes, now my running buddy and instructor, would meet Mom and form a distant love affair that made me feel even more enveloped in community. Eddie was a dear friend during that time, and that would matter a lot.

I also became pregnant. I was seeing a nice and noncommittal criminal defense attorney at that time. We were reckless and I—thirty years old, pregnant for the first time in my life, and at a new stage of adulthood—was faced with a serious decision. Mom had been very clear with me at a young age that a fetus was not a child, and I should not hesitate to come tell her when I was ready for birth control or needed an abortion. I never needed help with an abortion until, to my utter horror, I was old enough to be less reckless. The relationship was not serious, and there would be no marriage discussion. I was not a teenager or a student. I had my degrees and a job and the ability to afford to keep a child as a single parent. Now the question was, should I?

As in all things, I told my mother as soon as I took the pregnancy test in the bathroom in her house. She and Bruce were now separated and living apart. Dan was living in Brooklyn with his artist wife and working for a community organization. It was just Mom and me. She looked me straight in the eyes, with one of the most serious looks I remember her having, and asked, "What are you going to do?" I assume she could sense my ambivalence. I replied honestly, "I don't know. Maybe I should keep it." She leapt. "No, you shouldn't! It's hard to be a single mother. That's not what you want."

I knew she wasn't wrong. I didn't think that made her necessarily right, either. I had been recruited by the US Department of Health and Human Services, and it would pay me a low six figures, which was a huge change after earning $30,000 for the fifth year in a row. I didn't want the job. I didn't see myself as a government insider. I had also always known I wanted a family. Two kids and a husband. My own family, for all its imperfections, traumas, and difficulties, was a deep joy to me, and I wanted to continue building that joy. My mother wanted that, too. She longed to be a grandmother and had always force-fully told me not to start a family until I was at least thirty years old. Well, here I was.

I didn't want to be a single mom. I didn't want to leave civil rights work. I was just beginning to feel truly a part of it and to find my voice in it. Mom and I talked again. She made it plain. "I won't help you." She would love me and visit me and all those things. I knew she would love the child. But she wouldn't be a stand-in for the father the baby would not have. Mom was always honest and direct, loving with boundaries. She would insist that if I made the choice, I owned the consequences.

Part of me was hurt and angry. I felt the welling up of old anger about Mom being off duty, about my parents, when they were together, not being traditional parents, and how I longed for a normal family. To me, her being an active, supportive grandparent was being normal. I also knew that Mom was wise. She knew that if she volunteered to help, I might make a differ-ent choice and come to regret it. I would never regret the child, but that wouldn't be the same thing as regretting the choice.

I had an intense moment of examining my pain from my childhood, but I also recognized I never regretted my child-hood. It made the good parts of who I was, as well as the flawed parts. It taught me compassion, and resilience. For all my par-ents' shortcomings, they had shown me what it meant to live as fully as possible and for something bigger than me. I wanted that badly. I had a taste of what it felt like to be part of some-thing bigger and meaningful, and I didn't want to lose it just as I was beginning to drink from its cup. The nectar was sweet with the saltiness of struggle. I also wanted to have children, but not at any cost. Not at the price of my own sense of purpose, and not without a dad. I missed mine so much. I wished so much for his guidance, his approval, his love. Mom was telling me I could have both, that being a Wiley showed us how to have both, but not as a single mom.

I cried. I cursed to myself and at myself. I had the abortion. It would be the right decision.

CHAPTER 14

CHANGE

AT THE LDF, I was beginning to see parts of myself that gave me a new kind of courage, one I had not had when it came to continuing modern dance as a child. I was learning more leadership skills by doing, including using persuasion rather than angry outbursts. I still wouldn't have described myself as a leader back then. I still carried a voice from that self-hating child in my ear, the one who was unremarkable, but I also had my mom's teachings of humility and to see those most impacted by problems as leaders. Inside the Beltway was different. I was eagerly learning how to lobby Congress. I not only had the facts, but I had the ability to communicate them. Older and wiser leaders looked to me for my expertise and answers to questions posed by lawmakers. All this added up to a newly buoyed confidence in myself, along with new skills.

I remember one meeting in particular with Nancy Kassebaum, a Republican senator from Kansas. Ralph Neas, who headed the Leadership Conference at the time, was once a pro–civil rights Republican and used that position to reach the moderates and even conservatives willing to compromise to pass civil rights legislation. Kassebaum was one of those senators who might cross the aisle to provide the services we needed for low-income women of color. I met with her as part of a fairly large delegation that included Black civil rights and women's rights groups. She was gracious and listened politely with only an occasional question, but she asked why we needed to take major action to revamp our health care system at all. I was ready for her. I was carrying Yvonne Mussington and her children with me. I was not the visual artist my brother was, but I could paint a picture with my stories of real people and the statistics that captured the lives I had described. She looked at me and said gently, "That is very persuasive."

Ultimately, I would learn the truth about politics. It didn't matter. This was going to go down on party lines. But I could see the importance of trying and why connection could be more powerful than conflict at times.

Having no movement behind us made our efforts difficult. At one point Wade Henderson, the top lobbyist for the NAACP, decided we needed to have a Sunday day of action for health care in Black churches across the country. He recognized that we needed to build some pressure and momentum for our legislative demands, and that required regular folks speaking up. Because the NAACP had chapters all over the country and the

Black church remained a central institutional base for the organization, he went to work putting out the call. Some churches participated, and the *Washington Post* ran a story about it. It wouldn't be enough.

Despite years of fighting, we also lost the St. Luke's Hospital case due to laches, which is one of those arcane, judge-made procedural rules that essentially means *You waited too long to bring this lawsuit.* It was an obvious way to avoid dealing with serious civil rights claims. I was outraged. A small but active group of community leaders had given the hospital every chance to make a different choice, and free lawyers were engaged, but the hospital won because it had more resources than community members and because underresourced, nonprofit civil rights lawyers need time to build complex cases.

Litigating remained my calling because I continued to recognize it as an important tool. It did matter that we took the case because the community didn't stand alone. We added to the pressure community members applied to push the hospitals to provide maternal and NICU services in Harlem. I also still loved the challenge of the courtroom, but I felt I still had to learn to litigate well. I loved LDF, but it had few resources to train us newly minted lawyers.

One day I made my way to the office of a lawyer who was more experienced, though not a manager. She was a voting rights lawyer named Sherrilyn Ifill. Wickedly smart and with the kind of steely strength and unapologetic directness that made her a magnet, Sherrilyn would many years later become the head of the organization. At the time I was there to commiserate, and she told me the story of her first serious voting rights trial, one she had to figure out on her own. She confided that it was so stressful that she suffered physical symptoms from the stress. It was awful to hear, but oddly reassuring because Sherrilyn had survived and thrived, and was an inspiration. I found myself both itching and simultaneously terrified to get into the courtroom, knowing I might wait years to build our complex cases into readiness for actual courtroom experience.

Jane Booth, who headed Legal Aid's civil appeals and law reform unit, was tapped to become the head of the civil division at the US attorney's office. She recruited me with assurances that I would be trained to litigate, get tons of trials including civil rights enforcement cases, and could return to LDF a seasoned attorney. It was 1994 and I jumped at that chance, thinking I could help bring the weight of the federal government to bear on the change we needed. Though we were not in movement times, the federal government had real power to bring justice and rights to more people, and I could become a better lawyer doing it.

At the US attorney's office, I refused to take a job as a prosecutor in the criminal division because too often many Black and Latino young people and women were getting harsh sentences for low-level drug offenders. At LDF, we called prosecutors the "persecutor's office." The prestige and career-making potential of a job in the criminal division did not entice me. I knew I wanted to learn to litigate civil rights cases, including police brutality. My rejection shocked the head of the criminal division, who made me an offer along with the civil division. He said, "We do the work of the angels." I knew he believed it. I didn't, with the exception of corruption cases. If I could have gone into the public integrity unit directly, I might have said yes. The civil division was my path, and I would be the only Black attorney of fifty in the division. Their sole Black attorney was leaving the office as I was coming in, and I derisively began to refer to my position as "the Thurgood Marshall seat," since Marshall had been the only Black Supreme Court justice and was replaced by the second, Clarence Thomas.

My supervisor was an excellent lawyer, I'd heard. She was also one of those humorless and stern women who decided her job was to break her new supervisees down into a million pieces, to rebuild them in the proper image of a lawyer with the Southern District of New York. Her feedback was fair, but she was derisive in tone and dismissive in demeanor. Her cold and casual, taciturn face could feel withering in its judgment. Every letter had to be reviewed and could be slashed and handed back with a statement as hard as a physical slap in the face: "This is not the quality of an assistant"—my title in short form. It felt isolating and abusive.

I knew it wasn't personal. She made everyone she supervised feel that way, at least for a period of time. I was not singled out, but it didn't matter. I was the only Black attorney, the only civil rights lawyer, in the office. I had natural locs and wore funky clothes, like my favorite dress, a light pink knit A-line, with a double-breasted pink wool blazer I had miraculously found and bought separately. I refused to fit in, so that I wouldn't lose myself. I could not have been more culturally out of place if I had moved to rural Montana.

I was getting angrier as I was getting more demoralized, feeling that part of me from my troubling adolescent years. It was even more isolating than Dartmouth, where I at least had a social network of Black students. It wasn't that other attorneys were not kind to me. They were. It still felt like a judgmental environment, if not hostile. I felt an obligation as the only Black attorney to defy the low expectations the office appeared to have of Black lawyers since, according to some higher-ups, it was "so hard to find qualified Black attorneys" in New York City. New York City isn't Maine. There are a lot of Black attorneys. What I heard was *So few of you measure up.* Eventually I would be added to the office hiring committee as the few Black representatives of an entire race of people. There it appeared that "qualified" meant having graduated from an Ivy League law school, clerked for a federal judge, worked a requisite number of years in a white-shoe private law firm that someone in the office had also worked for, and been recommended by a partner who was respected by the right people.

I was about a year into a three-year commitment to the job when I and the sole Puerto Rican attorney figured out we were being assigned more employment discrimination defense cases than our white counterparts. I knew I would have to do some of this work, defending government agencies against discrimination claims, but I took the job because I was told I would get to go after civil rights violators in the name of the US government, not just defend claims against the government. Now it appeared that the two attorneys of color were being overassigned the defensive cases, which made it feel like we were being used as cover. To add insult to injury, a white attorney hired after me had been assigned a pro–civil rights investigation. I didn't begrudge him a case, but how was I less ready for one? I decided to advocate for myself.

I went to the deputy who headed the civil rights unit, and asked outright for a proactive civil rights investigation. He expressed some sympathy and advised me to go to Jane Booth, who had hired me and made all the case assignments, to ask for a civil rights investigation, where the government would be the plaintiff. He said he would support it, so I did.

I was polite and deferential. After all, I respected her

leadership at Legal Aid, and she had recruited me. I thought of her as an ally. I had also learned to be more diplomatic and prepared, and less of a human flame-thrower. First, she declined because I hadn't been in the office long enough. I pointed out that a white male attorney who was hired after me had already been assigned a civil rights case. Next, she blamed my lack of experience on the subject. I noted that I had come to her from LDF and the ACLU before that. I had already been a civil rights lawyer and he had not. She continued with some other arguments that felt to me equally unsupportable and I felt I batted them back. By the end of the conversation, in which my polite demeanor was visibly souring, she ended with a simple, "Well, you're not ready." She was done discussing it.

I was done, too. To me, it felt that the woman who recruited me did not believe I could do the work. I am incapable of hiding my feelings so, while I had remained calm and said nothing inappropriate, I marched out of her office in a gathering storm. The clouds darkened around my head with each step back down the long corridor, passing white face after white face. By the time I arrived at my open office door, I threw myself, my locs, my chunky-heeled shoes, and my less than assistant-like suit into my chair. I began to curse loudly, and I didn't care who heard me because I was quitting.

What happened next changed everything. My next-door neighbor was a very smart guy and a bit of a curmudgeon, but always kind. He came into my office and sat down in one of my two guest chairs opposite my desk. He said slowly and with an uptick in his voice on the last word, "What happened?" I began to tell him loudly. Very loudly. Somewhere in there I am pretty sure I said, "That bitch..." Then another nearby office neighbor entered. And then a third. These were attorneys who

I considered nice and vaguely distant acquaintances. At some point during all this, one of them had the presence of mind to shut my door.

The first attorney's response shocked me. I expected to receive a kind and condescending *You'll get there, be patient* speech. Instead, this attorney said he agreed. I loved him from that day on. He declared, "I have a trial coming up. I'm going to ask that you be assigned as my second seat." That was a big deal. Trials were what I came for. It was not a career-making case, but it didn't have to be. I had won motions to throw cases out. I had not yet had my first trial. As an elite office where the leaders are constantly protecting its reputation as the "Sovereign" Southern District of New York—the "best" of the nation's US attorney's offices—the worst thing was to have a lawyer who lost trials. The others chimed in and pledged equal forms of support, with indignation at the injustice of it all. They went from acquaintances to trusted friends.

They gave me enough of a lifeline. I resolved, with their encouragement, to stay for another two years and see my commitment through. Just as I had pledged to myself that I wouldn't let my judge down, I now told myself that I would make sure Jane and my supervisors would be sorry to see me go when I resigned on my terms. I didn't want them to defeat me, not that it was their intent. But it was a possible result if I couldn't dig deeper. I couldn't become proof that it was "hard" to find "qualified" Black lawyers and I couldn't let myself sink into self-doubt that I could litigate well.

Within a month I was trying a case. My colleagues came to watch, including my borderline sadistic supervisor, who actually complimented me for cross-examining a witness well. I was subsequently sent to the Department of Justice's trial advocacy training for two weeks in Arizona. I performed so well there that the instructors sent word back to my superiors that I was a high performer. I did an advanced trial advocacy training and those instructors asked that I consider coming back as a trainer. That was the greatest compliment I could ask for. The training feedback to Jane would raise my stock valuation. I would be asked to second-seat a trial of a much more senior lawyer, a kind and smart man, who had not yet tried a case despite his years of service. I was, essentially, being tapped to help him navigate his trial.

My reward for this success was to be added to the team on a big civil fraud case that roiled my innards. The case emanated from David Dinkins's mayoral administration. The agency responsible for visiting homes where children might be neglected or abused had an obligation to do home visits based on federal dollars given to the foster-care agency. My office had brought a civil fraud case based on evidence that caseworkers falsified their reports, claiming to have completed home visits that were never made. The remedy in a civil fraud case was to reclaim millions of dollars from an overstretched and under-funded agency responsible for the health and well-being of almost exclusively Black and brown children. In my view, while the behavior of the foster-care agency was wrong, it was the result of a systemic problem that required funds and fixing, not taking money out of the system. Of course, as the junior attorney I was given the grunt work of thumbing through forty boxes of dusty documents in search of evidence in a case that troubled me. It would get worse, though. I would be assigned to take the depositions of the Black people being accused of fraud. It was horrible sitting opposite Black civil servants who had impossible jobs and basically calling them liars—and it was clear to all of us that I was the one taking the depositions for that reason.

During this period, I was so unhappy and so distrusting of my emotional state that I married a lovely man I had no business marrying. We met in a Fire Island house share I got pulled into by a law school classmate. That friend was the only person I knew in the house. Jonathan had recently broken up with his first wife and made his interest clear. He was smart, attractive, and kind, and he was interested in working on homelessness and affordable housing. His father was an economist and his mother was a librarian. He felt closer to my interests than anyone else I was meeting, and I was depressed. After dating for a short time, he made very clear that he was interested in marriage, which was a change from the men with various commitment issues I had known.

I had my doubts. I also had some friends, one Black woman in particular, who wanted to know what was wrong with him. What she meant was: What was wrong with *me* for not counting my blessings and rushing him down the aisle? This was not my parents' romantic, determined, *us against the world* nuptials. I doubted my own emotions, assuming something was wrong with me because he was great. It would be the second time in my life I got rare bad advice from Mom. I had already convinced her to move to New York, and she and I were living together on different floors of a brownstone she had found in the neighborhood I loved, Fort Greene.

I remember us sitting side by side in her high-ceilinged, bright living room on the parlor-level floor. I casually asked, "Do you think I should marry Jonathan?" Just as casually she responded, "Marry him! If it doesn't work out, you get divorced!" I admit I was shocked. When I had asked Mom about finally divorcing Bruce, with whom she was clearly not happy, she had said she didn't believe in divorce. Of course, I understood that didn't mean she would never get a divorce—she'd been divorcing Dad, after all. Instead, she meant she wouldn't easily cut and run and saw no reason to divorce Bruce. It was a kind of pragmatism over expectation of happiness.

Subconsciously, I was looking to Mom to tell me the truth: *I don't think you love Jonathan, so no, you shouldn't marry him.* I didn't get what I expected but I was too lost, too distanced from myself, to understand that I was looking for permission to walk away. I would only realize that after marrying him in 1997 and quickly acknowledge what I couldn't quite admit to myself: We were not a match.

I was no longer following my calling, married to a man whom I shouldn't have married, and I was lost. But I did not sit still. At the end of my three years at the SDNY, I quit as planned. A friend, who had been the Karpatkin Fellow before me, and one of the ACLU board members I had known there were now in high positions at the Open Society Institute, which billionaire George Soros had founded. I had been recruited to work at the fledgling foundation before I went to the US attorney's office. At the time, I had declined because I wanted to litigate, not grant-make.

Now I was burnt out after working seventy-hour weeks for the previous three years. I knew I wasn't going back to LDF. I had enjoyed litigation. But after three years at the US attorney's office, I no longer felt it to be a calling. I wanted to find my way back to race and poverty work, but now I was unsure what to do and where to do it. At the ACLU we felt stymied on our Louisiana case. At LDF I was reminded of the importance of organizing to the cause for change, which litigation could help support, but it was not the primary tool that it had once been. But even in my parents' day, it was the organizing that was so critical to bringing about changes in the law, along with pivotal court cases. Mom was proud of me for the path I had chosen, and she told me that regularly. I was glad I had chosen it, too. But being a Wiley always came back to being strategic, engaging the ordinary people who couldn't see a doctor when they were sick, or couldn't get childcare or afford housing. I needed to find a way to use all that I had learned from litigating and all I loved about the storytelling to support community activism. Dad had left chemistry, and I would leave litigation.

The foundation gave me the perfect way to leave. I would work part-time in the general counsel's office on employment issues and spend the rest of my time advising U.S. programs on race and poverty. The president of the foundation, Aryeh Neier, would also send me to the South Africa Foundation to help develop and establish a criminal justice initiative in that country. Changing jobs and traveling to South Africa would be much more of a profound personal journey than I imagined. It helped me realize how unhappy I was, that I needed out of my marriage to Jonathan, and that I needed to look deep inside myself. South Africa—a country still reeling from the traumas of apartheid, poverty, crime, and violence—would be the place I would confront my own traumas and change my life from within.

CHAPTER 15

CONFRONTING AND CREATING

THE YEAR WAS 2000, the beginning of a new millennium, and it was a bright, hot weekend in the countryside a few hours' drive from Cape Town. I watched the rough beauty of the Western Cape province, the southernmost tip of the large country, pass me by and wondered what would come next. We reached the low, rocky hills permitting scrub-like growth by the dusty roads off the paved highway. The light had a quality that was bright, piercing, and poignant. I felt I could see everything with a different clarity, even as I wondered what unexpected sights might appear.

That was often my experience in South Africa, and maybe even in life. I think I'm seeing the world with perfect clarity only to realize something unexpected has been staring me in the face. I was used to being an outsider in many of the settings I was in. South Africa would be another example. I was a foreigner, and as a Black American I was privileged even with white racists in a way Black South Africans understandably resented. I had spent the better part of two years by choice at the Open Society Foundation South Africa (OSF-SA) as, in essence, an inside outsider: a New York head office staffer sent to our sister foundation in the network of Open Society Foundations, which is what country-level foundations in the Soros global network were called. The discomfort could be eye-opening, even if it was sometimes challenging. It pushed me to look at my own ideas about my identity, what I could offer and how I could help, while getting out of the way of Black South Africans seeking to lead themselves.

I started the year 2000 reevaluating myself, my path, and my purpose after three years away from litigation. Jonathan and I had called it quits by 1999, although we were still friendly, and now I was reconnecting with an old friend and flame, Harlan Mandel. I left the foundation at the end of 1999, but I decided to stay in Cape Town for the first three months of 2000, living off savings. That was a big deal for me. Savings were a rare treasure in my family and in my life, and they were to be guarded at all costs. It would be the first time in my life I would not have a paycheck or a plan.

I knew that I needed to take a break and reflect on what I wanted to do next. What I did know was that Harlan and I would decide to commit to each other and to starting a family. I also knew that to determine my next steps, including my personal life, I had to fully explore my feelings about Dad. Back in New York, I had periodically been in therapy. One therapist, an older white, no-nonsense woman, who was very sharp and truly kind, teared up as I described Dad's death to her with my usual practiced recounting. I was very touched by that. Then, as if she was grabbing my shoulders with both hands and shaking me, she looked at me and announced, "You have PTSD!" I admit to being shocked. No one had told me that before.

Now I would explore, in earnest, my trauma, because regular talk therapy didn't seem to pierce my protective shield. I didn't even know what exactly had to be broken down, because I still felt pretty well adjusted. But I had come to consider that my inability to fall apart at the seams might be a problem. What I was clear about was that my distance from who I had been and who I might now become required a reckoning. I had an emotional account past due with myself.

I was volunteering at the Legal Resources Center, the LDF of South Africa, helping them set up a constitutional law program, but that was only two days a week. The other days I was exploring myself. I had a friend there, a crime prevention consultant, whom I met because of his community mediation work. He was white, had an Afrikaner father who had been abusive to his mother, a very common experience in South Africa, and he spent a good deal of his time exploring his own experiences. As we shared our past traumas, he became a kind of guide to healing methods I had never considered before.

I started seeing a hypnotherapist whom he had worked with in the past. I was deeply skeptical because of the stereotypes I had from movies, but he assured me it was more like deep relaxation rather than any talisman waving, trance-inducing control mechanism. The therapist was a white, blond-haired woman who lived in an upper-middle-class suburban home. In other words, she and her surroundings were almost comically traditional. Like my previous therapist, she was very kind and open. She understood that I was trying to explore my relationship with Dad and come to terms with that and with his terrifying death. With what could be more aptly described as guided meditation, she encouraged me to think back to his death. I never regretted the sessions, but after a few, we agreed to stop. It wasn't getting me anywhere, perhaps because it felt like we were just doing what I had been doing off and on my whole life: replaying his death. The boat, the sky, my brother behind the boat's wheel. The splash. The screams. They neither plagued me nor left me. They live with me like so many gray clouds, neither good nor bad, neither calming nor distressing.

My friend had another recommendation. A sweat lodge. I remember thinking, *Wait, there's some South African tribes that share a practice with Native Americans?* The answer was no. This was an example of white South Africans practicing a Native American tradition. I was deeply skeptical about this appropriation. I was already a Black American and not a Black South African, and now there was this strange cultural tradition practiced by people who did not inherit it. I feared it was a self-absorbed endeavor undertaken by people who felt guilty about their privilege, adopting a cultural performance over meaningful self-searching. I was nervous but decided I had nothing to lose.

The lodge, a cozy, modest home with a few simple bedrooms and a tent for sweating out back, was run by two women. It was a good thing, because I didn't realize, until we arrived and sat in a circle as the women explained the rituals, that I would be naked in a tent with four men. It was particularly discomforting that two of them were much older, although I don't know why. The other one, about my and my friend's age, was "coloured," a common term in South Africa meaning of mixed racial heritage. I had never met them before and would not see them again after the sweat, although I didn't know that at the time. I froze immediately and considered my options. I had driven there and, theoretically, could just jump back in my car and head back to Cape Town. Still, I took a deep breath and decided that I would stay. I was at a place in my life where I was going to accept the uncomfortable challenges, and this was apparently one of them.

We had arrived in the morning because, as I would learn in the circle, while the sweat would be at night, there would be some rituals in advance. This journey into the actual tent would begin with spiritual preparation. We were instructed to walk in a direction, but different directions from one another—north, south, east, or west. We would not discuss or plan which direction we would choose. We were simply instructed to go, walk for a while, consider what came up for us on the journey, stay for a long period, and return.

I walked out the door and saw the high hill behind the house, and I instinctively chose to climb it. There was a clear, scrabbly path visible, and the hill didn't look unreasonably steep or high. I began the hike easily enough. It was beautiful to be rising upward through the yellow dust bound by the roots of various low shrubs. Before long and seemingly suddenly, there was no more path. I looked around and saw no clear way to reach the top, judging myself to be about halfway. It wasn't an appealing place to stop and sit with myself but I had already come too far, and it was too soon to turn back.

Since the shrubs looked low and the distance manageable, I decided just to pick my way through them. How hard could that be? I placed my feet carefully to save my bare legs from too many scratches by the angry shrubs guarding the hilltop. I had been wearing shorts because it was hot. As I climbed, the slope got steeper and the brush felt more threatening. The rain-deprived dirt and gravel crumbled beneath my feet, and I found myself increasingly reaching for the ground as the incline became more vertical and my footsteps less sure. My heart was thumping harder, not just from the effort, but because when I turned around and looked down, the valley below looked distant and a fall dangerous.

As I kept going, I became more panicked, so much so that I froze. Going forward and backtracking both looked life-threatening to me at that moment. My thoughts were racing in circles. I just kept moving forward because it was less scary than stopping. I was frantically looking around, hoping to perhaps pick up a life-preserving path again. I looked around once, twice, maybe a few more times, with mounting terror. Suddenly I saw it. It was narrow but it would serve as a path, traveling up to the summit. Was it there all this time? In that moment it felt like it had appeared because I needed it.

I broke into a slight jog to escape my fear and, far more quickly than I thought I would, I reached the top. I had arrived. Safety. Almost miraculously. I collapsed down on the ground and surveyed the view, which quickly soothed me with its quiet beauty. I began to feel at peace. The sky was still bright and the light was vivid without being cutting as it illuminated the landscape all around. I sat with myself, after my climb and all the fears and determination and questioning. I was here at this sweat lodge to connect with my feelings about Dad, about his death, about how I had been shaped by it, and how I had ended up fearing for my own life. It left me thinking about him. In fact, "thinking" is the wrong word. It left me with him, feeling him, seeing images and strips of memory floating unbidden in and out of my mind. Dad was always a love, a mystery, an idea, and an absence. Now he felt more like a presence.

My mind, more than my thoughts, turned to the women who were not Wileys. The Hill women, not the Whittle women. It was my mom's mother, her sisters, their parents crossing the South to the Southwest in a covered wagon. They were still so alien to me, not because they were deceased but because they were white, from a slave-owning South and a barren, wildcatting, cattled Southwest that hated Indians and Mexicans as much as Black people. My mother was both descendant and outlier. Her strength and her gifts were undeniable. We inherited something steely from these women who would have been dangerous to me and who sought to control her. The woman who encompassed my greatest sense of protection came from women who embodied my greatest sense of threat. I couldn't feel any emotional connection with those strangers, even though we shared a bloodline. I could find some gratitude for the grit my mother took from them, and ultimately used to determine her own views and future. I could make peace with that. I loved Mom, and I could be grateful to them for her strength and the strength she used to help me learn strength. I could embrace what I received without embracing what these women otherwise represented.

After our walks, the men and I came back together to share our experiences. We learned that the directions we chose had meaning. I had chosen north, which I learned was the direction that represents the ancestors. It wasn't just me. Each participant had a similar need that was appropriate to the symbolic nature of the direction they traveled. Now as the earth was turning her back on the sun, we would be turning to one another in the bareness of our journeys and with a vulnerability I had never given myself permission to have.

In the dark, with only the light of the fire outside the sweat lodge, we shed our clothes and were guided in. I thought stripping would be hard and it was, but not as hard as I thought. By this point, we had spent almost a day together sharing about ourselves. It helped that women were leading us in the sweat. The tent was big enough for the six of us, but just barely. We sat cross-legged and relatively close. One woman was the guide inside the tent, while the other tended and fed the fire outside, adding heated rocks as necessary to maintain a high temperature inside that would continue to burn off layers of our emotional force fields. I remember the heat more than the chants or the guiding questions from our leader.

The sweat had rounds. I think there was a question during each, but I can't remember if that's true. I grew up in the high heat and humidity of DC, and the first round felt like an extreme version of the summers of my youth. We didn't have air-conditioning, so every night I would shower and not completely dry myself. I would lay down on top of my sheets with a fan I had perched beside my bed so that it could blow directly on my body and would fall asleep hoping that, once asleep and dry, the heat wouldn't wake me.

After the first round, we got a break as the tent flaps were opened to allow the heat to escape and the outside air to come in. It was a great relief to be embraced by the arms of cool air, but I remember thinking that the experience so far was hot but not so hard. I would be very wrong. There would be four rounds, and each was progressively harder. We were suffering. The heat was peeling back all pride, all resistance, all controlled thoughts. The layers I had been building up over the decades were melting away despite my efforts to wrap them around myself like a blanket. It was too hot for blankets.

By the third or fourth round, most of us were unable to sit upright, instead lying in fetal positions. I had started singing "Amazing Grace" without thought, tears running down my face as I thought about those women who would judge me, shun me, and whom I owed for what strength I had. I was making peace with them, thanking them, but not needing them. Mom didn't need their acceptance because she had their strength. Neither did I. It turned out that Dad's death was not what I needed to make peace with.

I was not healed, but I was better. I now believed Dad's death had no hold on my life. I had never really felt that way, but everyone kept telling me it must. Now I knew that the strongest holds on me were more connected to the trauma growing up with the societal sickness of racism. Fear of the climb, panic when the path seems to end, and the loneliness of death would be repeated in different ways on my journey through life. I knew I would keep having to climb. Resilience is a march of faith, a gratitude for the gifts, including the gifts of hardship, and a willingness to move forward despite the fear and the questions that would come again. I was ready for the next climb. That climb would be family. My own.

I always knew that I wanted Mom to live with me. I wanted that three-generation, close-knit family with children enveloped in love. But it wasn't just about my children. I always felt my emotional and intellectual life was richer with my mom in it, sharing in all my experiences, guiding me with her wisdom. When Jonathan and I were engaged and getting married, I had convinced Mom to sell her house in DC, and she had moved in time for our wedding.

Now, at thirty-six, as I was planning my return, having split amicably with Jonathan, I was connecting with Mandel, my friend from law school. We had a kind of *When Harry Met Sally* story: We were strictly platonic friends in law school; he would marry the woman he was seeing then and move to LA. We often joke about how Cathy Albisa and I didn't make the cut for the wedding invite list. We did not stay in touch, but when he moved back to New York about four years later as his marriage ended, we would be reunited by a mutual friend while I was still at LDF. We dated for about six months, and during that time, he became one of my best friends, as well as a quiet love, which I didn't realize until it ended. We broke up within the first few months of my hardships at the US attorney's office as he grappled with the demise of his marriage.

When we dated in 1994, he had announced that I would not meet his parents. He was born in a working-class, Jewish neighborhood in Manhattan but grew up in the Long Island suburbs. His mother was a homemaker and a Holocaust survivor, and his father a real estate lawyer. By the time we were dating, they had moved to a Park Avenue apartment on the Upper East Side. I always wanted Mom and Bruce, but especially Mom, to meet all my boyfriends. I expected they would know who was in my life, whether serious or not. Harlan's soon-to-be ex-wife was a Southern belle and exceedingly not Jewish. His parents had always wanted their son to stay in the tribe. Harlan didn't say it then, but the implication of *and you aren't even white* hung in the air.

My own parents navigated the rough waters of interracial marriage at a very different time. Their decision to marry was swift and certain, but the actual wedding took place months later. Mom was still taking classes and working for the dean of the Maxwell School when drama broke out on campus. There were precious few Black students, and they were mostly male athletes. On the pages of the campus newspaper, an undergraduate dean had chastised and seemingly threatened white women undergrads for the offense of dating Black male undergrads. The campus was abuzz with the debate about the article and interracial dating. Mom's coworkers were buzzing, too. A friend of hers, a white woman, began actively defending the dean's position against interracial dating and marriage with another colleague. When Mom left the room, she would later learn that her other coworker had informed the mouthy antimiscegenist that Mom and Dad were engaged to be married. There was tension between her and this woman after that but not one they would discuss. For my mom, there was nothing to say.

My parents were scaling two opposite sides of a wall to be with each other, refusing to behave as if there were any wall at all. They did not ask for acceptance or permission. At the same time, Dad instructed Mom to stay as far away from the controversy as possible. Dad was faculty and Mom was a graduate student, after all, and they were bracing for a backlash to their marriage. They were clear what side of the fence they were on, but they also saw no reason to go out of their way to engage in the controversy.

It's a surprising response coming from my activist mother and determined father. They always struck me as the people who confronted what they thought was unjust. And I mean "confronted." With arguments, protests, and direct action. It shows how I can't fully walk in their shoes, to understand the amount of social pressure and consequences they were willing to stare down and the potential costs. I imagine myself cursing some people out, but that is an easy fantasy of the world I grew up in, one that is much less costly than theirs. It would not have been far-fetched for my parents to face significant consequences. Could Dad have lost his tenured faculty position for being with a white graduate student? Could Mom have been excused from her graduate courses? I'll never know, but I know I didn't have to face these types of questions.

My parents eloped. They traveled to Massachusetts, where a white ordained minister Mom knew, who was also a philosophy professor at Amherst College, was willing to marry them. Mom wanted a church ceremony, not a civil one, even if it wasn't a big wedding. She would have been happy to marry in a Black church, but they weren't members of one, and few Black churches would marry people who were not members. Ironically, despite them bracing for it, my parents faced no backlash after their marriage. People who had strong feelings before expressed no views, at least not publicly. Daniel Patrick Moynihan, who later became a kind of nemesis for Dad and the Ladies, was then an assistant professor at Syracuse. He and his wife invited Mom and Dad over to dinner shortly after their marriage. It was an explicit statement of acceptance to others.

The more central tension had been family, specifically Mom's. Dad's parents were displeased, but they didn't try to dissuade him. They were not ideologically opposed. They were just being practical. On the other hand, my mother's parents, particularly my grandmother, were significantly more outspoken, threatening to end their relationship with their daughter. Her parents were modestly middle class and Mom cared little for money; therefore, "disowning" her meant severing the emotional relationship. My grandmother was terrible, organizing everyone she knew to call and write to Mom, admonishing her for the horribly misguided decision to marry a Black man.

Mom was welcomed into Dad's family. Nana and Papa arranged a family dinner for the newly married couple with all the siblings and their spouses. It was a warm welcome, although my uncle Al's wife, Aunt Jean, a gorgeous woman who was always well dressed with perfectly coiffed hair or a wig, proclaimed my mother's hair "white trash hair" and offered to take her to a beauty salon. My mother declined the offer, but she always laughed about that story.

During my almost two years in South Africa, Harlan, with whom I had remained friendly, would visit periodically for work. His work in a media democracy organization brought him to South Africa for meetings. What started as two old friends grabbing a meal turned very quickly into a rekindling of old feelings. By 1999 we were dating again, and on New Year's Eve we knew the new millennium would be, for us, the beginning of a family. I'd declared that I would not remarry after my time with Jonathan. I hated so much the social expectation that came with the marriage, the ownership some people felt that they had over the breakup. I had a few friends, Black women themselves searching for husbands, who were judgmental about my divorce. One had wondered what was wrong with me for hesitating to marry and expressed her dismay that I would give up a good husband. It felt freeing to be able to say about Harlan, "Oh no. We're together, but I'm not his wife." We would be partners. Harlan, having gone through a divorce, was comfortable with not getting married as long as it was clear what commitment we were making to each other. We were clear. I was clear.

Harlan met Mom for the first time before I was back in

North America. Mom knew everything about Harlan and had for years. Now she knew that we were planning to spend our lives together. I suspect that because I had every intention of having a three-generation household, Harlan and Mom wanted to make sure they could each embrace my vision. It would be some months before I was back in the United States, and neither of them seemed to think it made sense to wait before meeting. I had little say in the whole matter, which seemed funny to me at the time. Mom liked him upon meeting him. Her specific words were, "I can see why you chose him." That was Wretha-speak for *Good job, sweetie!* Even I was taken aback when they began house hunting together without me. Harlan had an apartment in Manhattan, but it was only a one-bedroom like my garden apartment, which Jonathan and I had shared in the Brooklyn brownstone Mom bought in 1996. Mom thought we should find a new house to occupy more comfortably as a two-family home. I returned home at the end of March 2000. Finding that house turned out to be a good thing, because, despite my assumption that it would take a while to get pregnant in our midthirties, I would learn I was pregnant almost immediately. We were all thrilled and wonderfully unprepared. I was consulting to bring in a little money, which was perfect because I wanted the freedom to stay at home for the first year of my baby's life.

Things were falling into place perfectly. We found a Victorian that needed a ton of work in central Brooklyn, but it was a beautiful wreck. Dan, no longer Danny, already knew Harlan, and I already knew Harlan's sister from when he and I dated in the mid-1990s. Now the only piece of the puzzle not yet in place were Harlan's parents. He needed to tell them I existed. Like my parents before me, we had given his parents no opportunity to weigh in on whether we would be together. He went to see them without me and told them about me, showing them pictures of us together, the life we were starting. It was his way of letting them know that this was a decision and not a discussion. He was extending them an invitation into our lives together and into the life of their forthcoming third grandchild. I loved him for that clarity but also the boundary he held. He had chosen a side, if there was to be one, and it was beside me.

Their response, delivered through his mother, was swift and unequivocal. They would disown him if he did not marry me, which was its own almost comical contradiction. The fact of my pregnancy forced her to demand what she least wanted. It was a toothless threat in the sense that Harlan had put himself through law school, incurring debt despite their ability to pay his tuition, so that they would not be able to dictate what he did with the degree. He chose debt over dependence.

Harlan was pained and angered by his mother's response, though he wasn't surprised. She apparently said something vile on a call with him. To this day, he has not repeated it to me because it was too ugly and made him ashamed of her. I pressed him gently on more than one occasion. In my world, hearing the ugliness was an important way of dealing with it. I wanted to help him deal with it. But I also understood and ultimately let it go. This was his beloved and complicated mother, and I couldn't quite put myself in his shoes. Instead, I made a decision. I was going to work hard to help Harlan and my unborn child have a relationship with his parents. I had grown up with a loving grandmother who possessed that same ugliness. Despite her own emotional deformities, she had given me so much.

My grandmother was an active part of our lives and a precious one, even with her clear prejudices. There were only two instances when her racism appeared. Both happened when I was in high school, almost an adult. She was in her eighties. Both times I was just sitting with her at the kitchen table having casual conversation. On one occasion, I made a reference to being Black while she was visiting us. It was an offhand remark that was natural for me. My grandmother was incensed and agitated. She began sputtering, "You are *not* Black!" I found it so absurd that it was almost comical. I was more curious than upset. I said, "Well, then what am I?" It was half challenge and half real question. What did she see me as? She looked down at the table, unable to find an answer so she simply repeated, "You are *not* Black!" I replied, "Okay, Grandmother" in that *Yeah, right* tone of sarcasm.

This was my first understanding of why my mother would never let me travel to Abilene and why she almost never went. She never spoke badly about her family, even years after she left Texas. But she returned only three times in the half century since her departure; once for her father's funeral, once for her mother's eightieth birthday, and finally to bury her mother. She made it clear that she would never take my brother and me to Abilene. I remember asking her when our stranger of a grandfather died whether we would all go there. She simply said, "No. You will never go." I didn't question it. I was only twelve but some part of me must have understood.

On another occasion, during the period I lived with my adopted Black family on the weekends, Grandmother was visiting, and my friends wanted to meet her. I was sitting in the kitchen talking to Grandmother about nothing important. It somehow turned to her making a comment about "the Nigras back home." I stared at her, wild-eyed and incredulous. I had never heard such a word leave my grandmother's lips, even as it was registering that she must have heard these terms daily and used them as often. I responded in the only way I knew how: directly. I said, "Grandmother, you can't say that. My friends are on their way over and I won't be able to pull them off of you if you say that." Her response was, "Oh, is that bad?" I simply said, "Yes, Grandmother. That's bad." She never used the word again. My grandmother could be funny and charming as she would be when my friends came over.

Even with her bizarre contradictions, my grandmother was a wonderful part of my life. She infuriated my mother in ways it was impossible to miss. She would say she had to walk five miles to school each day in shoes that were too small, only to have my mother roll her eyes and later tell me that was a lie. My grandmother once told me my grandfather had been physically abusive. I didn't know him so I had no way of assessing her whispered secret. My mother gave a groan and an eye roll on that lie. Grandmother was unhappy and domineering, and not above lying for attention and to manipulate others. She was a product of her society. It was an ugly society. But she was her best self for me almost always, showering me with *I love you*s, hugs, kisses, and her humor. Even more remarkable, she never made me feel one bit less loved than Danny or her two blue-eyed granddaughters in Abilene.

My child would have my mother, but I wanted them to also have their other grandparents. My child, my children, deserved to know their roots. All of them. My unborn child's grandmother was a Holocaust survivor, which marked something in Harlan as the son of a survivor, and they deserved some connection to that history. Equally important, Harlan loved his mother. I loved him, so I needed to try and be part of the solution. I would do my part to open the door and hold it open. She had to decide whether to walk through it, and if she didn't, I would not have any regrets because I would know I tried.

Like my parents before me, I knew this wasn't about me. Ellen, his mother, didn't know me. She was rejecting an idea, a fear, not Maya Wiley. Her trauma was different from my own, and I would not be able to walk in her shoes. What I could do was consider my own, very different, experience of bullying—strange and sometimes disapproving looks from white people—to help me find empathy for the shame and fear that drove her to blind stereotyping and desperate attempts to control her children, and appearances.

Harlan's father, Newton, asked to have lunch with us some months before I gave birth. It was clear that he wanted a relationship. He wanted to meet me. It was an olive branch and we grabbed it. We met at the Sea Grill, a restaurant at Rockefeller Center where Harlan and I would never have otherwise dined. Harlan, Mom, and I had already settled into the dust-filled heap of our beautiful house, trying to repair it and make it more livable. Honestly, we were deliriously happy, and his parents' intransigence had done almost nothing to dampen our joy.

Newton immediately asked me how I was feeling. He seemed sweetly stiff, his tone and demeanor swinging between sincere interest and excitement and stern statements. It started with, "You have to get married or your child will be illegitimate." I was grateful he didn't say *a bastard*, although I was quite sure Ellen had. I looked down at my fish and let Harlan be the one to give the eye roll. The two lawyers became enmeshed in a ridiculous debate about how to protect the legal rights and relationships in the absence of marriage. It was obvious that Newton was delivering demands as instructed by his wife. I doubt he disagreed on substance, but he had no real interest in pressing the point. I remained uncharacteristically quiet, which was hard for me generally, but this was not my fight. In fact, it was so clearly beside the point. It got harder when he asked me to convert to Judaism. I simply said I wasn't Jewish, and Harlan hopped in to close the door on that demand, too. What also allowed me to remain stoic was Newton's obvious discomfort. This was not the pain of an accuser. It was the pain of a father. A grandfather. A man who, it soon became clear, was pleading with us to help him get his wife to a place that would enable him to have a relationship with his unborn grandchild and with us. Tears began to stream down this emotionally detached real estate lawyer's face.

I felt for Newton, even as I resented his insistence on our marriage and his conversion demands. I could see Harlan in his father, and because I loved Harlan, so I had love for that part of his father that reminded me of Harlan. But it was not enough for me to be someone I was not. Wretha and George's daughter wasn't built that way.

I still had a sincere hope that we could turn this around, though. Harlan was angrier. His father knew better but was not doing better. He was enabling Ellen's emotional blackmail. Newton's family, including two of his siblings and nieces and nephews, were mostly on Long Island, and they had an annual summer reunion. We went when I was still pregnant. Newton and Ellen refused to attend. I was greeted by all with kindness and acceptance. Newton's family made clear that they had chosen sides, and they were a bit gleeful to be on ours. As Sherry, Harlan's sister, once explained, Ellen had a way of doling out insults.

Naja Ann was born shortly after. She was greeted by Mom, Bruce, Dan, and one of my close friends. Sherry and her family were thrilled. I knew she was fighting with her mother on our behalf, not that we asked her to. I decided to send Ellen and Newton some photographs with a simple note, introducing Naja to them. I acted as if it was the most normal thing in the world for me to send it, because it was how I felt. I was not going to react to their dysfunction, but out of my own happiness. Harlan was grateful. Ellen wrote back. It was a formal letter, thanking me for the photographs and declaring that she hoped I would make our child legitimate. Ellen was sticking to her guns, but I knew that she could not hold out.

As I expected, Newton refused to hold ranks. After speaking with us at a family funeral, we came together at a family event in Long Island not long after Naja was born. It would be the first time Harlan's extended family would meet baby Naja. Newton came, plopped himself on the couch and welcomed Naja into his arms with the deepest and most genuine smile.

The break in the dam came with a Passover Sherry was hosting at her house. Ellen agreed to attend with Newton. It was a big deal. I knew that I had to be prepared for Ellen to attack or disrespect me. I don't handle that well. I did something I learned to do in South Africa. I imagined meeting her and her saying the most hurtful things I could think of. I imagined her calling Naja a bastard, saying I wasn't good enough for her son, disparaging my background and expressing that I had no place in the family. It wasn't that I expected her to be that outwardly cruel, but if I was prepared for the worst, breathing through my guided meditation, I could respond as my best self and not from hurt and anger.

In each instance of imagined insult, I considered what I knew of her. She had witnessed Kristallnacht. Her father's furniture store had been vandalized, and he had been picked up by the Nazis and taken to Sachsenhausen, the euphemistically titled "work house" that was the prototype for their concentration camps. He was there for two weeks. Ellen was a small girl, seven or eight years old. I had been nine when I lost my father. Not knowing what was happening to him must have been terrifying. Her mother must have been frantic. He would escape to Ecuador, and she and her mother would end up in Brooklyn, where her mother would work in a sweatshop and she, speaking no English, would be emotionally abused by the woman they rented a room from.

I backed up every blow with the memories I imagined her carrying, the fear of anything that would make her son vulnerable to that kind of hate, and her desperation for acceptance and safety. She could not see me, but only her pain and her fear of shame. I also knew that there had to be a part of her I could like because she had raised two people I loved. I had to look for that person, who was deeply imperfect but had something wonderful underneath her scars.

We were already at Sherry's when the doorbell rang. Newton trailed a woman I had only known in pictures. Short, barely over five feet, elegant in a formal suit, hair dyed auburn and styled in the same short, curled style she had worn for years, completely made up, painted nails. She had her chin raised slightly in the air, which I read as a defense mechanism. She would be better than anyone who might seek to hurt her. And she would hurt them first.

I was smiling as I greeted them and offered to take their coats. It was the simple home training I had been taught by my mother. I would have done it for anyone. But I wanted to show that I was going to treat them as I would treat anyone else, even if they hadn't done the same for me. Ellen was disarmed.

She had expected me to behave as she would have in my shoes. She was well behaved, watched her husband hold five-month-old baby Naja, and Harlan's sister's children, her other grand-children, who were four- and seven-year-old boys, relishing their "Aunt Maya" time. Everything shifted then. I could feel the tension evaporating into the air and I knew it was going to be fine. And it was.

We went from one big change to another with dizzying speed. September 11, 2001, was an event we could not fathom. We had just arrived home from a late-summer vacation. Naja was beginning to pull herself up and make tentative efforts to move her shoed foot a step as she held on to a knee or a chair. I had a consulting project or two, but nothing that took my atten-tion from Naja. Our reliable NPR went to static. As we began to catch on that a plane was hanging out of one of the World Trade Center towers, we struggled to understand the sheer horror. We did what many people did. With Naja in tow, we went to higher ground, Fort Greene Park, because the need to witness was so deep because what we were hearing was incomprehensible. By the time we got there, there were two building-size pillars of jet-black smoke rising where the twin towers that marked our skyline had been. Hundreds of people were there, silent. Watch-ing. Crying.

Over time, as the panic to find friends and ensure everyone was okay began to ebb, and as the days stretched into weeks, it would be clear that the tragedy, the thousands of lives lost, would not be the end. Cathy's apartment on the Lower East Side was too close to the World Trade Center for comfort and, as far as we were concerned, as much a part of Ground Zero as the twin towers and the financial district. The smoke and smell remained in the air, the streets were patrolled by police who looked more like the army, and a sense of foreboding lingered because it truly felt as if there could be another attack. But equally striking was how Chinatown and the Lower East Side were somehow outside the "perimeter." We were terrified for Cathy and her oldest boy, my godson, and the community as a whole. Our city as a whole.

Billions of dollars would flow into the city to rebuild, but it would soon be clear that the geographic focus would be Wall Street. The number of undocumented workers who lived in the outer boroughs, as well as in Manhattan, would not be helped. In the predominantly Pakistani community that bordered our own in Central and South Brooklyn, women in head scarves pushing baby strollers were being threatened and men were being disappeared from their homes, the victims of a new form of profiling and Islamophobia. George W. Bush would initiate a war against Afghanistan. Later, with false claims of weapons of mass destruction, he would invade Iraq. It was dizzying.

Jocelyn Sargent, a dear friend from the Open Society Institute in 1994, and I had been kicking around the idea of launching a nonprofit policy strategy organization. We were both starting families, so it became a five-year plan while we worked at the foundation. Jocelyn, a political scientist, focused on Black political participation, and I focused on race and poverty. We found ourselves in what I began calling the Plessy office, playing off of the infamous Supreme Court decision, *Plessy v. Ferguson*, which upheld racial segregation under the Constitution. The foundation had placed us, their two Black hires, in a single shared office. It was the best thing that could have happened to me. Jocelyn was from Texas—like Mom, descended from sharecroppers, and the daughter of a single mom—and we shared a worldview and a philosophy that has bound us together to this day.

After three years of friendship and conspiratorial efforts to move the foundation to address the need for multiracial organizing in the South, we both moved on. We had been looking for an organization that would support organizers with research and provide advice on transformational policy. We wanted to empower local leaders and groups in communities of color so they could make lasting change in their communities while addressing issues of racial injustice. Like my parents before me, I wanted to start an organization that would get down and dirty locally and build from there.

After we left the Open Society Foundation, I suggested that maybe we should finally enact our plan. I had long toyed with the possibility of founding an organization but had feared that I was trying to be my parents instead of myself. But as I moved further away from the litigation path, all I had seen and all that I had done gave me a different vantage point. Now I watched my city burn. I watched people in my borough suffer. I watched new organizing groups sprouting up in communities of color around the city. A few I had supported at the foundation formed a new multiracial coalition that included Asian communities in Chinatown and Queens as well as Black people in Brooklyn—it was important, and I wanted it to succeed.

I watched as Mayor Rudy Giuliani and Governor George Pataki, both Republicans in a Democratic city and state—white men in a distraught city of people of color already struggling to survive—called for affordable housing in the financial district. This would create homes for people earning close to $100,000 a year. It was an outrage. A network of labor unions and community organizations that had formed after 9/11 was calling for

REMEMBER, YOU ARE A WILEY

housing for first responders, the largely white firefighters whose
ranks were not available to most Black and brown people. They
were heroes, and we all cried for their bravery and their loss, but
what about everyone else? Their intent was good. One academic
who was active in the matter tried to convince me that this
race-neutral approach would help people of color. I knew better. It served the false "deserving"-versus-"undeserving" view of
who should benefit from affordable housing.

I called Jocelyn and told her the time was now. We couldn't
wait five years. Naja was in her bouncy seat sucking her fist and
watching me, and as I sat looking at that beautiful moon face
with plate-size ebony eyes, I knew what I would do. I banged
out a proposal. I had tunnel vision. Jocelyn jumped in unques-
tioningly. I started reaching out to friends and allies who might
help with resources. An old friend of my mother's, a white
woman and lefty who ran a small foundation, half snorted and
said, "Oh yeah, you can raise three dollars for that!" I froze at
the sarcasm and cynicism. I knew it was hard to ask foundations to back a new venture being started by two Black women.
I wasn't looking to be praised. I was looking for advice and
guidance.

I called my former boss at the foundation, and he agreed
to give us $75,000 out of his discretionary fund. He added, "I
doubt you'll be able to succeed, but I'll give you a little money."
I felt I got both the backhand and a helping hand. I knew we
might fail, but wished he had said, *It will be difficult, but I'll help
you try.* Another ally scoffed and said something just as doubtful
without offering advice. People are often unaware of how they
communicate and for far too many women, particularly women
of color, particularly back then, such skepticism could be crippling. While I found doubt and the occasional disrespect from

others highly motivating, it still hurt. I would rather fail at trying than fail to try.

The Center for Social Inclusion (CSI) would be born the summer of 2002, less than two year's after Naja's birth. We wanted to research the many issues facing communities of color, from education, to public transit, broadband, and food justice, guided by and working with community-based organizing groups in communities of color. We'd bring what Dad and Mom did naturally and sought out in Professors Cloward and Piven and others. We would bring our know-how to craft with them, not for them, the policies that would help them achieve their vision for change. CSI was the unplanned child of a devastating moment that had the potential to be transformative or to further trap the city and the country in an us-versus-them vise-like grip of fear. Twenty billion dollars in federal aid was coming to the city, and yet groups were asking Jocelyn and me to research how much less money foundations were giving them. I understood. It was enraging and wrong. But it was hardly the right strategic fight in that moment and was much less likely to produce real dollars directed to their causes, which included affordable housing and employment opportunities. For an organization like the Center for Social Inclusion to provide support, our partners had to be willing to partner with us, but the intertwined traumas of struggle, disinvestment, and the often racial nature of determining worth could be crippling.

Jocelyn and I turned our attention to the South, where the majority of the nation's Black population lived. We visited so many of these states and met with the leaders and groups who were fighting on multiple fronts for environmental health, to improve school systems, for criminal justice reform, and to build more policy power in state capitals still run by very conservative and mostly white lawmakers. We knew it mattered for a national strategy to, as my dad had, obtain more resources for public education, environmental health, and everything else they were fighting to get. But change at the federal level was also critical because, as I would not so jokingly say, we could still win the Civil War if we tried—the promise of an inclusive country was still being undermined by the South. Dad had looked South, too, during his work with CORE. I would do it in a more tailored and tactical way, working with the groups that were ready and willing. I did so often without the structure of a national head office and with no desire to get them into a "chapter" membership relationship with CSI.

I still worried about whether I was doing this for the right reason. My parents had been very focused not on their own self-aggrandizement, but on the empowerment of others. I felt pulled to their legacies. I also knew I wanted to ensure I was following their moral compass. One night, in the midst of these thoughts, I had a powerful dream: I was sitting at a large table. Dad was sitting at the head of it. Above him was a framed poster with his own face. There were signatures all over it, including a former organizer who had worked for NWRO and revered Dad. This person ran an organization similar to CSI in some ways. It was clear to me that the poster was an homage to a lost hero. Dad was being remembered and revered after his passing. And yet, he was sitting at this table beneath the poster.

I asked Dad whether I was doing the right thing, playing out my competing thoughts and my fears. Dad listened patiently. He never spoke in my dream. He only nodded at me, and the message was as clear as an unequivocal statement. The meaning was *Everything you have said is true. Now do it.*

Then I awoke. I've never had that experience before or since.

I told Mom about the dream. She shrugged and said, "Oh. Yeah. He has appeared to me in dreams, too." I said, "*What?*" I couldn't believe my ears. Then she said, like she was talking about the weather, "And it was always about work." Her consternation about his failure to appear on more personal matters was both funny and totally weird. All I could do was laugh and tell her I loved her.

By 2005 my mother started to worry us. We had our second baby, Kai, in 2003. Mom was definitely Kai's favorite family member and her twin! One day we had gone out for the day without Mom. When we got home hours later, we found several messages on the home answering machine from her. She had driven to a store and locked her keys in the car. I have done this myself, so it only struck me as odd because she knew we wouldn't be at home. Why was she calling the house phone? She spent all her quarters calling us from a pay phone repeatedly. She didn't use a single one of those George Washingtons to call the AAA, which she had been a member of for decades and had called in the past for everything from a dead battery to a flat tire. We came home and heard the messages, and Harlan went to pick her up.

Then there was the time she was going to the movies with an old friend, Ren. They were meeting in Manhattan to go to the Quad Theater near Union Square. About an hour after she left, Ren called me looking for her. He had been waiting at the theater and she hadn't shown up. I wondered if she had subway trouble. We checked in periodically. A few hours later she returned home. By this time I was worried. She simply laughed, when I asked her what happened, and said she went to Grand

Central Station, where she thought she was meeting Ren. He did take the Metro North train in from Westchester, so it wasn't completely absurd. But when she got there and realized she had made a mistake, she couldn't recall where she was supposed to meet him. This, too, was strange. She knew she was going to the movies. And her response to her own confusion was to sit down and stay put, and then she eventually came home. I asked why she hadn't called me, or Ren on his cell. It hadn't occurred to her, she said.

Before these more troubling incidents, I had come across Mom sitting down, looking distractedly out into space. This was normal. Mom used to do this at the dinner table all the time when I was in high school. She called it "being in oblivion." It was her mind turning and contemplating her day at the end of it. I often ignored these moments because they were very in character. On this particular day, I asked what she was thinking about. I wasn't worried, just curious. She said, "I'm contemplating cognitive decline." At the time, I thought little of it. Mom was growing older, was still an avid reader, and was enjoying her grandkids. Mom was in great health, taking walks, going to the mountains and hiking and so much more. I had chalked this musing up to her aging gracefully. These later incidents changed that.

A close friend had recently learned that her mother had Alzheimer's, and the more she discussed her mother's Alzheimer's behaviors the more I wondered about Mom. Mom was still very rational and intelligent, so, like all things in our family, it became an open discussion. I told her I thought we should get her evaluated. I was not at all convinced about the diagnosis. Having done some research, I knew it could be vascular, a vitamin deficiency, or something unrelated to the incurable disease that was eating the brains of others. My mother came from a long line of women who lived long lives. My great-aunt, my grandmother's youngest sister, was still alive and would live to be one hundred. My grandmother lived to be ninety-one. I was sure Mom was destined for two more healthy decades on earth.

It took me some months to convince Mom we should go. She had never been one to avoid what was hard in life, but now she was both agreeing and dissembling. In 2006 I took her to Columbia Presbyterian's Memory Disorder Center. The doctor looked like he had walked off a soap opera set. He had wavy dark hair and a certain confidence mixed with attentive concern. He had been written up in *The New Yorker* for his Alzheimer's research using MRI technology to track the disease. We liked him. He laid out the journey of testing by elimination since there was no one Alzheimer's test.

I remained convinced that a treatable vascular disorder would be the culprit. But it would be one of the first things ruled out after vitamin deficiency. We would make three trips to the center. I was also actively running CSI, with staff and projects, and traveling regularly to South Carolina and Mississippi. My work life was constant and my home life busy, but both felt fairly well balanced. Things were going well, and Mom would be fine.

On the final visit, the doctor confirmed our worst fears: Mom had Alzheimer's. I was stunned, even as I recognized I had already known despite my denial. Mom was stoic and considered. He would explain all the things that would not ultimately matter. It would kill her. But I would lose her slowly, painfully, over the following seven years or so.

We had a family meeting. Dan came over. Mom announced

that she would end her life at the appropriate time and asked for our help and support. Dan protested rationally. I simply said that I understood, but I could not help her. I knew Dan felt the same way. We had watched Dad die. I could not do this thing she asked, even as I felt like I was failing her.

Mom was fiercely independent, and her brain was what had enabled that independence. She said she would rather have cancer. I understood that, too, but I couldn't let her go. I wanted every last moment I could have with her. Next, she announced that she did not want to live in a nursing home. That was one thing I believed I could do, and I told her that she would be at home, with us.

It is impossible to recount the next six years of her decline. We were relatively lucky. She wouldn't wander from the house, preferring to stay indoors. When she became incapable of finding words and would carry on conversations we could not understand, it grew harder. She thought my brother was her favorite cousin at some point. But she never forgot she loved us, even if she wasn't completely sure who we were. Naja and Kai still brought large smiles to her face and I could count on their ability to coax her to the dinner table.

Eventually she couldn't be left alone. I had one then later two home health aides and was contemplating hiring a third to sit up with her all night because she had started to wander the house in the dark. I was becoming less available to Naja, now a middle schooler, and Kai, now in elementary school. I was working all day, then rushing home to make dinner. Wrangling Mom to bed made it difficult to manage getting them there, too. Mom's gerontologist finally convinced me that I had to put her in a nursing home, and I knew he was right. Dan would find a great place for her, and she would go quietly. That didn't matter. I was devastated, and I sank into a kind of functional depression. I had failed her. I had lost her.

She would live in the home until her death, which would come about a year and a half later, in early 2013. It was a Tuesday. I remember that with the clarity of a branding. It pierces the skin of my memory with a searing heat. I usually visited her on Sundays—alone because it was too hard for my kids to see her there. I couldn't blame them. It had to be frightening watching their once-elegant and grounded nana in that place. The fluorescent lights seemed to strip the rooms and hallways of the soft life-affirming glow of our bulbs at home. The thin air was scented with urine. Some residents, one woman in particular, walked the hallways dragging their feet in open-toed slippers, disoriented and disturbed about something unknowable. It somehow created a whirlpool of sensory signals that the disintegration we had slowly absorbed for years now ended in a communal pile of living remains.

I went on Sundays because they were my least busy days. I wanted to be reliable. I wanted her to have the structured experience despite her fractured memory. I needed her to catch my rope. Desperately. But I was also ashamed because I hated going for all the reasons my children did. I had to commit myself to going each week, forcing myself out the door. And I knew that I couldn't just run out after fifteen minutes.

That particular week in January, I had missed my Sunday visit. I had a free afternoon that Tuesday, and I realized I could leave work a bit early to see Mom in the late afternoon. I'd still be home in time to make dinner as I did every night, keeping her post-Dad tradition alive.

The nurses were such a gift. They always seemed happy that a patient was getting a visitor. Most of them didn't, which added to the sadness of the place. This day, the nurse who greeted me said "She's not feeling well today" rather than a hello. My interactions with the nurses always began as if I hadn't just arrived. It was a kind of comfort. A way of saying, *Don't worry. You are part of this.* It was as if they knew that I felt I had let Mom down, and they were trying to make me feel I was part of her care. I asked what was going on with Mom and the response was casual: "Just a cold. But she doesn't feel well."

She was in the activity room, which was where I always found her. The television was always on in there, and the residents sat around a very large, rectangular table that filled most of the room. It was not fancy, but she seemed to feel most comfortable there in the company of the other residents and with a nurse always present. I entered the tight room and saw Mom sitting in the middle of one side of the table. Her back was to the row of windows that ushered in some natural light denied in the long windowless corridor. It was her usual spot. Even with her shoulders stooped under the weight of her disorganized mind, she was tall. And she was white. A pale, white-haired woman in a sea of mostly Black and brown faces to match the nurses. I knew this suited her just fine. That she would prefer it to the obvious, segregated alternative. That was some solace.

Her head was uncharacteristically bowed, almost as if she dozed. I thought she might be asleep, but as I took the chair beside her, she lifted, turned her head toward me, and smiled briefly but knowingly before bowing her head again. She sniffled. Yes. A cold laying her low. We sat in silence that way for a while. I have no idea how long, but probably not more than a half hour. Mom was not interacting. The mother hen of the group was a resident, a lovely Latina with a thick accent, who always gave me updates on my mother based on her own observations. She said, "Your mother no feel good. She okay but she got gripe [a cold]." I spent about a year wondering how this woman with Alzheimer's had such mental clarity and acuity. One of the nurses finally told me that she didn't have any dementia at all. She lived on the ward before it became the Alzheimer's floor, and she didn't want to move.

Mom had a cold. We all agreed. I left to let her rest. Before I did, she acknowledged me for only the second time that visit. She wearily raised her head again, with lidded eyes, and managed a smile. "I love you," she said. I kissed her cheek. "I love you, too, Mom." I left, relieved as I was each week that she still knew she loved me. We both still held an end of this thin rope.

I had been home for only about forty-five minutes when the phone rang. It was the nursing home. A nurse I didn't know said, "Your mother is having trouble breathing. Do you want us to send her to the emergency room?" I was stunned into silent confusion for a heartbeat. "What?" I'd heard her, but I couldn't understand her. My mom had "a cold," she repeated, as if that would help me. I went into litigator mode, demanding that she explain the circumstances. She told me she didn't know more. She wasn't a ward nurse. She would have the doctor call me. "Please," I said.

Forty-five minutes later an unfamiliar doctor called to say, "I'm sorry. Your mother has died." In the frozen seconds that followed, those words robbed me of the flow of oxygen to my brain and blood to my extremities. I held only the absolute absence of all thought and feeling. It felt like being suspended in midair, in a soundless, empty room, with some vague awareness that I was about to fall on a hard floor. No net. No one would catch me.

That lasted a split second. Then the anger. My pain has

always been wrapped in anger to protect myself from its force. I went for him. What happened? I just saw her! She had a cold two hours ago. How is she now dead? Why didn't anyone explain to me when I asked about the emergency room? As quickly as the questions had poured from me, the last dammed the flow and I was left with myself. Alone. My anger was not at them. It was at myself. By demanding information before I made a decision, had I condemned my mother to death? Would she have lived if I had said yes? Anger again. Why did they think it was merely a cold? Why were they unprepared to help me make an informed choice?

The next day the medical director of my mother's nursing home, a lovely man, called me. He was Sri Lankan with a British accent and always referred to my Mom as "Mummy." He said my name with a gentle and soothing upward lilt that punctuated it with a question mark. "Maya? Mummy went peacefully. She was not in a lot of pain. We can't know for certain without an autopsy." Soothing upward lilt. "But I'm telling you it was congestive heart failure." The emergency room would have been terrifying for her, he told me. And she would have died anyway. I cried and thanked him.

CHAPTER 16

POLITICS

DURING DAD'S SHORT LIFE after NWRO, as he searched for what to do next, he was asked to speak at an African Liberation Day. It was April 1972, and the rally was at the foot of the Washington Monument—an ironic copy of the Egyptian obelisk and a totem to a founding father who professed to support the abolition of slavery even as he firmly held on to his own slaves. Here stood my father: the man who had Mozambican anticolonialist Eduardo Mondlane at his home, who was an innovator and erstwhile first mate at CORE, who organized and elevated Black women on welfare, who was excited, comfortable in this all Black gathering, and who still struggled for recognition as a Black leader. He mounted the platform for featured speakers. A group of Black women began heckling him for having a white wife, themselves enmeshed in their own struggle for recognition.

A friend who was there described him as visibly shaken. He tried to address the need for Black men to support Black women, but his words fell on deaf ears. The chant turned to "Talking Black and sleeping white." I can feel the pain of that blow, given all the endings in his life and his search for his new beginning, especially with the growth of his own Black activist self over the previous decade. Public repudiation could not have been easy, even for him. He had a Black girlfriend at that time. What did he have to do to be seen as he saw himself?

I could see myself in his shoes the day I planned my run for New York City mayor. It was the summer of 2020. My journey to remain unapologetically Black had been very different from his, and yet it had taken me to a Jewish man and another mixed family. Deep down I believed I would receive the same treatment, and Dad had seemed to me so much stronger and surer of himself than I was. I had my own demons around racial identity in a racist America. I also knew I was not Black like my father. I was Black like me. We had different experiences, even if I could relate to some of his and would find myself taking a leap he considered.

Once, I asked Mom what she thought Dad would have done in the next chapter of his life had he lived. She told me he'd toyed with running for public office. She said it with disdain. When I pressed her a bit on her feelings, she said that she could not imagine being a spouse to a politician. Mom's third-party political organizing had been focused more on pushing the professional politicians to the left than on supporting a candidate for office. I was in high school at the time, and I took it as a guidance. It sounded like a horrible life, full of fake smiles and false promises, constantly trying to please the wrong people while failing to help the right ones.

I had no clue that cofounding and running the Center for Social Inclusion (CSI) for more than a decade would become the beginning of a long and unexpected path to politics. It began a twelve-year period of my life leading a hybrid organization focused on dismantling "structural racism" at a time when john powell had just coined the phrase, and a small group of leaders, including the Aspen Institute and the Applied Research Center, agreed we would push it out into the public consciousness. It would take the brutal murder of George Floyd in the midst of the COVID-19 pandemic to make "structural racism" a term used on cable news, but it would happen.

It also began my television exposure on MSNBC, thanks to Wade Henderson and the Leadership Conference on Civil and Human Rights. We were working on transportation equity together. When he was invited onto *The Melissa Harris-Perry Show* on MSNBC, which aired on Saturday and Sunday mornings, he asked for me to join him as a guest. That was the start of everything. I would become known for my commentary on the George Zimmerman murder trial. I enjoyed being a guest, and it was a very important opportunity to help others understand racism and poverty and their interconnectedness. That was one way I could contribute to what I was witnessing as a renewal of movement times. With Trayvon Martin's death, we were seeing the decentralized organizing of the Black Lives Matter movement.

I would begin to join Chris Hayes's morning show, as well as Ari Melber's first show, where I appeared with Ari, Touré, Krystal Ball, and S. E. Cupp. The New York City public advocate, Bill de Blasio, was an MSNBC fan. The public notoriety, coupled with my work at CSI, put me on his radar screen, unbeknownst to me.

In December of 2013, the newly elected mayor, and the first Democrat to win that office in two decades, had mutual friends contact me to see if I would come into the administration. I was stunned. Why me? De Blasio wanted people who would think outside the box and help transform government.

CSI had grown to a staff of thirteen people, and we had been making a name for ourselves in a somewhat unintended way. To advance organizing strategy, we learned early on that we had to bring people together across organizations or within them, and examine what they wanted to change, and bring information, then analyze and research how they might affect real, tangible changes. This was long-term work and not straightforward. It required a kind of pedagogy of analysis and thus created a structural racism–training workshop. Increasingly, the workshops were turning into municipal work. Foundations and local groups asked CSI to come in and conduct trainings on how government policies shaped structural racism, and how to build strategies to tackle this issue meaningfully and in coalition. Our work in the South was often local and focused on municipal government, like addressing Black-owned land use policy in Lower Richland County, South Carolina; rebuilding New Orleans after Hurricane Katrina; and crafting public transit strategies in Birmingham, Alabama. With local wins, we knew we would be able to change national policy, particularly when there was a friendly federal administration in office.

I was also becoming restless about our inability to impact people more directly and more tangibly. It was a restlessness that my father felt when he transitioned from CORE to creating

NWRO. When I met with the mayor, I was already looking to work on issues and implement policies in ways people would actually feel.

Even after working in de Blasio's administration, I didn't think I would ever run for office. If I hadn't worked in City Hall and had the opportunity to more directly impact policy, I don't believe I would have. It was clear just how much heat there was in the very hot kitchen called the mayor's office. The difference, however, a mayor can make in the direct experiences of residents is palpable. It felt like we were moving toward movement times to reform policing, and that was important. I could see how working in local government would allow me to enact change. When I left City Hall, I went into academia because from a university perch I could combine a public platform with all that I had learned in policy advocacy and city government to work with the next generation of movement leaders and the government alike. It seemed the best of all worlds at a time when New York City had a progressive mayor and, I thought, we would have the first woman president of the United States.

Then Donald Trump became president, and Trumpism released the ugliest of what America had in her. Would I have chosen to run for office if there had been no President Donald Trump? I will never know. One thing I knew for sure: If my kids had been younger, I certainly would not have placed myself in politics, putting them more centrally in the crosshairs of political attack and risking the invasion of privacy that came with public office.

When I decided to run for mayor, I was clear that it had to be on my terms, but I also had no idea what that meant beyond holding on to myself. I would need to be clear who I was and why I was in the race, and also why I was trying to win. I had to be clear about what I wanted to do for people after being elected.

I stood on that step that sunny but cold and windy October 7, 2020. TV cameras were lined up behind a row of seats. As I waited to deliver my announcement, I remembered that I was standing there as a Wiley. I was a Black woman who had never run for public office. But now I was about to proclaim myself a candidate for mayor of the largest city in the country, one of the most challenging cities in the country to run. A city that had never elected a woman of any race to run it. A city reeling from trauma and loss after the tens of thousands of deaths from COVID-19. A city that had not recovered from Eric Garner's killing or the murder and gun violence plaguing too many communities after long, dark months of quarantine and the constant blare of ambulance sirens. A city that had a homeless crisis and an affordable housing crisis so much vaster than any other city by virtue of its gargantuan size. I believed so deeply in the city. In its people. Our resilience has always been a strength. I also believed, sincerely, that I could help pull us all together to address these issues.

As a Wiley, I had been taught that what matters most is delivering real change alongside the people who need it most. Throughout my run, I engaged with people to shape my platform through virtual "town halls" open to anyone who was not the press. I planned to address housing affordability and ensure that New Yorkers—like the Black and Latina nurses at my mother's nursing home and the classmates from my kids' schools—would not be pushed out and disappeared like my childhood friend, Charlene. I also knew that recovering from COVID would mean tackling homelessness and the eviction plight looming for far too many, a pre-COVID crisis that had

312

been growing as rapidly as the disease itself. But I would look to do things differently. If we subsidized rents, we could keep people in their apartments, rather than subject them to eviction proceedings that might land them in the overcrowded city shelter system.

As a trauma survivor myself, I knew we had so many traumatized children in our public schools before the pandemic and many more after that terrible time. We could have mental health care for kids in schools if we made it the priority it deserved to be. We could spend money on these critical health services if we recognized that we didn't need to hire more police officers to help prevent violence. This city needed solutions that would not just aid New Yorkers but could help heal them by addressing so many of the problems that the pandemic exacerbated. I wrote my policing reform plan personally because I had already thought long and hard about it. I had taken the time to explore possible solutions with experts, including hearing from the Black people who had experienced police violence and violent crime. I knew, like my parents before me, that most people directly experiencing all our public safety failures wanted practical solutions, not political ideology. I had a clear ideology and a plan to build it off the pillars of pragmatism grounded in the desires and demands of the people suffering the most.

I would not allow my campaign to make any plan public that I couldn't explain or didn't believe would be possible. I held back our housing plan and repeatedly sent it back to my team until I was sure there was a way to pay for it and clear authority to enact it. It could be hard to make these plans work, but they had to at least be possible. As a Wiley, I knew everything worth doing was hard. Not everything worth doing was possible. I remembered clearly hearing my father frequently say,

"Make a plan and make it happen." I was simply not able to do anything differently, not only because this was drilled into my head but also because the planks for my own strategic flooring were cut from my family tree.

When I was planning my announcement speech with a team made up of my small, but deeply committed and supportive inner circle, one said, "You have to talk about your father's death." I was immediately angry. I understood the political point. I could humanize myself to people, show the public that I understood their trauma and could connect with their pain. I could be a bringer of hope because I, too, had survived trauma. It made sense. Ever since I was that knobby-kneed nine-year-old girl on a beach already figuring out how to move on, I knew I was resilient.

My anger stemmed from my fear that I would betray my father and my Wiley roots if I did anything that had even a whiff of self-indulgence, of using my dad's death for political gain. That was a feeling I could not bear. I would not sell my father's story for political office. At the same time, I knew the value to me of being my full self, including all my experiences. I could do this, but only if I could find a way to stay true to myself. I knew that I had to write it.

In many respects, this was my first and greatest test of how to navigate running for office as Maya Wiley. I talked with the nice and competent young speechwriter the team found for me. I was already struggling with the very idea of someone telling me what to say. I, not anyone else, owned my words. It was an all-too-rare privilege, as a Black woman, to be able to have a public platform and to make it authentically mine. I could not give myself completely over to this stranger to write that part of my story, even though I could talk openly about Dad's death.

When I read out the words, I had to know that I was talking to people from my heart. I had to do, perhaps for the first time, what I could not do as that middle schooler, when my friend had so insensitively expressed disgust at my flat recounting of my father's tragic, devastating drowning. I could think about the families who lost a mother, a teacher, or a grandparent to COVID and know what that felt like, not because I knew better or was better, but because I knew pain and knew how important it was to not feel alone. It was about us and not about me. I could do that. Make it about us. Make it about hope and action and change. For those reasons and more, I could promise compassion in public office. I was not the typical candidate. I was a Wiley. I could be that.

ACKNOWLEDGMENTS

When I set out to write a book, I had a very different book in mind. I wanted to write a book about social movements— the years, usually decades, of activism and organizing behind the hashtags of #BlackLivesMatter, #FightForFifteen, and #TimesUp. Movements can't be willed into being, but they ignite as part of hard foundation laying. I was so excited by the surge in transformative and strategic protests and the policy possibilities that could produce lasting change. Instead, here I am, trying to figure out how to thank all the amazing people who supported, cajoled, challenged, inspired, and loved me on this journey of a memoir. If it were not for my kind and collaborative book agent, David Vigliano, I would not even be struggling with how to acknowledge all the wonderful people who deserve thanks. It was David who supported me so wholeheartedly, as he hopped on my rickety boat to some uncharted shore called a book. He just believed in me and in whatever I wanted to say. But he didn't just come along for the ride. He helped to let out the sails and look for land. He told me to meet with many book editors and just talk to them about my ideas. The social movements book was on the top of my mind, but it was

Knopf's Vicky Wilson who would set me on course, pushing me hard to consider that I was avoiding my parents' legacy. She was right.

Course set and now terrifying personal project under-way, there was then the task of telling my partner of over two decades, Harlan, and our fierce and fabulous young adult children, Naja and Kai, that I was going to lay myself—and therefore them—bare. They have always supported me, and this would be no different. They immediately gave me more than permission. They threw their love onto me like a life jacket, shrugging at any thought that I would get it all wrong. My brother, always patient, always thoughtful, always challenging, tolerated my disappearing on him to work this through, overwhelmed and terrified that I might disappoint him. He did what only my big brother can. He told me what I got wrong, including the critical details of his height at certain ages, the reminder of forgotten adventures like the one with leeches (don't worry, as it's not in the book), and most of all his understanding. He commiserated with me and even expressed his regret for my ridiculous and unfounded feelings for which he was not responsible. He is and will always be my oldest friend.

Getting a book to proposal and getting through the self-doubt and circling in the bay of chapter organization and crafting was so much harder than I would know. It was the amazing Thomas Flannery Jr.—Tom—at Vigliano & Associates who did so much more than hold my hand through proposal writing. He believed in the book and dug into the narrative arc with me. He pointed to possibilities and advised me to hold back when appropriate. He never doubted me or the book and never stopped encouraging me.

When it came time to send the book proposal out into the

world of publishing, it felt like tacking across waters quieted by the lack of wind. I could not create or direct the winds to get the book to shore. But David and Tom helped keep me on course as I tacked back and forth between meetings with publishing houses, which was both wonderful and nerve-wracking. Joining a Zoom call with Colin Dickerman and Maddie Caldwell at Hachette's Grand Central Publishing was like the blessing of a cooling breeze that promised to carry me to my destination. They just got it. They got me. They got the book. It was the kind of meeting that made me want to be in their company, and that is a blessing for the journey that is a book. The gift that has been Maddie Caldwell, my book editor, is impossible to overstate. She sent me the most beautiful email after our first meeting, before Grand Central had agreed to be my publisher. It was the kind of note that promised the best kind of faithful commitment. She said she could tell that I wanted to "change the way we think about the foundations of leadership." She was all in, and that meant that she would challenge me. I wrote to her at one point in our long editing adventure during a rare moment when I could put words to my feelings for the gift that is Maddie. I wrote, "I feel very lucky to have you as an editor. Starting there because, throughout this process, you have consistently shown me the value of a thoughtful and penetrating editor that knows how to push in a way that is deeply sensitive and also quite clear and easy to get." She demanded my vulnerability when she thought I was shying away from it. She did not hold back when she thought I needed to be clearer about what I was trying to say. Yet she never did anything with any hint of criticism. She knows it's hard to express vulnerability, to dig down beyond the obvious surface of the waters into the dark deep below. She was a guide, a partner, and a friend throughout the process.

The entire team at Grand Central has been wonderful. For the design team that came up with the cover that makes me cry and remember and cry some more, I am grateful. For the other behind-the-scenes team members, from compliance to copyediting, audiobook production, publicity, and so much more—Elisa Rivlin, Morgan Spehar, Laura Essex, Melanie Schmidt, and Roxanne Jones—along with the marketing team and all the countless people I didn't get the pleasure of meeting who helped guide this book to the shore, I am so grateful.

There is no way to thank all the people in my life who supported me through this book process, but I will acknowledge dear friends Liena Zegara, Patrick Gaspard, and Cybele Gaspard. And then there is Jean Alexander, the wife of my stepfather who isn't my mother! Families are what we make them, and Jean is family. She was my companion on my research adventure to historical archives and my constant champion. There are too many other countless friends, bosses, mentors, teachers, professors, colleagues, and leaders to name all the people I credit with helping me to remember that I am a Wiley. I wish I could, because I have done none of it alone.

I will end these acknowledgments with where my story truly begins: with George and Wretha Wiley. They shared with me their passion, their compassion, their wisdom, their strategic sensibilities, and their persistence for a just, fair, peaceful, and poverty-free, multi-racial world. They were the ones who set me on a journey. Dad didn't get to see it all, but I carried him with me every step of the way. Mom saw so much of it and she continued to be a guide. I am also so thankful to have had my stepfather, Bruce Hanson, in my life. I am so grateful to have had all of them as parents. And to the ancestors on both sides of my complicated family, the ones who would be guides and celebrate me and the ones who, in life, would have disowned me or disavowed me, I acknowledge them all. I am not a "book without a source or a tree without a root," as the proverb goes. I embrace the roots and thank the ancestors for being the sources that made me who I am. That made me a Wiley.

ABOUT THE AUTHOR

Maya Wiley is president and CEO of the Leadership Conference on Civil and Human Rights, the nation's oldest and largest civil rights coalition. She is a former legal analyst on MSNBC. A lifelong civil rights advocate and a civil rights attorney, she mounted a historic performance in New York City's 2021 Democratic mayoral primary, contesting to be the first woman mayor on a reform platform. Prior to that race she served as senior vice president for social justice at the New School and as a member of the graduate faculty at its Milano School. She was the first Black woman to serve as counsel to a New York City mayor, and her expertise and compassionate approach was (and remains) almost unprecedented in the world of advocacy, activism, and politics. Maya serves as the Joseph L. Rash Jr. Chair of Civil and Human Rights at the University of the District of Columbia School of Law. She lives in Brooklyn with her partner, Harlan, their three cats, and her revolving door of young adult children, two of whom are biological and the others are happily inherited.